CHURCH, STATE AND CIVIL SOCIETY

At a time when secular liberalism is in crisis and when the civic contribution of religion is being reassessed, the rich tradition of Christian political theology demands renewed attention. This book, based on the 2001 Bampton Lectures, explores the relationship of the church both to the state and to civil institutions. Arguing that theological approaches to the state were often situated within the context of Christendom and are therefore outmoded, the author claims that a more differentiated approach can be developed by attention to the concept of civil society. The book offers a critical assessment of the effect of the First Amendment in the USA and, in a concluding chapter, it defends the case for continuing disestablishment in England and Scotland.

DAVID FERGUSSON is Professor of Divinity at the University of Edinburgh.

CHURCH, STATE AND CIVIL SOCIETY

DAVID FERGUSSON

CAMBRIDGE
UNIVERSITY PRESS

PUBLISHED BY THE PRESS SYNDICATE OF THE UNIVERSITY OF CAMBRIDGE
The Pitt Building, Trumpington Street, Cambridge, United Kingdom

CAMBRIDGE UNIVERSITY PRESS
The Edinburgh Building, Cambridge CB2 2RU, UK
40 West 20th Street, New York, NY 10011–4211, USA
477 Williamstown Road, Port Melbourne, VIC 3207, Australia
Ruiz de Alarcón 13, 28014 Madrid, Spain
Dock House, The Waterfront, Cape Town 8001, South Africa

http://www.cambridge.org

First published 2004

Printed in the United Kingdom at the University Press, Cambridge

Typeface Adobe Garamond 11/12.5 pt.   *System* LATEX 2$_\varepsilon$ [TB]

A catalogue record for this book is available from the British Library

ISBN 0 521 82239 4 hardback
ISBN 0 521 52959 X paperback

Contents

v

Preface

The present book is a revised version of the 2001 Bampton Lectures delivered in the University Church of St Mary the Virgin, Oxford. I am grateful to the Bampton Electors for their invitation to deliver the series and to those who hosted me during eight visits to Oxford. A particular debt of gratitude is owed to Professor Ernest Nicholson, then Provost of Oriel College, to Miss Elizabeth Llewellyn-Smith, then Principal of St Hilda's College, and to Dr Richard Repp, then Master of St Cross College, for their generosity and encouragement. The opportunity to visit two former teachers, Basil Mitchell and John Macquarrie, also added to the enjoyment of my time in Oxford.

The material from eight lecture-sermons has been converted into book-length chapters during a period of research leave at the University of Edinburgh, and I am grateful to my colleagues for making this possible. Since returning to New College in 2000, I have been assisted by occasional conversations with many friends along the way. Particular thanks are owed to Duncan Forrester, Will Storrar, Larry Hurtado, Graeme Auld, David Reimer and Jane Dawson. I am also grateful to Jason Curtis for preparing the index.

The study has also benefited immeasurably from the detailed comments of four anonymous referees whose reports were solicited at an early stage by Cambridge University Press. Their constructive criticisms have reminded me that there is no such thing as a bad review prior to publication. Although I cannot name them, I am pleased to record my gratitude.

The delivery of the Bampton Lectures coincided with a time of transition in our lives. This involved a period of commuting between Aberdeen and Edinburgh. As ever, I am grateful to my wife and our two sons for their forbearance and support.

CHAPTER ONE

The politics of scripture

I just want you to know, my friends, that I stand here to speak from this Holy Book. It is important for you to recognize that what I am going to say is not based on any ideology, political or otherwise. It is based on this Holy Book.

(Desmond Tutu)[1]

The present study is governed by two overriding convictions, one negative and the other positive. The relationship of church to state has often been cast in terms of the relations that obtain between two dominant institutions existing in a close and exclusive partnership. With the end of Christendom, this is now outmoded. A more differentiated approach is required that positions the church in positive relation to a range of other institutions within civil society, thus more effectively presenting its public significance. To this end, however, a rich tradition of Christian social thought can be appropriated for contemporary political conversation. Hence the attention devoted to historical materials is neither a preamble nor a diversion; it is integral to the argument.

These two ruling convictions are supported by a range of further considerations. As secular liberalism experiences various crises, especially the ordeal of 'value pluralism', attention can be diverted to early modern arguments for religious tolerance. These provide an account of social diversity that is articulated along distinctively theological lines. With the concept of 'civil society' now attracting fresh scholarly interest, the social contribution of churches can be positively assessed without recourse to the options of sectarian isolation or public dominance. This is reinforced by attention to the experience

[1] *The Rainbow People of God* (London: Doubleday, 1994), 166–7.

of non-western churches which have become socially significant but without aspiring to function as national or state institutions. And in the background to these arguments, an ecclesiology emerges that in important respects stresses the increasingly congregational, voluntarist and ethically formative dimensions of the church in western societies. The case is supported by familiar arguments against establishment, although it will be claimed finally that the concept of 'disestablishment' is neither univocal nor unproblematic.

PATTERNS OF DISSOCIATION

Most people over the age of about forty have little difficulty in providing anecdotal evidence for the decline of mainstream Christianity in western European societies. The opening of retail stores for business on Sundays; the availability of leisure alternatives to church attendance; shifting patterns in domestic and family life; the affirmation of pluralism as a positive social good; less media coverage of the ethical pronouncements of church leaders: all these are symptomatic of a growing dissociation that has taken place in our lifetime between the beliefs and practices of the Christian churches and those of civil society. With the help of sociologists and historians one can detect these trends already at work more than a century ago, but the momentum that they have gained in living memory is striking. The statistical decline in baptisms, church attendance, weddings and even now Christian funerals confirms the intuition that ours is a society less interested in traditional expressions of religious faith, less sensitive to ecclesial practices, and less informed about Scripture, prayer and the sacraments. Even the faithful themselves have become uncomfortable with arrangements that quite suddenly seem outmoded, the relics of a bygone era of establishment. The attack by secularists on the regular BBC Radio 'Thought for the Day' slot on the flagship news programme seems persuasive to many who remain committed to the ethical and social relevance of religious resources.[2]

---

[2] Clifford Longley confesses that 'my own misgiving about doing "Thought for the Day", the difficulty of attracting Catholic contributors, and the distaste of the National Secular Society are not entirely disconnected. For it is surely a legacy of a Protestant and Erastian understanding of Church and society which now seems obsolete'; *Tablet*, 9 August 2003, 2.

Callum Brown, in his recent book *The Death of Christian Britain*, has painted a provocative picture of how rapid and recent has been the dissociation of contemporary society from the ethos of the churches in the past generation:

> It took several centuries to convert Britain to Christianity, but it has taken less than forty years for the country to forsake it . . . In unprecedented numbers, the British people since the 1960s have stopped going to church, have allowed their church membership to lapse, have stopped marrying in church and have neglected to baptise their children . . . [A] formerly religious people have entirely forsaken [*sic*] organised Christianity in a sudden plunge into a truly secular condition.[3]

In some measure, this lament is part of a wider social story. Institutions and organisations which commanded the commitment of mass memberships are generally in decline. Our corporate life is increasingly fractured and fragmented. The Royal Society for the Protection of Birds can now boast many more members than all of the United Kingdom's main political parties combined.[4] The pressures towards the atomisation of social life can be detected in shifting patterns of family life with more people living alone than ever before, in working practices which place us increasingly in front of computers, in leisure pursuits which are more various and accommodating of individual preferences, in meal times and moments of relaxation spent not in conversation but in front of a television screen. These trends have given rise to a body of literature which complains in Tocquevillian fashion of a loss of moral identity and social cohesion, the evaporation of community spirit, deracinated elites, and the dangerous dissociation of growing numbers of citizens from the political process.[5] Voter apathy, a familiar ailment, is now difficult to remedy. With the process of fragmentation, there arises a different set of pathologies. These are no longer the repressive conditions produced by societies and homes demanding a narrow conformity. Instead, the psychological ailments

---

[3] *The Death of Christian Britain* (London: Routledge, 2001), 1. In citing Brown's work at this juncture, I do not intend to endorse his particular take on the secularisation thesis. However, the evidence he cites for the rapid changes that have taken place within the last forty years is striking and ineluctable.

[4] *Times Higher Educational Supplement*, 22/29 December 2000, 24.

[5] E.g. Robert Putnam, *Bowling Alone: the Collapse and Revival of American Community* (New York: Simon & Schuster, 2000).

of western culture are generated by the loss of those stable ideologies and moral standards that once defined the self. The resultant effects include cynicism, privatism and self-preoccupation.[6]

In this new social landscape, we seem to be faced with two ecclesiological options. These are withdrawal or assimilation. This disjunction is probably most plausible to those living in the USA and in those western European societies which have suddenly departed from familiar patterns of establishment. The social pre-eminence of churches has disappeared in a more pluralist culture that esteems individual lifestyle choices and tends to perceive religious commitment as now restricted to a private or subcultural domain. The former option of withdrawal has been described pejoratively as 'the sectarian temptation'.[7] The church can maintain its identity by corralling its members into tightly defined subgroups within which they are socialised in the ways of authentic Christian life forms. The maintenance of tribal identity is thus secured albeit for a small minority who are willing to make this commitment. The other alternative is merely to position the church in the slipstream of cultural developments, where it will provide an ongoing religious dimension or variant to whatever moral and social choices are made by individuals.[8] On the assumption that there will always be some spiritual aspect of human life, the churches can thus survive by meeting the shifting needs and aspirations of our contemporaries. The decision of the Church of Scotland minister at Dornoch Cathedral to preside at the wedding of Madonna and Guy Ritchie and to baptise their child was presented, albeit unfairly, as symptomatic of an ecclesiology in which the church will bend in whatever direction the winds of cultural change happen to blow.

Each of these options thus described contains elements of caricature, and neither is sociologically possible nor theologically supportable. The stark alternatives of withdrawal or assimilation present modern culture as monolithic. You are either for it or against it.

---

[6] This is argued by Charles B. Guignon and David R. Hiley, 'Biting the Bullet: Rorty on Private and Public Morality', in Alan Malachowski (ed.), *Reading Rorty* (Oxford: Blackwell, 1990), 339–64.

[7] E.g. James Gustafson, 'The Sectarian Temptation', *Proceedings of the Catholic Theological Society of America* 40 (1985), 83–94.

[8] My colleague David Wright sees this as increasingly the reality of establishment churches; 'The Kirk: National or Christian?', in Robert Kernohan (ed.), *The Realm of Reform: Presbyterianism and Calvinism in a Changing Scotland* (Edinburgh: Handsel Press, 1999), 31–40.

Yet this is surely to simplify what is a highly complex phenomenon requiring a discernment that will sometimes confirm and sometimes reject developments in the worlds of art, education, science, medicine, social-welfare economics and politics.[9] It would be surprising if one were in favour of either everything or nothing. Nonetheless, a range of critical questions is raised for contemporary theology by recent cultural dissociation from the church, by modern ideologies of pluralism and by the politics of state neutrality. These are not new problems. In one form or another, they have generally beset Jewish and Christian communities, who in turn provide us with a rich heritage of resources for critical reflection. Attention to these is required for an adequate and informed response to these changing cultural conditions.

THE KINGSHIP OF YAHWEH

Much early Christian thought in this area (as in others) is rooted in centuries of Jewish reflection. For the Hebrew Bible all thinking about political authority and power is profoundly related to the claim that 'Yahweh is king.' It has been pointed out that the Hebrew word for 'king' – *melek* – is found over 2,500 times and is the fourth most frequently encountered term in the Hebrew Bible.[10] The affirmation of Yahweh's kingship is thoroughly political to the extent that it embraces the social, economic and cultural life of the community. This is celebrated in the enthronement Psalms and reveals the extent to which not only is the life of Israel sustained by the kingship of Yahweh but also the natural world and the other nations of the earth. The world is firmly established by Yahweh (Psalm 96:10). Yahweh will judge the world with righteousness and the peoples with equity (Psalm 98:9). Yahweh loves those who hate evil and guards the lives of the faithful (Psalm 97:10). Yahweh the most high is awesome, a great king over all the earth (Psalm 47:2). Despite the Christian temptation to spiritualise these passages or to project them on to a distant eschatological state, it is clear that they are of intense political significance.

---

[9] A similar point is argued to great effect in John Howard Yoder's critique of H. R. Niebuhr's typology in *Christ and Culture*; 'How H. Richard Niebuhr Reasoned: a Critique of *Christ and Culture*', in Glen H. Stassen, D. M. Yeager and John Howard Yoder (eds.), *Authentic Transformation: a New Vision of Christ and Culture* (Nashville: Abingdon Press, 1996), 52.

[10] Horst Dietrich Preuss, *Old Testament Theology*, vol. II (Edinburgh: T. & T. Clark, 1996), 21.

Brueggemann suggests that the rhetoric of divine kingship has two functions in the thought of Israel.[11] Negatively, it destabilises any government or regime which claims an absolute authority. This is true of Pharaoh and Nebuchadnezzar at either end of Old Testament history. Yahweh alone determines who rules proximately on the earth, and brings low those who walk in pride (Daniel 4:37). Yet positively, Yahweh's kingship offers compassion, healing and the deliverance of justice. 'The Lord upholds all who are falling, and raises up all who are bowed down' (Psalm 145:1).

Given the significance attached to the kingship of Yahweh one might expect to find monarchical models of government legitimated in terms of their mediation of this higher kingship. In part, this is true. Israel has a monarch as do the other nations. His task is to maintain the security of the nation against external threat and to execute the will of Yahweh amongst the people. Nevertheless, there are strands within the Hebrew Scriptures which are highly critical of the monarchy as an institution. Gideon renounces the kingship in Judges 8:23 for it is Yahweh's right alone to rule the people. In Judges 9 Jotham tells a parable in which the olive, the fig and the vine all renounce any claim to be king over the trees only for the worthless bramble to take up a position of supremacy. This is a deeply anti-monarchical story, which led Martin Buber to insist upon prophecy rather than kingship as the authentic political voice of Judaism.[12]

Monarchy is conceded, as it were, in 1 Samuel but not without reservations which are subsequently articulated by the prophets and the histories, which record at best mixed outcomes. There are repeated efforts to position the monarch under the claims of divine law. Thus the king, like any other citizen, is subject to Yahweh's law. It is this which legitimates his rule and brings prosperity to the nation. Nathan is able to confront David for despising the word of Yahweh (2 Samuel 12:9). Solomon is rewarded for placing wisdom above all other gifts: 'If you will walk in my ways, keeping my statutes and commandments, as your father David walked, then I will lengthen your life' (1 Kings 3:14). Yet he also will become the object of divine anger for turning to foreign deities (1 Kings 11).

---

[11] Walter Brueggeman, *Theology of the Old Testament* (Grand Rapids: Eerdmans, 1997), 38–240.

[12] 'At no other time or place has the spirit been served in the human world with such militancy, generation after generation, as it was by the prophets of Israel'; Martin Buber, *On Judaism* (New York, Schocken Books, 1967), 194.

The tension between the ideal of kingship and the empirical reality is maintained through much of the Hebrew Scriptures. Psalm 72 is a prayer for the reign of a king which petitions Yahweh for justice, military success and economic prosperity. In Jeremiah, despite his suspicion and bitter experience of kingship, the reign of Josiah is held up as an example of just kingship according to the law of Yahweh: 'He judged the cause of the poor and needy: then it was well. Is not this to know me? says the Lord' (Jeremiah 22:16). The king remains an ideal. He can mediate Yahweh's sovereignty in the responsible use of power towards the goal of communal well-being.[13]

Following the exile in 587 BCE, Israel's life is no longer shaped by king, temple and city. In some places, this is interpreted as a judgement upon the failure and corruption of the monarchy, for example in Ezekiel's prophecy against the false shepherds of Israel (Ezekiel 34). The inability to use power responsibly is indeed perceived as a cause of its withdrawal by God. Yet hope for a time of renewal is expressed in terms of the restoration of the Davidic monarchy. The root of Jesse becomes a signal to the peoples of a new era (Isaiah 11:10).[14] This remains a political hope. The king who comes to Jerusalem in Zechariah 9 commands peace to the nations. His dominion is from sea to sea.

Despite this hope, from the time of the exile the political situation of the Jewish people remains radically altered. In Babylon there is a strong maintenance of Jewish identity but also an accommodation with the state and civil society. This is expressed most famously by Jeremiah's injunction to 'seek the welfare of the city' (Jeremiah 29:7). His discourse appears to have been written to counter unrealistic hopes of an imminent return to Jerusalem and to criticise false prophets: 'But seek the welfare of the city where I have sent you into exile, and pray to the Lord on its behalf, for in its welfare you will find your welfare.' A positive commitment to the peace of the city is advocated and acknowledgement made that the welfare of Jews there is bound up with that of the civil community. Yet the language of exile is still restrained and an eventual return to the homeland anticipated. This creates dissonance and makes a full assimilation into Babylonian society impossible.

[13] I am indebted in all this to the discussion in Brueggeman, *Theology of the Old Testament*, 611ff.
[14] This passage is sometimes read as a post-exilic addition to the text.

By the first century there is not so much exile as dispersion. It is estimated that there may have been 5–6 million Jews throughout the empire. Philo reports that there are about a million Jews in Alexandria alone during the first century.[15] Throughout the empire, Judaism had the status of *religio licita*, thus enjoying the position of a recognised religion. The synagogue (or prayer house) served as a meeting place for daily and sabbath prayer, for religious instruction and communal gathering. So the faith could be maintained and upheld within societies displaying a measure of tolerance and hospitality, albeit with a tension never permitting total assimilation.

JESUS AND THE DOMINION OF GOD

In Israel at the time of Jesus we find a range of attitudes including withdrawal, resistance and forms of accommodation. The Essenes adopted a strategy of detachment either within urban communities or in remote sites such as Qumran. Their separate identity was maintained by an elaborate system of purity, ethics and initiation. They did not recognise the Jerusalem priesthood. Violent resistance was sporadic, and recent scholarship suggests that resistance movements took a variety of forms deriving from the example of Maccabean revolts in the second century BCE. The issue of taxes raised one problem. In paying taxes, they owed allegiance to a foreign power. According to its sacred traditions, however, Israel was to be ruled by a king of divine appointment. Submission to Rome could be seen, therefore, as effectively violating the first commandment. Faithfulness was to be exhibited in outright resistance to foreign overlords, and God would vindicate the faithful either in this world or at the end of time. There was such armed resistance to the rule of Herod's son after the death of his father in 4 BCE and in the example of the Sicarii.

The assumption that resistance to Roman rule was restricted to the Zealot party has been challenged by recent scholarship.[16] Examples of wider resistance amongst Pharisees and other groups are available, while it is now doubted whether a discrete Zealot grouping existed

---

[15] However, John Barclay notes that this estimate is probably much exaggerated; *Jews in the Mediterranean Diaspora* (Edinburgh: T. & T. Clark, 1996), 41.

[16] In what follows I am indebted to Marcus Borg, *Conflict, Holiness and Politics in the Teaching of Jesus*, 2nd edition (Harrisburg, PA: Trinity Press International, 1998), 43–65.

before or about the time of Jesus. Herod's desecration of the Temple with the eagle of imperial Rome in 4 BCE was attacked by two Pharisees and forty students. For destroying the eagle they were executed, a political event that precipitated widespread public protest. Tensions with Rome were ongoing; resistance was sporadic, involving a range of groups from a broad cross-section of the Jewish population. Torah and Temple dominated Palestinian Judaism, so that varying threats to these institutions brought about forms of protest, sometimes violent, from a range of individuals and groups. The neat packaging of priests as collaborators, Pharisees as quietists, Zealots as guerilla fighters, and Essenes as sectarian escapists obscures the complexity of the historical situation. It may also have the effect of marginalising the importance and necessity of political criticism within Judaism.

It is within this complex political, social and religious context that Jesus is to be understood. In some respects, the group to whom he may be closest is the Pharisees. The intensity of their conflict indeed may be explained by the sheer proximity of ideology.[17] By positioning himself between outright resistance and total withdrawal, Jesus follows a path mapped out by other movements. His eschewal of violence in the Sermon on the Mount sets him apart from more violent trends in first-century Judaism, while his eschatological vision of the coming reign of God prevents any political or military orchestration of the ideal society. In response to the divine rule of compassion and forgiveness already being inaugurated in his teaching, people are called to live obediently and gratefully. This was a social movement directed not merely at individuals but at Israel as the people of God. Its radical inclusiveness made for indistinct and fluid boundaries. Yet it was a corporate movement, a new community adumbrated by the calling of twelve disciples. Although this vision of divine grace and inclusion, together with its eschatologically urgent demand, brought Jesus into conflict with the regnant interpretations of Torah and Temple, the proximity of his position to that of Pharisees and priests should not be overlooked.

In attempting to reshape the *polis* of Israel, the outcome of Jesus' ministry was confrontation with some of these religious forces and

---

[17] Borg points out that the closer the relationship between the antagonists the more intense is the conflict; ibid., 153.

execution by the civil authorities. Jesus may not have actively sought confrontation with the Roman authorities, but his willingness to suffer crucifixion for the rule of God indicates where his highest allegiance lay. His fate and that of many of his followers reveals the inability of Christianity to function as a form of civil religion, a religion whose primary purpose is to reinforce the life of a civil community. There is never a perfect coincidence of civil and theological loyalties. The possibility of conflict is always present, and in such a situation one's highest allegiance is to God. This is dramatically represented in the trial before Pilate as narrated in the Fourth Gospel. Here the clash of allegiances is personified in the encounter of Christ with the Roman procurator. Pilate is ostensibly the judge yet the story attests Jesus as the judge of Pilate whose kingship is derived from God and conceded only in a provisional manner.[18]

The credal confession *crucifixus est pro nobis sub Pontio Pilato*, often quoted in this context by Donald MacKinnon,[19] is a reminder that Jesus was a victim of the *Pax Romana*. The procurator charged with maintaining the peace of Palestine perceived Jesus as a threat. Here the *Pax Romana* and the reign of God collide. To this extent it is hard to disagree with Klaus Wengst when he argues that 'anyone who prays for the coming of the kingdom of God, expects it very soon, and sees the sign of its dawning in his own action, has no faith in the imperial good tidings of a pacified world and human happiness in it'.[20] The peace of Rome, enforced by military means under the imperial authority, was of course not devoid of legal, economic and cultural benefits. Yet the fate of Jesus under Pilate meant that any subsequent endorsement of Roman authority by the early church could only be provisional and temporary. It might generate the conditions under

---

[18] This is emphasised by Bultmann in a commentary written in the midst of the German church struggle. The neutrality of the state is no longer possible when the state becomes pressed by 'the world' to execute the Revealer. Hence Pilate is placed under judgement by Jesus. Bultmann concludes that an atheistic state, i.e. a neutral one, is impossible although an unchristian one is possible in principle; *The Gospel of John*, trans. G. R. Beasley-Murray (Oxford: Blackwell, 1971), 661. The first German edition appeared in 1941.

[19] E.g. *Borderlands in Theology* (London: Lutterworth, 1968), 87.

[20] Klaus Wengst, *Pax Romana and the Peace of Jesus Christ* (London: SCM, 1987), 55. The extent to which the community inaugurated in Jesus' ministry is effectively a religious, social and economic challenge to Roman imperial rule is stressed by Richard A. Horsley, *Jesus and Empire: the Kingdom of God and the New World Disorder* (Minneapolis: Fortress Press, 2003).

which the Christian faith could be practised and offered to others, but the possibility always remained that the followers of Jesus would provoke similar opposition and hostility.[21] Both attitudes towards the state can be detected in the New Testament and they issue from a single theological perspective.

The account of Jesus offered here is irreducibly eschatological, and thus at odds with some recent portraits that detach his vision from later eschatological materials. These are decried as interpolations of the early church. Instead we are presented with a sapiential teacher whose words have a timeless quality stripped of apocalyptic and eschatological associations.[22] However, the sheer weight of eschatological material in the synoptic tradition, together with the need to situate Jesus in historical relation to both John the Baptist and the early church, makes this difficult to sustain.[23] The gospels present Jesus as one who announces the imminent rule of God and enables a new quality of existence in those around him. This is neither a purely future eschatology in which the present is only a time of waiting nor a realised eschatology in which the future has already arrived without remainder. The present is given new significance in light of a future that is expected. It is eschatology in the process of being realised.[24] In its healing of the sick and exorcising of demons, Jesus' ministry has an inaugural quality, occasioning celebration in those who respond positively: 'As long as they have the bridegroom with them, they cannot fast' (Mark 2:19). If the content of the future necessarily remains

---

[21] Oliver O'Donovan argues in this context that the church's attitude to the Roman state could take two forms, both of which are found in the New Testament. Secular government could find a provisional authority by providing the conditions under which Christian mission was to be enacted or else it could be provoked into an assertion of itself in hostile reaction to the church: 'Either way the victory of Christ was the key to the relation'; *The Desire of the Nations* (Cambridge: Cambridge University Press, 1996), 156–7.

[22] E.g. John Dominic Crossan, *The Historical Jesus: the Life of a Mediterranean Jewish Peasant* (San Francisco: HarperCollins, 1991). For a recent reassertion of the eschatological Jesus in response to this movement see Dale C. Allison, *Jesus of Nazareth: Millenarian Prophet* (Minneapolis: Fortress Press, 1998).

[23] John Meier has concluded that 'the advantage and appeal of the domesticated Jesus is obvious: he is instantly relevant to and usable by contemporary ethics, homilies, political programs, and ideologies of various stripes . . . Yet, for better or for worse, this strange marginal Jew; this eschatological prophet and miracle-worker, *is* the historical Jesus retrievable by modern historical methods applied soberly to the data'; *A Marginal Jew*, vol. II (New York: Doubleday, 1994), 1045.

[24] Ben F. Meyer, *The Aims of Jesus* (London: SCM, 1979), 249.

indeterminate, its signs include healing, liberation and friendship for those who are oppressed in a range of ways. These are signs of the coming dominion of God and response to Jesus determines how one will fare in the future.

One may argue that Jesus expected the imminent end of the world and was mistaken in this respect. There are some passages in the New Testament that appear to support this view, for example Mark 9:1. In his early writings Paul also may have expected the world to end in his own lifetime (1 Thess. 4:17), only to revise this expectation in his later work (Phil. 3:10–11). But, whatever the perceived timetable of events for Jesus and the early Christians, the relationship of present to future is structurally unaltered. The present is never understood to be simply a pause, a momentary delay or an interval of suspended animation before the irruption of the divine rule and the creation of another world. For Jesus, the present is an occasion for living the new life in anticipation of the future. There is thus a present transformed and a future expected regardless of specific dates. Moreover, it is not the task of the prophet to perceive the precise form of the future through an act of clairvoyance. By the use of symbol and image, the will of God is interpreted and held forth, but it remains for future generations to determine in exactly what ways this has been fulfilled. This might explain why the early Christians robustly maintained the eschatological side of Jesus' teaching while remaining puzzled by the delay of the *parousia*. The resurrection, the birth of the church, the failure to convert all Israel and the continuation of historical processes over the long haul may not have been clearly foreseen in the ministry of either Jesus or his earliest followers. But subsequent believers could perceive in these events the fulfilment of the divine purpose. Ben Meyer writes,

The most historically charged event of late antiquity was the entry of Mediterranean Gentiles into the Christian movement. It was not, then, through a pilgrimage to Zion that Gentiles would come into the eschatological heritage of Israel; it was rather through an energetic missionary movement that this was already beginning to come about! To the eye of faith the visionary imagery of Jesus was being translated into time, place, and action by the world mission.[25]

---

[25] Ibid., 247.

The reign of God proclaimed by Jesus, moreover, has political overtones. The restoration of Israel is foreshadowed in the calling of twelve disciples. It is a new community that is already formed, one that is continued in the life of the church. And this community in its life and witness implicitly reverses many of the regnant assumptions about status, power and destiny in Graeco-Roman society. The figure of Jesus himself is crucial in this new *polis*. He proclaims God's rule, calls others to follow him, offers divine forgiveness, instructs his followers in prayer and moral precept, and finally enters Jerusalem in fulfilment of messianic prophecy.

The crucifixion under Pontius Pilate, as has already been argued, demands a criticism of all political action. Jesus' resurrection from the dead, pivotal for all the New Testament writings, is not an isolated event for him alone. With its connection to the expected dominion of God, it is fundamental to the church, the people to whom he is present. The risen and exalted Christ is thus the agent of God's future (1 Cor. 15: 20–8), the one who guarantees not so much personal survival and immortality, as the establishment of God's new creation.[26] This too is known and celebrated in the present, while providing the context for Christian moral insight and effort.

In all these respects, the life, death and resurrection of Jesus are politically significant. This of course cannot be seen in terms of initiating a revolutionary programme of resistance, of mounting a campaign of political action, let alone overthrow of Roman rule. Neither the means nor the resources for any of this were available. Nonetheless, as Christopher Rowland puts it, 'there is enough evidence to discern the contours of a different kind of polity which differed sufficiently to lead to a challenge to current arrangements and which consisted of the controversial assertion on his part of the right to articulate that difference'.[27]

In evaluating the politics of Jesus, much discussion focuses upon that ambivalent saying at Mark 12:17 and parallels (Matt. 22:21; Luke

---

[26] The integral connection of Jesus' resurrection to the expectation of a new age is usefully explored by John Muddiman, 'The Resurrection of Jesus as the Coming of the Kingdom – the Basis of Hope for the Transformation of the World', in Robin Barbour (ed.), *The Kingdom of God and Human Society* (Edinburgh: T. & T. Clark, 1993), 208–23.

[27] Christopher Rowland, 'Reflections on the Politics of the Gospels', in Barbour (ed.), *The Kingdom of God and Human Society*, 239.

20:25), 'Render to Caesar the things that are Caesar's, and to God the things that are God's.' This text has been used in diverse ways in the history of the church whether to justify political quietism, the Lutheran two-kingdoms doctrine or even revolution. Its original context is in response to the practical problem of paying the tribute tax, an additional form of direct taxation given by Palestinians to their Roman overlords. The denarius is a Roman coin which Jesus displays, thus suggesting that the Romans were to be paid in Roman money. Should this tax be paid? Does it imply allegiance to Caesar and the Romans who have occupied the Holy Land? And if payment is refused will this not shatter the uneasy peace that has been established? Jesus' response is to point to the coin with the image of Caesar's head, and then to offer his cryptic remark.

What does he mean? Perhaps we can approach this by looking at what he did not say. His answer would have disappointed revolutionary or sectarian trends within first-century Judaism. We are to render to Caesar. This was not easily consistent with either withdrawal from or outright resistance to the secular powers. On the other hand, obligations to Caesar and God are not to be perceived in a kind of equilibrium or equal measure. The money is Caesar's. Yet elsewhere Jesus is rather negative about money. Caesar may have the money; he can be given his coins. But more important is to give God what is due. This would be evident to a Jewish audience familiar with the first commandment. You shall have no other gods before me. 'What belongs to God is much more likely to mean the dedication of one's whole life: the seeking of his kingdom and righteousness. Obedience to God's will is not compromised by letting Caesar have the money which bears his name.'[28]

The fact that these loyalties can and often do compete also falsifies a bland spiritualising of this passage. This is a besetting temptation. Merely to assign to Caesar material goods and to God spiritual goods does not capture the force of the saying. Had this been Jesus' intention, the question of the Pharisees and Herodians would have lacked its potential to entrap. They already recognised the tension between the claims of the divine rule and the existing political order. What we

---

[28] F. F. Bruce, 'Render to Caesar', in E. Bammel (ed.), *Jesus and the Politics of His Day* (Cambridge: Cambridge University Press, 1984), 261.

have here is not so much a distinction between two discrete realms as a guide for assessing competitive claims.[29] The potential for conflict is always present, even though it is neither desired nor necessary. The inevitable prioritising of God's claim for a Jewish audience situates the subordinate and limited claims of Caesar. In different circumstances, this provides a range of interpretations but each proceeds from the primacy of God's claim upon us. Caesar's coins have their place; but our attitude to them should be determined by their relation to the divine priority.[30] What is clearly out of the question is any reading of the text that offers a spiritual constriction of the Christian faith by dissociating the religious and the secular as separate and essentially unrelated spheres.

THE FIRST CHRISTIANS

Two features of the ministry of Jesus are particularly significant in understanding how the early church viewed the civil authorities. His intention was not to overthrow the Roman state and to supplant it with an alternative *polis* in Palestine. Yet the eschatological commonwealth proclaimed, expected and enacted in Jesus' ministry is one in which the political hopes of Israel are fulfilled. In interpreting Christ as the fulfilment of Jewish hopes, the early Christians expected a polity that would realise the ideals of psalmist and prophets. In this rule, the earth would be transfigured, the nations would bow before God, and a time of healing and harmony would begin. In confessing the risen Christ as Lord, therefore, the church encounters the state in two ways. On the one hand, it seeks neither to overthrow nor to replace the state. It remains for the time being and can contribute in its own way by establishing the conditions for the enactment of the church's mission. Furthermore, in the limited and provisional terms outlined in Romans 13 and elsewhere, it may also contribute to the present anticipation of God's just rule. On the other hand, the church as a community already assumes some of the features

---

[29] This is argued by John Howard Yoder, *The Politics of Jesus*, 2nd edition (Grand Rapids: Eerdmans, 1994), 44.

[30] This is broadly the interpretation favoured by N. T. Wright, *Jesus and the Victory of God* (London: SPCK, 1996), 502–7 and Walter E. Pilgrim, *Uneasy Neighbors: Church and State in the New Testament* (Minneapolis: Fortress Press, 1999), 64–72.

of a new *polis*. The social and economic relationships between its members are transformed. Their highest allegiance is to this community as the household of God. They have another king, Jesus, who is risen, ascended and now present in their midst through the Holy Spirit. Their new citizenship *(politeuma)* is in heaven (Phil. 3:20). It is within the theological tension created by these two features of the early Christian context – a tension similar to that felt by Jewish communities throughout the Diaspora – that Christian attitudes to the state had to be articulated.

From this same fundamental attitude to the civic authorities, the Book of Revelation offers its perspective on the demonic possibilities of political rule. Where Christians are faced with the command to worship the emperor and conform to the social and economic standards of a corrupt culture, faith demands resistance. Any transference of categories from Christ to Caesar is in breach of the first commandment. Here the condemnation of the state and all its attendant offices and practices arises not so much from a different political theology as from the same fundamental subordination of human society to the rule of God, but in different circumstances. Whatever its Manichaean leanings, Revelation presents, presumably in the context of late first-century Domitian persecution, a critique of a state that arrogates to itself divine authority and oppresses the followers of Christ. The call for faithful witness, endurance and resistance is a valid expression of Jesus' earlier injunction to give to God those things that are God's. A necessary component of the canon, the description of the state in Revelation 13 is a cautionary reminder of the ever-present possibility for corruption in the wielding of political power.

In preserving the dominical saying about the respective claims of Caesar and God, the early church resisted the temptations of withdrawal and assimilation. By doing so, it developed a theology positioned between these polar opposites. Analysis of the early Christians in urban context reveals them to belong to different social groups. Many came from a Jewish background, while some had wealth and property. Wayne Meeks has suggested that many converts were those who suffered from 'status inconsistency' or 'status dissonance'.[31] This

---

[31] Wayne Meeks, *The First Urban Christians: the Social World of the Apostle Paul* (New Haven: Yale University Press, 1983), 22ff.

occurs when the categories by which social status is measured in the Graeco-Roman world are in some persons present in contradictory ways. Thus a person may be wealthy but of low rank, educated but a slave, or exercising a powerful role but female. Status inconsistency tends to occur when one's achievements (e.g. wealth, education or profession) are in tension with one's inherited status (e.g. race, sex or birth). A number of Paul's converts can be viewed as experiencing this conflictual identity. These included women of considerable means, wealthy Jews in a pagan society, educated free persons who were stigmatised by their former slavery, and Gentiles who had attached themselves to the synagogue without becoming fully integrated into Judaism.

While this socially dissonant group may be difficult to quantify, their presence in the church conveniently illustrates for us the tensions that early Christians felt between their loyalty to Christ and the church on the one side, and their obligations to the state and civil society on the other. Already conscious of the ways in which their lives defy conventional stereotypes, they convert to a faith that further accentuates these tensions. This is reflected in a range of New Testament passages. Tending to advocate, where possible, peaceful coexistence with the civil community, these also admit the prospect of friction and the encounter of outright hostility.

Most significant is Romans 13:1–7. One could provide an account of church–state relations on the basis of the history of the interpretation of this passage. Positions ranging from quietism to armed resistance have been advocated by appeal to these verses. Yet here again context is crucial to any correct understanding of Paul's exhortation. In his commentary, James Dunn makes much of the connection with the moral advice of the previous chapter, the Jewish antecedents of Paul's teaching, and the socio-political context in Rome.[32] Paul is writing to a small Christian community that is conscious of imperial power. The expulsion of Jews from Rome some years earlier would be in the mind of Paul and his readers. The demand for loyal conduct is partly driven by a desire to avoid a fresh edict. Hence the moral advice of Romans 12:18 is to live peaceably with all so far as it depends upon one. This is now taken up in the discussion of attitudes towards the

[32] J. D. G. Dunn, *Romans* (Texas: Word Books, 1988), 759ff.

political authorities. In maintaining that the justification for political obedience resides in the institution of the authorities by God, Paul is repeating a Jewish tradition already noted. Power derives from God and is admitted to human agencies for divinely appointed ends: 'By me kings reign, and rulers decree what is just; by me rulers rule and nobles, all who govern rightly' (Prov. 8:15–16). Although no account of the legitimate and illegitimate uses of civic power is developed by Paul, there must be implied here the thought that since power is held under the rule of God there is a right and a wrong use of it for which earthly rulers come under divine judgement. This is already the conclusion of Wisdom 6:4–5 and the dramatic narrative of Daniel 5, where the mysterious writing on the wall reveals that Belshazzar has been weighed on the scales and found wanting.[33]

Although Romans 13 appears politically quietist to some read-ers, the context of the preceding chapter indicates otherwise. At the opening of Romans 12, we read of the renewing of the mind in accor-dance with the will of God. Conformity with this world is set aside. Furthermore, the prospect of persecution is firmly in view in verses 14–21, which echo the teaching of Jesus in Matthew 5:16. Here a pattern emerges in which persecution and a declaration of civil loy-alty stand together. By eschewing sedition, Christians testify to the purity of their lifestyle. Thus their light shines before the world and they are vindicated in the sight of God.[34] This pattern is evident in the post-canonical period, for example in the martyrdom of Polycarp. In standing before the proconsul, he acknowledges that although he is taught to give all due honour to the authorities he will refuse to revile Christ before the mob.[35]

Admittedly, the argumentation of Paul is more philosophical and less christological in this portion of the text. This has even led some commentators to question its authenticity. However, the prevailing view is that its presence in the earliest manuscripts, its use by Irenaeus

---

[33] This tradition is outlined by Pilgrim, *Uneasy Neighbors*, 22–6.

[34] This is argued by Luise Schottroff, '"Give to Caesar What Belongs to Caesar and to God What Belongs to God": a Theological Response of the Early Christian Church to Its Social and Political Environment', in Willard M. Swartley (ed.), *The Love of Enemy and Nonretaliation in the New Testament* (Louisville: John Knox Press, 1992), 157–76.

[35] *Martyrdom of Polycarp*, 10.

at the end of the second century, its resonance with Jewish themes, and its coherence with the ethical injunctions of the previous chapter confirm its Pauline authorship.[36] Significant in this context is that Paul nowhere refers specifically to the state, the emperor or Roman power, unlike 1 Peter 2:13–15.[37] The vocabulary is more generally that of Hellenistic administration. The concept of the authorities in 13:1ff. (*exousiai*) refers to Roman officials; 'rulers' in 13:3 (*archontes*) is a reference to the local authorities rather than to the central political state; while 'servants' in 13:6 (*leitourgoi*) denote the representative of any administrative body. This linguistic range suggests that Paul's intention is not to outline a metaphysical doctrine of the political state and the obligations owed to it. Instead we are presented with a range of officials and institutions which under divine providence are capable of exercising some civic good. In maintaining their faith, Christians are urged to recognise the role assigned to them by God. As they must live peaceably with all where possible, so they should submit to those civil authorities that exercise their legitimate divine role. This is a low-key, qualified, but nonetheless positive account of the capacity of the civic realm.[38]

Elsewhere in Paul, the use of imperial rhetoric to articulate the claims of the Christian faith suggests a running criticism of secular constructions of power and authority. This imperial hinterland of Pauline theology may have been obscured by scholarly concentration on his controversy with Judaism. Yet, as has been pointed out, the opening contrast in Romans is between the justice of God and the corruption of human society, not between Jewish and Christian self-understandings. Like other Jewish sources, Paul's letter is 'a defiant

---

[36] E.g. Joseph Fitzmyer, *Romans* (London: Chapman, 1992), 664.

[37] Here I am following Ernst Käsemann, *Romans* (Grand Rapids: Eerdmans, 1980), 353. Käsemann is at pains throughout to argue against any metaphysical doctrine of the state advanced in terms of natural law or orders of creation. Nevertheless, the reference to the power of the sword presumably indicates that the state is not excluded from the scope of Paul's reference.

[38] Neil Elliot argues that its context is one in which Paul seeks to prevent any fresh outbreak of persecution upon vulnerable Jews and Jewish Christians in Rome. The avoidance of desperate resistance reflects both the eschatological hope of the church and also the injunction to live in the mean time both peacefully and resolutely in the imperial city; 'Romans 13: 1–7 in the Context of Imperial Propaganda', in Richard Horsley (ed.), *Paul and Empire: Religion and Power in Roman Imperial Society* (Harrisburg: Trinity Press International, 1997), 184–204.

indictment of the rampant injustice and impiety of the Roman "golden age"'.[39] In 1 Corinthians, with its contrast between the wisdom of the world and the foolishness of God, Paul rejects the standard strategy of rhetorical persuasion (1:17–20) and refuses to present his own character as proof of his authority (2:1–5). Yet in his discussion of the church in Corinth, Paul uses political concepts and analogies to describe the community into which his readers have been baptised. The discourse of unity, harmony and cooperation is employed, most obviously in the image of the body politic in 12:12ff. The formation of this community on grounds quite distinct from that of civil society provides a set of loyalties and standards which can function critically, as, for example, the refusal to participate in the worship of idols. The one bread and one body of the eucharist require a Christian rejection of pagan sacrifice (10:14–22).

Perhaps even more significant in this context is the use of imperial terms in Paul to characterise the person and work of Jesus.[40] The gospel (*euangelion*) of Jesus contrasts with the imperial good tidings by which the provinces are pacified through military force and celebrated in coins, buildings and festivals. For the church, peace is established only through God's anointed one, crucified by the Roman authorities. The rulers of this age are doomed to destruction (1 Cor. 2:6–8). Now vindicated, exalted and reigning in heaven, Jesus, not the emperor, is the one to whom the highest allegiance is owed (Phil. 2:6–11). From this position of pre-eminence, he will destroy every ruler, authority and power (1 Cor. 15:24).

While this christological transfer of imperial language does not signal a programme of revolutionary uprising against Rome, it does provide a relative weighting of loyalties. Proclaiming the rule of Christ and awaiting patiently its final manifestation, the church has the task of living as a pure, disciplined and godly community. Where possible, recognition is to be accorded to the civil authorities and their capacity in this scheme for obeying the will of God through the

---

[39] Neil Elliot, 'Paul and the Politics of Empire', in Richard Horsley (ed.), *Paul and Politics* (Harrisburg, PA: Trinity Press International, 2000), 37.

[40] Here I have drawn upon Richard A. Horsley, 'Rhetoric and Empire – and I Corinthians', in Horsley (ed.), *Paul and Politics*, 90ff. Horsley argues that 'in his use of key terms and symbols from political public oratory and imperial ideology, Paul was thus proclaiming an alternative gospel of an alternative emperor as well as building an alternative assembly in the city of Corinth'; 91.

promotion of justice. Christians are to live peaceably with others and to bear witness through their virtuous conduct. Yet this sober and qualified description of state authority derives from a prior account of the person and work of Christ, the nature of the church and its eschatological expectation. It is not that these exist in some bipolar relationship to an understanding of the state that proceeds from a semi-independent doctrine of creation. The moral and political dispositions of the Christian are worked out in terms of a commitment to Jesus, membership of the church and expectation of God's final rule.

CONCLUSION

This brief exploration of the Scriptures suggests that for both the Old and the New Testament human life under the rule of God is inescapably political. It has a covenantal, social dimension that is fulfilled not merely by the practice of individual holiness but by the observance of standards of justice. The well-being of individuals cannot be abstracted from the common good. These belong together. An apolitical faith makes no sense at all.

This is combined with a recognition of the necessity of political office and authority whether that be the king of Israel, the Roman emperor or other more local forms of civic rule. Under the providence of God, these afford provisional opportunities for promoting human well-being, including the cause of Jewish communities in the Diaspora and Christian congregations scattered throughout the Roman empire. The impossibility of a religiously unitary society (outside Old Testament Israel) requires some theological coordination of the religious with the civil. Yet this should be understood in terms of a prevailing theological framework informed by the central notion of the rule of God. In this respect, the different practical attitudes to the state in the New Testament can be regarded as reposing upon something approaching a single, consistent theological outlook.

The treatment of secular powers in Scripture should caution us against the assumption that in this domain of theology we are concerned only with two metaphysical entities – the church and the state – both ordained by God and existing in equipoise. While this impression may have been created historically by some standard

Catholic and Protestant theologies of the state, there is little scriptural warrant for it. Unquestionably, there is an array of secular forces – emperors, kings, queens, local rulers, administrative officials, civic bodies, socio-political institutions – yet these are not to be reduced to one single, mystical entity called the state. Moreover, Jewish and Christian loyalties are not fundamentally divided. There is one loyalty to God and therefore to the community under God's rule. By divine grace, secular forces, institutions and rulers may fulfil the will of God and therefore be worthy of support and respect. But acknowledgement of this possibility arises from an undivided loyalty to one end alone. The notion that we have differentiated though correlative duties to God and country is absent from this outlook.

Nonetheless, whatever its potential under providence, each form of secular rule is subject to standards of prophetic criticism and the central example of Jesus before Pilate. For Paul, the reign of the crucified and risen Christ implies a new community by which imperial practices are judged. The sober, almost monotonous criticism of the kings of Israel is transposed into a criticism of the wisdom of the world in 1 Corinthians and the outright rejection of imperial corruption in Revelation. This leads neither to a light-headed escapism from the challenges of the secular realm nor to a Manichaean condemnation of everything outside the ecclesial sphere.

This chapter began by suggesting that the two possibilities of withdrawal or assimilation were caricatures. If this exploration of Jewish and early Christian views is plausible, then it can be shown that both are theologically excluded. In his prison cell Dietrich Bonhoeffer read the Bible from cover to cover, and more thoroughly than at any other time in his life. Near his death in 1944 he wrote: 'The theme of redemption takes us back into the world and its history . . . The Christian has no last line of escape available from earthly tasks and difficulties into the eternal, but, like Christ himself must drink the earthly cup to the dregs . . . This world must not be prematurely written off; in this the Old and New Testaments are at one.'[41]

---

[41] *Letters and Papers from Prison*, 3rd edition enlarged (London: SCM, 1971), 336–7.

CHAPTER TWO

Church and state: theological traditions

When Christianity takes itself seriously, it must either forsake
or master the world and at different points may try to do both
at once.   (Roland Bainton)[1]

EARLY CHURCH TRAJECTORIES

Despite its apparent hyperbole, the above statement reveals trends
and tensions that are deeply embedded in the Scriptures and traditions of the church. The dominion of God demands forms of life
that respond to divine justice and goodness. These, however, are never
fully realised. This generated an eschatological hope that came to be
measured and reassessed by the life and crucifixion of Jesus, now risen,
ascended and present to his community. What arrives in the life of the
church is both an anticipation of the coming rule of God and partial
fulfilment of this by the grace of Christ's resurrection. In this tension
between the now and not yet of Christian existence, there is a perpetual reserve and criticism of all earthly forms, yet also a recognition
that these forms, within their limits, can be providentially ordered.
The church is never without blemish nor is it coextensive with the
world. But by the action of the Spirit both may in surprising ways
conform in some measure to the will of God. In this dialectic setting,
we find theologians of the early church expressing the faith in ways
that reflect their own historical circumstances. With varying degrees
of dissonance, they write about the tensions, competing loyalties and
dispositions of Christian living. Nonetheless, despite obvious differences, much of this early Christian writing on the state and civil life

---

[1] *The Medieval Church* (London: Nostrand, 1962), 42.

arises from a shared theological orientation that can generate attitudes ranging from respect and honour to contempt and outright rejection. In this respect, the early centuries may be little different from the canon. In an attempt to indicate the diverse yet often coherent series of doctrinal reflections, there follows a brief and cursory inspection of patterns of thought from different periods of Christian history.

In the writers of the first four centuries we are faced with what has been called the paradox of alien citizenship. Christians inhabit and contribute in their own way to the *pax Romana*, yet their belonging to the household of faith places them at a critical distance even to the point of alienation. In this respect, commitment to the two polities does not run smoothly in parallel lines. Any position which argues for a strict separation of the spiritual from the temporal must break down. The possibility of conflict is embedded in the contrast between the two polities and the different loyalties they command. In any case, the early church could hardly forget that Christ had been crucified under Pontius Pilate. Points of tension were soon to emerge – the imperial cult, the exposure of infants, sexual morality and military service provided occasions when Christian commitment would collide with the practice of its host society.[2]

'Christians are distinguished from other persons neither by country, nor language, nor the customs which they observe,' writes the anonymous author of the *Epistle to Diognetus*. 'But inhabiting Greek as well as barbarian cities, according as the lot of each of them has determined, and following the customs of the natives in respect to clothing, food, and the rest of their ordinary conduct, they display to us their wonderful and confessedly striking method of life.'[3] In his book *Broken Lights and Mended Lives* Rowan Greer points out that this is never developed into a theory or clear vision of what Christian citizenship involves and he suggests further that this is not something that is ever possible. The paradox can only be displayed in different ways under varying circumstances.[4] Thus Justin and Origen can

---

[2] For a selection of primary sources see Agnes Cunningham (ed.), *The Early Church and the State* (Philadelphia: Fortress Press, 1982).

[3] *Epistle to Diognetus*, 5. All quotations are from the *Ante-Nicene Fathers* translation.

[4] *Broken Lights and Mended Lives: Theology and Common Life in the Early Church* (University Park, PA: Pennsylvania State University Press, 1986), 141–61.

appeal to the moral integrity of Christians when judged by criteria recognised throughout the pagan world. Their lives are not subversive but supportive of the highest standards known and espoused generally: 'Christians are benefactors of their country more than others. For they train up citizens, and inculcate piety to the Supreme Being; and they promote those whose lives in the smallest cities have been good and worthy, to a divine and heavenly city.'[5] Justin and Origen may thus be said to seek the welfare of their cities. Yet in their different ways they make extraordinary sacrifices for the faith – Justin is martyred and Origen leads a life of profound ascetic discipline.

In Tertullian, writing in about 200, the paradox of alien citizenship becomes even more strained. He claims that Christians participate in the economic and social life of the empire and contribute to its well-being. They live virtuous lives, and their intercessions are effective in preserving the peace of the world. Respect is shown towards the emperor whose authority derives from the God of Jesus. Tertullian even claims that 'on valid grounds I might say that Caesar is more ours than yours, for our God has appointed him'.[6] Tertullian's rejection of Gnosticism and his determination to embrace both Old and New Testaments must prevent a simple demonising of secular agencies. There is one God of creation and redemption, of Israel and the church. Tertullian's writings reiterate earlier themes about God's providence, and the potential of political and economic life for divine service. Yet the abiding sense is one of alienation. We become conscious of the witness of the martyrs. The Christian life must escape the pervasive filth and pollution of the pagan world. Military service is perceived to be deeply problematic.[7] Christians are to shun idolatrous activities, astrological speculation, gladiatorial sports, together with a range of trades and professions associated with these. The philosophers have only a partial and imperfect grasp of the truth. They disagree with one another, reach mistaken conclusions and teach immorality. Even Socrates, formerly extolled by Justin, is condemned as demon-possessed.[8] So Tertullian famously asks 'what indeed can Athens have

[5] Origen, *Against Celsus*, 8.74.   [6] Tertullian, *Apology*, 33.
[7] This is discussed in Oliver O'Donovan and Joan Lockwood O'Donovan, *From Irenaeus to Grotius: a Sourcebook in Christian Political Thought* (Grand Rapids: Eerdmans, 1999), 2ff.
[8] *A Treatise on the Soul*, 1.

to do with Jerusalem? What concord is there between the academy and the church? . . . We want no curious disputation after possessing Christ Jesus, no inquisition after enjoying the gospel!'[9] The church is an ark that rescues the faithful from a lost world, and even those within are not safe from shipwreck or from being washed overboard into the suffocating waves.[10]

It is clear that the paradox of alien citizenship is less pronounced by the end of the fourth century. Within a settled social order where the Christian faith, though not unrivalled, is in the ascendant, the threat of violent persecution is reduced. Greer draws attention in this context to the writings of John Chrysostom. There the heavenly commonwealth that awaits us is presented as an ideal by which to measure existing realities. Yet the continuities are now greater. The family, the city and the nation embody the love of God for us and our love of one another. While monastic ideals are able to exercise a critical standard by which to judge secular life, the realisation of a heavenly citizenship on earth is present in a manner hardly conceivable for Tertullian. The example of the martyrs now becomes a hallowed memory celebrated in pilgrimages and homilies.[11]

Greer argues eloquently for the concept of alien citizenship. It creates a positive tension by which the purity of the faith must be maintained while also being translated and adapted to shifting socio-political circumstances. Moreover, the one paradox can blossom in different ways at different times. 'Monk and priest, ruler and private citizen alike have the possibility of living their varied lives in the light of this common vision.'[12] It is an inevitable corollary of faith in Christ's victory and his eschatological rule. Nonetheless, *pace* Greer, it becomes harder in the subsequent history of the church to present the identity of Christians in terms of their status as aliens. At most, 'alien' is a predicate to describe the tensions that arise from maintaining the faith amidst circumstances that can be indifferent, threatening or hostile. In becoming a cosmopolitan and increasingly international movement, Christians cannot be described as 'alien' in any ethnic sense. Admittedly some groups, particularly in the context

---

[9] *On Prescription against Heretics*, 7.   [10] *On Idolatry*, 24.
[11] For an introduction to Chrysostom and a selection of his sermons and writings see Wendy Mayer and Pauline Allen, *John Chrysostom* (London: Routledge, 2000).
[12] Greer, *Broken Lights and Mended Lives*, 160.

of the radical Reformation, could revive scriptural notions of the 'resident alien' by consciously applying this to the ecclesial community. However, most Christians would find it difficult to construct their civic identity in terms of an 'alien' status. Under certain conditions, loyalty to the church creates estrangement; if this is never experienced, that loyalty itself may be questionable. Our baptism into the church is accompanied by obligations and commitments that override those of patriotic loyalty. Nevertheless, there usually remains affection for one's native land, its customs and its institutions. It may be more apt in this context to speak of a subordinated or stratified citizenship, instead of an alien identity.[13]

The discipline and integrity of Tertullian's position as representative of the martyr church are often compared favourably with the post-Constantinian world of church–state relations.[14] At or shortly before the battle at Milvian Bridge in 312, the conversion of the emperor has been portrayed as a watershed at which the church lost its former purity and integrity.[15] In the tribute of Eusebius to Constantine on the thirtieth anniversary of his accession to the throne we are presented with a vision in which, to use Bainton's expression, the church has mastered the world. One might equally well say that the world has mastered the church. The reign of God is now universally acknowledged. The whole of society is ordered according to the wisdom of the faith. As there is one God and one Logos, so there is one emperor and one empire throughout the earth. The present is compared favourably to the past. The establishment of Christianity is the goal which early generations sought. Drawing upon Origen's thought that the Roman empire providentially supplied the conditions for the successful spread of the faith throughout the world, Eusebius notes that it has now been achieved. This view is sometimes thought to be normative for every national church. The fusion of church and state in the civil order is thus traced back to the Constantinian settlement, often with the result that Constantinianism takes its place in today's great roll-call of heresies.

---

[13] I owe this point to conversation with Nicholas Wolterstorff.
[14] E.g. Alistair Kee, *Constantine Versus Christ: the Triumph of Ideology* (London: SCM, 1982).
[15] For a historical interpretation of Constantine and his reception in the writings of Eusebius see Timothy D. Barnes, *Constantine and Eusebius* (Cambridge, MA: Harvard University Press, 1981).

It can be plausibly argued, however, that in the history of the early church the position of Eusebius is strikingly egregious. In claiming that the emperor bears the image of the Word of God in a pre-eminent way by which he can rightly exercise divine sovereignty on earth, Eusebius flouts all the cautionary words in the Hebrew Bible about kingship and its need to be regulated by the law and the prophets. The king is only one other human being, susceptible to error and prone to sin. The political reserve that this demands is entirely absent in the eulogy to Constantine. Imported into Christian doctrine, we have here something akin to the imperial cult of paganism.[16] One has also to recognise that much subsequent reflection on the church–state relationship was not seduced by this way of thinking. In this respect, it can be seen as an aberration from the Christian mainstream.

A deflation of the Eusebian view is found in Augustine's mature theological reflections on the relationship between the earthly and the heavenly cities. Yet his early political theory tends to follow more classical lines. In emphasising the divine order that is mediated throughout the cosmos by a range of institutions, Augustine is able at this juncture to blend theories from classical writers with the types of argument that we can find in Origen and Eusebius. The tradition of Plato and Aristotle emphasises the importance of the *polis* in the essential order of things. It is only within the properly ordered city state that human beings can flourish and together achieve their essential well-being. While the great philosophers may have differed in their perceptions of this order, they nonetheless offer a positive account of political authority as making a necessary contribution to the good of all citizens. In stressing the concept of order, doubtless influenced by his neo-Platonist leanings, Augustine locates secular power in a cosmic system which flows downwards in a series of hierarchies from God. This tradition of Hellenistic thought is shared by Eusebius and enables philosophical ideas of order to be integrated with the notion of a Christian emperor exercising the rule of the divine Logos throughout the earth. In his study of secular power in Augustine, Robert

---

[16] Greer stresses the despoiling of pagan themes in Eusebius' panegyric; *Broken Lights and Mended Lives*, 151.

Markus is able to show how this train of thought is characteristic of his theology until the late 390s.[17]

Thereafter, however, other themes begin to dominate Augustine's political thought. These arise from his immersion in Scripture, his sense of the church as the community of the elect gathered across the ages, and the doctrine of sin that emerges in the Pelagian controversy.[18] Although the *City of God* was written following the sacking of Rome by Alaric's Goths in 410 and in the face of apparent imperial collapse, these developments in Augustine's work were already under way at least a decade earlier. Here the notion of the state as a restraining ordinance is presented. Political forces were incapable of producing societies in which human fulfilment could be achieved. Individual happiness could not be secured by moral and social endeavour. At most, secular forces could minimise disorder by restraining the worst effects of sin and evil. This would often be done through brutality and violence. Although necessary, political power is inevitably compromised and of limited value. Subordination to the authorities is here constructed along post-lapsarian lines. As slavery represents the control of one person by another so political rule is an aspect of our concupiscent condition. Instead of the natural order of the paterfamilias, social relations are distorted and dependent upon force. While this does not place them outside the scope of divine providence, the relation of political rulers and subjects must inevitably be situated within the disordered and fractured world of Adam's descendants. There now recedes from view the idea that human law images the divine law. The earthly legislator works in the dark where compromises must be made, errors committed and regret for decisions experienced, even in the most peaceable of states. Although sometimes

---

[17] Robert A. Markus, *Saeculum: History and Society in the Theology of St Augustine* (Cambridge: Cambridge University Press, 1970), 72ff.

[18] John Rist also sees Augustine's more realistic political theology as reflecting his personal experience of North African Roman culture: 'If the culture of classical Athens forms the background to Platonic and Aristotelian beliefs about the educational role of the better human societies, the bleak and brutal hierarchies of Roman North Africa are the setting for Augustine's more pessimistic estimation of the edifying power of the state'; *Augustine: Ancient Thought Baptized* (Cambridge: Cambridge University Press, 1994), 225. For further discussion of Augustine's political theory in relation to his classical predecessors see Janet Coleman, *A History of Political Thought from Ancient Greece to Early Christianity* (Oxford: Blackwell, 2000).

justified, the evils of war must be acknowledged.[19] We find in the *City of God* a curiously modern unmasking of the weaknesses and limits of all secular power, however wisely executed. The disorder within the human soul is magnified in societies, each an arena for competing interests, greed and lust for power. As Rist suggests, the 'implication for political science is that Augustine is concerned not with the best regime . . . in the classical manner, but with the basic flaws that must be discerned in each and every form of political society'.[20]

The city of God (*civitas Dei*), to which Christians belong, is an eschatological polity to which we are called by baptism into the church. In its task of preparing souls for the city of God, the church nevertheless makes use of the peace of the earthly city (*civitas terrena*). Secular power has a place within the divine economy. It makes its contribution to the true peace of the heavenly city. As a restraining ordinance that controls the worst excesses of evil and sin, the secular is used by God, and Christians are enjoined to seek the peace of the city not so much on account of self-preservation as through love of their neighbours.

There is much of enduring value in this account. The critical reading of secular power and the recognition of its necessity and value offer an alternative to the Eusebian account that resonates with earlier patristic and biblical themes. Later theologians, as we shall see, were able to draw upon this Augustinian tradition in ways that could check political excess. The account presented here is able to situate both state and church within an overarching theological scheme embracing election, creation, fall, redemption and eschatology. Augustine does not merely seek to position the church in relation to the state, but offers a comprehensive theological vision in which the purpose and contribution of each can be understood in relation to the other. This distinguishing of the functions of church and state was to prove significant in the Middle Ages, particularly in the Christian West, where the Augustinian tradition provided a conceptual framework that prevented the fusion of secular and ecclesiastical power. The offices of pope and emperor remain distinct; the Gelasian formula indeed argued that the roles of priest and king were combined uniquely by Christ and that it is thereafter impossible for anyone

---

[19] *City of God*, 19.5–7.   [20] *Augustine: Ancient Thought Baptized*, 217.

else to hold both offices. Their reunion awaits the coming of Christ again. Therefore, a separation of the two is an eschatological sign that acknowledges the fallibility of human beings and the need for the division of power. Today we might describe this as a system of checks and balances.

On the other hand, the weaknesses of the Augustinian account are at least twofold. The limiting of legitimate secular force to a restraining function is too restrictive; its capacity for promoting social good and thus in its own way anticipating the divine rule tends to be downplayed by the account of sin and eschatology offered. If not ignored, the more positive possibilities of divine rule mediated by political agencies, as outlined, for example, in the Psalms of enthronement and in much of the Wisdom literature, are overwhelmed by the doctrine of the Fall. The refusal to construct political authority as part of our divinely intended natural state represents a departure from aspects of Hebrew thought, and not just the classical tradition. A further weakness, ironically in light of the foregoing, is that Augustine attaches too much to the legitimacy of political force in dealing with Christian heresy. The dominical injunction to compel people to come in (Luke 14:23) is used to coerce non-compliant Donatists. Under specified circumstances, state persecution becomes a legitimate instrument for the promotion of the Catholic church. Pressure can enable one to recognise what has been overlooked and may thus be the cause of genuine conversion.[21] This argument would be used later in the forceful suppression of heretics by the church.

THE *BONUM COMMUNE* IN THE MIDDLE AGES

The charting of political thought throughout the Middle Ages is well beyond the scope of this study, not to mention the competence of its writer, yet the development of a cluster of significant ideas in the thirteenth and fourteenth centuries requires some comment. The

---

[21] '[T]he Lord Himself bids the guests in the first instance to be invited to His great supper, and afterwards compelled'; Augustine, *Letter 185 (Treatise Concerning the Correction of the Donatists)*, 7.24. On whether Augustine's advocacy of coercion is inconsistent with his political theology see the excellent discussion of the proposals of Robert Markus and John Milbank in John R. Bowlin, 'Augustine on Justifying Coercion', *Annual of the Society of Christian Ethics* 17 (1997), 49–70.

rediscovery of Aristotle was one factor in producing an account of political society that offered a more positive vision than that projected by Augustine. Although not to be neglected, the restraining function of the state was not exhaustive. As a political animal, the human person naturally entered into a network of social relations with other persons. Without the knowledge, practices and goods made possible by these exchanges, human fulfilment could not be attained. This generates the important notion of the common good (*bonum commune*) and also a richer, more stratified account of political society that accommodates a range of intermediate communities between the level of the monarch and that of the family.

Thomas Aquinas, following Aristotle's *Politics*, notes that human beings, more than all the other animals, are naturally social and political. The companionship of fellow humans is required to secure the necessities of life. Furthermore, knowledge is acquired not so much through instinct as through cultural transmission, so that the practical science of politics must be considered an art.[22] Citing supportive texts from the wisdom literature of the Old Testament, he can claim that political rule is necessary for human companionship and cooperation to flourish.[23] The purpose of government is to lead human persons to those social goods that are essential to their nature. Consequently, there is provided a standard by which just and unjust political rule can be measured. In favouring kingship as the best form of government, Aquinas deploys familiar theological arguments that perceive in a single, personal authority the image of the divine monarchy over the whole cosmos. Nonetheless, the end served by the earthly monarch is that of the common good.

The key concept of the common good is explicated by Aquinas in different ways, for example with reference to related notions such as order and justice. It is clear in all this that the common good is reducible neither to the interest of the collective nor to an aggregate of individual interests. It is a concept that expresses the underlying conviction that the end of each person is fulfilled only where a range of social goods is realised. In the shared enjoyment of these social goods,

---

[22] 'Commentary on the Politics of Aristotle, Book One', in *Selected Political Writings*, ed. A. P. D'Entrèves (Oxford: Blackwell, 1959), 195–7.

[23] See 'On Princely Government', 1.1 in *Selected Political Writings*, ed. D'Entrèves, 3. Only the first book of this treatise is now regarded as authentic.

the well-being of individual persons is fulfilled. (Since our political life is subordinated finally to our supernatural end, Aquinas' theology can avoid a state absolutism in which the existence of the individual is submerged within corporate existence.) At its best, this blending of individual and corporate goods affirms the significance of the person whose identity and *telos* cannot be described without recourse to social categories. In promoting that common good, political society may thus exercise a role in fulfilling the divine law and expressing God's providence in ways that go beyond the more negative characterisation in Augustine's *City of God*, although even here the peace created by the earthly city is not without some value.

Aquinas' more positive reading of political society needs to be contextualised within the circumstances of European society in the mid-thirteenth century. For Thomas, the organic unity of church and political society is settled and affirmed in his writings. There is a consonance of interest and a coordination of temporal and spiritual functions as each serves the divine law. In this respect, the temporal must serve the spiritual just as the body serves the soul, while kings in Christendom must remain subject to the Pope as to Christ himself.[24] While recognising that faith cannot be coerced by political force, Aquinas reasons that infidels may sometimes be resisted by warfare in order to prevent their placing obstacles in the way of Christian faith. Those baptised into the faith may also require to be corrected by physical coercion if other means fail.[25] And heretics incapable of reform should be executed for the safe provision of others who may be eternally harmed.[26] In this social vision, Jews, although tolerated, do not have the status of full members of the community.[27] However, Aquinas recognises that, in so far as political rule is natural and necessary for human well-being, some forms of pagan rule may be lawful: 'The distinction between the faithful and the infidel, considered in itself, does not invalidate the government and dominion of infidels over the faithful.'[28] This argument was impressively deployed by Francisco de Vitoria, an early sixteenth-century Spanish Dominican theologian, to defend the legitimacy of those forms of government

---

[24] *Summa Theologiae*, 2a2ae, 60.6.   [25] *Summa Theologiae*, 2a2ae, 10.8.
[26] *Summa Theologiae*, 2a2ae, 11.3.
[27] 'On the Government of Jews', in *Selected Political Writings*, ed. D'Entrèves, 85–95.
[28] *Summa Theologiae*, 2a2ae, 10.11.

found amongst American Indians but already threatened by imperial expansion.[29] It might also be noted that this position effectively challenges the high papal assumption of Innocent III that the regal authority derives its dignity from the pontifical.[30]

The concept of the common good and the contribution made to it by political society remains. It provides a valuable resource for contemporary Catholic social teaching and one that resonates with insights already taught by Scripture. It is significant, moreover, that the recovery of Aristotle coincides with a stronger sense of community and civil society in the second half of the Middle Ages. Rarely present in the political literature of the early Middle Ages, the concept of *communitas* is used to describe a variety of forms at a level between national or imperial powers and those individuals whom they govern. The *communitas* can denote the whole population of a town but also an association that is based upon the taking of an oath.[31] This led to a proliferation of forms and an increasingly loose and varied use of the term. By the fourteenth century a variety of communes had emerged in the form of craft corporations, colleges, confraternities and professional associations. These tended to construct their identity on the basis of quasi-theological language drawn from familiar descriptions of the church and its monastic traditions. Both a widespread awareness of group identity and also a desire on the part of individual citizens to manage and govern themselves in these communal forms

---

[29] '[T]he barbarians undoubtedly possessed as true dominion, both public and private, as any Christians. That is to say, they could not be robbed of their property either as private citizens or as princes, on the grounds that they were not true masters. It would be harsh to deny to them, who have never done us any wrong, the rights we concede to Saracens and Jews'; Francisco de Vitoria, 'On the American Indians', Question One, Conclusion, in *Political Writings*, ed. Anthony Pagden and Jeremy Lawrence (Cambridge: Cambridge University Press, 1991), 250–1.

[30] 'Just as the founder of the universe established two great lights in the firmament of heaven, the greater light to rule the day, and the lesser light to rule the night, so too He set two great dignities in the firmament of the universal church . . . the greater one to rule the day, that is, souls, and the lesser to rule the night, that is, bodies. These dignities are the papal authority and the royal power. Now just as the moon derives its light from the sun and is indeed lower than it in quantity and quality, in position and in power, so too the royal power derives the splendour of its dignity from the pontifical authority'; 'Letter to the prefect Acerbius and the nobles of Tuscany' (1198). This is reproduced at http://www.fordham.edu/halsall/source/innIII-policies.html.

[31] Here I am following Jeannine Quillet, 'Community, Counsel and Representation', in J. H. Burns (ed.), *Cambridge History of Medieval Political Thought c. 350–c. 1450* (Cambridge: Cambridge University Press, 1988), 520–72.

are now generated. This offers the possibility of a richer and more complex relationship between church and society. The church is no longer to be related simply to the monarch but also to a web of inter-related social groups, organisations and institutions that shape the lives of individual citizens in ways that are capable of promoting the common good. At the same time, these groups and organisations are themselves shaped in important ways by church practice and tradition. As I shall argue later, this has potential for development in a post-Christendom context in which the organic unity of church and state has disintegrated.

Accompanying this social development is a new emphasis upon popular sovereignty in writers such as John of Paris, Marsilius of Padua, Duns Scotus and William of Ockham. The political community serves its members by seeking to advance the common good. In doing so, it has legitimate powers to form and enact laws, to appoint and advise its rulers, and even to remove them should they threaten the very existence of the societies they ought to serve. Power is perceived to reside within the political community as a whole under the rule of God; it is not mediated from above, as it were, by a chain of command linking God first to the church, and then through the church to the secular monarch.[32] Particularly in the work of Marsilius, this leads to a curbing of papal power and a greater separation of religious and civic functions. The needs of civil orders are best met by strong secular rule, free of ecclesiastical interference. This is coupled with the argument that ecclesiastical rule is likewise to be exercised on the basis of popular will, that is, the whole community of believers.[33] While these models of popular sovereignty were also pressed into the service of an integrated social vision in which individuals, communities, societies, rulers and church all served a single divine purpose, they would later provide important resources for explaining political legitimacy in societies that could be considered pre-Christian, non-Christian or post-Christian.

There emerges from this an account of political authority that resonates with scriptural themes and that continues to commend

---

[32] A selection of writings from the key thinkers of this period together with a useful introduction is found in O'Donovan, *The Desire of the Nations*, 389–548.

[33] Marsilius of Padua, *Defensor Pacis*, translated and introduced by Alan Gewirth (Toronto: University of Toronto Press, 1980).

itself in the modern period. Power derives from God, and is to be exercised responsibly in accordance with divine law. Since its proper use is directed towards the common good, it is best ratified by the consent of all the community. While the people can acknowledge and even control the legitimate use of political power, they neither create it nor alter its function. Its creation and purpose are already established by God.

REFORMATIONS: MAGISTERIAL AND RADICAL

In the early Middle Ages, the Gelasian formula, although distinguishing temporal and spiritual rule, perceives these to be coordinated in a single organic whole. Here the priority is given to the spiritual rule and, *ipso facto*, the offices of the church. The Justinian code similarly coordinates the roles of priest and politician but tends to assert a hierarchy that works in favour of imperial power.[34] In adopting elements of these frameworks, while also introducing a stronger sense of individual freedom and religious tolerance, Luther can be viewed as providing a transition between the political thought of the late Middle Ages and the early modern period.

Neither his most original nor his best, Luther's political writings nonetheless provide an important example of the attitudes displayed by the magisterial Reformers in the sixteenth century. The assertion of religious liberty and the spiritual independence of the church are enunciated by Luther in the face of civil threats to the Reformation movement. Yet these are balanced by a need for state support. What we find in Luther are arguments that look curiously modern but are set within an Augustinian framework. These are blended with medieval assumptions which argue that the just ruler has a duty to maintain the security and well-being of the church.

Especially after his excommunication by the papacy in 1521, Luther depended upon the civil protection and patronage of Frederick the

---

[34] 'If the priesthood is above reproach from any quarter and stands before God with confidence, and if the imperial authority organizes the commonwealth committed to it rightly and fittingly, there will be a balanced harmony to ensure whatever may be of value to the human race'; Justinian, Novella 6, 'On the Selection of Bishops, Presbyters, and Male and Female Deacons and the Penalties for Departing from the Procedure Herein Prescribed', cited in O'Donovan, *The Desire of the Nations*, 194.

Wise, Elector of Saxony. In an address of the previous year, 'To the Christian Nobility of the German Nation', he urged the emperor and princes of Germany to reform the church. This was a plea for liberation from ecclesiastical tyranny, and it required civil support for its implementation. Luther it seems had greater confidence in the ability of the state than in the church of his day to be an instrument of divine agency. (He has not been the only person in the employment of the church to have held this view.) What Luther desired was the reform of Christendom, the whole of the civilised Christian world, rather than the mere creation and protection of a new church. This goal was shared with the other magisterial Reformers and sets them apart from the radicals who sought either the takeover of the civil authorities, or a greater separation.

Luther's most explicit teaching on political authority is found in the short treatise 'Von Weltlicher Oberkeit' (On Secular Authority) published in 1523. This work was prompted by the Duke of Saxony's prohibition in 1522 on the buying and selling of Luther's translation of the New Testament. As a consequence, there are some sharp criticisms of the limits of political authority and a vigorous defence of religious toleration, a cause which Luther did not always champion, it must be said. One can discern clear signs of Luther's Augustinianism. God has ordained that there be a secular government to hold the wicked in check and to maintain outward peace.[35] Commanded to love his or her neighbour, the Christian is bound to respect the secular authorities since the sword is indispensable to the peace of the whole world. Respect for the state is commanded by Scripture. So, following Romans 13, Luther could argue against radical rebellion or a disengaging from civil life. In this context, the function of the state is primarily negative – it is to restrain, where necessary by the use of force. Thus a kind of peace is maintained. This is required in a world that comprises saints and unredeemed sinners. 'Frogs must have storks.'[36]

While civil protection is sought, state interference in the life of the church is criticised. The secular authority has no competence beyond outward earthly matters. It cannot legislate for the soul; where it does,

[35] 'On Secular Authority', in Harro Höpfl (ed.), *Luther and Calvin on Secular Authority* (Cambridge: Cambridge University Press, 1991), 1–43.

[36] Ibid., 30.

it trespasses on God's government. Moreover, the state cannot coerce religious obedience. Faith is a free act that God works through the Holy Spirit. No one can be compelled to believe by secular forces.[37] These arguments, already present in the humanist literature of the sixteenth century, would later be rehearsed by advocates of religious tolerance. (Sebastian Castellio, an early exponent of religious tolerance, was able to include in his compendium of texts remarks of Luther in defence of spiritual liberty.) Luther's statement of the limits of legitimate secular power is also combined with some scepticism concerning the virtues of rulers. They are to be carefully watched and never idolised:

You should know that a prudent prince has been a rare bird in the world since the beginning of time, a just prince an even rarer one. As a rule, princes are the greatest fools or worst criminals on earth, and the worst is always to be expected, and little good hoped for, from them, especially in what regards God and the salvation of souls.[38]

The expression 'the two-kingdoms doctrine' (*Zweireichelehre*) has often been used to describe Luther's political theology.[39] Its weakness, according to Barthian criticism, has been to separate the temporal from the spiritual as if these run in parallel lines, thus excluding the possibility of a distinctively Christian criticism of social and cultural life. This challenge to the two-kingdoms doctrine (or at least one construction of it) was most forcibly made in the context of the German church struggle of the 1930s in the face of Lutheran quietism. Yet Luther's own political thinking reveals shifts and trends which are more complex than this criticism implies. In subverting the authority of the papacy, Luther assigns to the civil magistrate a greater measure of freedom in relation to the church than is found in much medieval political theory. To do this, he recalls Augustine's dialectic of the two cities, the city of God and the city of the world. Commentators have also drawn attention to assumptions shared with the late Middle Ages. The civil ruler still has a responsibility to maintain the cause of true

---

[37] Ibid., 25–6.　　[38] Ibid., 30.

[39] See Bernhard Lohse, *Martin Luther's Theology: Its Historical and Systematic Development* (Edinburgh: T. & T. Clark, 1999), 154. For an assessment of the different interpretations and applications of Luther's political thought see Jürgen Moltmann, 'Luther's Doctrine of the Two Kingdoms and Its Interpretation Today', *On Human Dignity* (London: SCM, 1984), 61–78.

religion and to this extent to preserve the ideal of a Christian society. Despite Luther's language about two realms – the temporal and the spiritual – corresponding to the two parts of the person – body and soul – which suggests a strict separation, his thought develops so as to maintain a strong interest in the political activity of the Christian and the more positive role of the state. His response to Thomas Münzer and the rebel peasants must be seen as a defence, rightly or wrongly, of a partnership between church and state with serious political and military consequences. Furthermore, as Bernhard Lohse points out, the stress on the three estates of church, marriage and the state reveals a greater degree of complexity than the metaphor of the two kingdoms might suggest. Within the estate of marriage and the family, the economic life of the community finds its focus. This is the sphere in which the Christian is called to serve God and neighbour, and it effectively corrects any impression that Christian action is confined to the church. There is a civic realm in which God's calling is to be enacted. The command to love one's neighbour requires that the Christian is active in the secular as well as the religious sphere. The metaphor of 'two kingdoms' needs to be complemented by the concept of 'two governments' to avoid any impression that the Christian inhabits only one kingdom or that the divine rule is restricted therein.[40] The secularising of vocations implies a social domain outside the church in which the divine will is to be fulfilled. In this context, furthermore, the state may be thought of not merely as a negative ordinance with the function of restraining evil; it has the potential to provide various social goods in conformity with the gospel of Christ.

However, the concept of not merely serving God in the secular realm but actually transforming that same realm is more characteristic of Reformed, as opposed to Lutheran, theology. The statue of Zwingli outside the Wasserkirche in Zürich depicts him holding the Bible in one hand and a sword in the other.[41] This represents a union of church and civil society in which temporal and spiritual concerns are fused. The ideal of organising the whole of society according to

---

[40] This is argued, for example, by Heinrich Bornkamm, *Luther's Doctrine of the Two Kingdoms* (Philadelphia: Fortress Press, 1966). See also Paul Althaus, *The Ethics of Martin Luther* (Philadelphia: Fortress Press, 1972).

[41] See W. P. Stephens, *The Theology of Huldrych Zwingli* (Oxford: Oxford University Press, 1986), 282–310.

the Word of God and following Old Testament precedents runs deep in the Reformed tradition. Yet, in Geneva, Calvin articulates a distinction between civil and religious government that is reminiscent of Luther and may have been set out as a corrective to the more theocratic model that obtained in Zurich.[42] The office of the magistrate was ordained by God for the maintenance of peace and justice within the territorial boundaries of the state. The magistrate was authorised to exercise force in carrying out this task. By contrast, the government of the church was spiritual and to be exercised by office bearers appointed from within the church. Calvin here establishes a position which rejects Anabaptist withdrawal from civil society on the one side, and state control of the church on the other. In this respect, it is incorrect to label his position theocratic. Nonetheless, it is not hard to see how this charge has arisen. In both his theology and Genevan ministry, Calvin sought a close partnership between church and civil authorities. The magistrate had a duty to uphold not only the second but also the first table of the law which outlines our duties to God. This entailed the civil protection of the Reformed churches, the suppression of serious heresy and the prohibition of the mass. The partnership between church and civil society characterised Reformed churches at other times and places. The *Scots Confession* of 1560 sets out the standard Reformation teaching about the divinely appointed office of political rule. It insists explicitly that judges and princes are 'to maintain true religion and to suppress all idolatry and superstition' and then proceeds to cite Old Testament examples of godly kings who complied.[43]

The First Book of Discipline,[44] produced at the same time as the *Scots Confession*, was an attempt not only to reform the church but to create a godly society. State recognition and defence of the Reformed cause were sought, while the church resolved to participate in a system of comprehensive education, poor relief and the moral discipline of all citizens. In cases of serious criminal offence requiring imprisonment or the death penalty, the state was expected to act in order

---

[42] *Institutes*, IV.20. Cf. Eberhard Busch, 'Church and Politics in the Reformed Tradition', in Donald McKim (ed.), *Major Themes in the Reformed Tradition* (Grand Rapids: Eerdmans, 1992), 180–95; Alister McGrath, *Reformation Thought*, 3rd edition (Oxford: Blackwell, 1999), 219–34.

[43] *Scots Confession*, Chapter XXIV.

[44] James K. Cameron (ed.), *The First Book of Discipline* (Edinburgh: St Andrew Press, 1972).

to supplement the disciplinary function of the church. At a local level, the Kirk Session emerged as a disciplinary body within each parish, levying fines and engaging in the public rebuke of those who, for example, broke the sabbath rest or were found guilty of sexual immorality. Indeed the Kirk Session in Aberdeen solved the problem of how to raise sufficient funds for poor relief by fining everyone found guilty of fornication, and then directing the revenue accordingly.[45]

The deficits of this tradition will be noted in due course, but it does acknowledge in the context of the sixteenth century that every society must have a religious identity which shapes its social ethos. Attempts to order the civil realm according to the Word of God, whatever their drawbacks, were at least able to advance the causes of health care, education, and social welfare. In England, there remained, under the conditions of the Reformation, an integration of church and civil society which found its classical expression in Richard Hooker's *Laws of Ecclesiastical Polity*. Hooker's thought marks something of a return to Aquinas' use of law and reason rather than the strict biblicism of the Puritans, and in doing so argues for the benefits of a Christian polity in which the political and religious ends of human existence are harmonised.[46] The celebrated claim is hence made that 'there is not any man of the Church of England, but the same man is also a member of the Commonwealth, nor any man a member of the Commonwealth which is not also of the Church of England.'[47] The presence of Jews and recusant Catholics in England rendered this at most an ideal, but it reflects an aspiration, akin to Bucer's Strasbourg, Calvin's Geneva and Knox's Scotland. The medieval vision of an organic unity of church and state thereby translated into the countries of the Reformation.

Despite centuries of social, economic and political change, the national churches of Europe continue to reflect some of the theological ideals of the magisterial Reformers and their medieval heritage. The integration of church with society finds expression in the parish

[45] Cited by Ann Pagan, *God's Scotland: the Story of Scottish Christian Religion* (Edinburgh: Mainstream, 1988), 202.

[46] For a comparison of Hooker with the magisterial Reformers see Duncan B. Forrester, 'Luther, Calvin and Hooker', in Leo Strauss and Joseph Cropsey (eds.), *History of Political Philosophy*, (Chicago: Rand McNally, 1963), 277–323.

[47] Richard Hooker, *Of the Laws of Ecclesiastical Polity*, ed. Arthur Stephen McGrade (Cambridge: Cambridge University Press, 1989), Book VIII.I.2, 130.

system in which the ordinances of religion are extended to all citizens, in the acknowledgement of the church's function by the state, and in the complex ways in which our institutions have reflected this unity. The effort to create not only a pure church but a godly society reveals a loyalty to biblical themes in which the whole of social existence is set under the rule of God. It also recalls the duty of the political ruler to promote the common good (or the common weal) under the law of God. But while the magisterial Reformation gained a measure of success, particularly in the countries of northern Europe, the movements of those on the radical fringes frequently provoked hostility whether in Lutheran, Reformed or Roman Catholic territories. In recent years, much greater historical and theological attention has been devoted to the radical Reformation. In part, this is a proper reaction to a neglect of the social history of the Reformation in contrast to the history of its ideas, but it is also born of an increasing awareness that in the post-Christendom period the church of today has something in common with that of the radicals.

The radical Reformation was far from a monolithic force and this makes appraisal of its theological significance a hazardous enterprise. It was a grass-roots movement that functioned largely in opposition to the magisterial Reformation. A range of reactions to civil society from violent resistance through accommodation to passive withdrawal can be discerned.[48] Their political vision was rooted typically in notions of local autonomy and community control. Each community had the right to hear the gospel preached in its pure form and to regulate its social life accordingly. This included the right to appoint a minister and to determine the use of ecclesiastical revenues. In this situation, the rejection of the widespread practice of infant baptism was significant. It signalled a political freedom, the rejection of civil society as Christian, and the nature of the church as a free assembly of confessing Christians. The moral laxity of the magisterial reformation was frequently noted. Menno Simons spoke of the 'great comfortable sects' of Roman Catholics, Lutherans and Zwinglians, each depending upon the power of the sword.[49] For Denck, there could not be genuine

---

[48] There is a useful selection of political writings from the radical Reformers together with an introduction to their thought in Michael G. Baylor (ed.), *The Radical Reformation*, (Cambridge: Cambridge University Press, 1991).

[49] Quoted by Timothy George, *The Theology of the Reformers* (Nashville: Broadman Press, 1988), 285.

faith without moral improvement. Hut criticised the moral failures of the educated clerical elite.

After the Peasants' War and the defeat in 1527, the Anabaptist movement developed in different ways. In cantonal Swiss villages there was an attempt to take over the civil order including its means of self-defence. Others called for non-resistance and separation. This is the position advocated in the Schleitheim Articles of 1527 composed by Michael Sattler. Christians were to shun the ungodly world by avoiding the religious services of the mainstream, the swearing of oaths, the holding of public office, participation in processions and the frequenting of wine shops.[50] The success of this movement involved a renunciation of every attempt to master the world. If society would not be Christian, at least the church could be. Christians could gather into purified communities that were marked sacramentally by the baptism of believers and the administration of the Lord's Supper. Discipline was exercised not by force but by the 'ban' that involved exile and excommunication of those unable to meet the moral demands of Christ's gospel.

A frequent criticism of this movement is that it required a sectarian withdrawal from society that is neither practical nor commended by the New Testament. Some accommodation has to be made with the civil authorities, to whom respect in any case is due as the holders of a divinely appointed office. The best rejoinder to this challenge is to argue that the radical movement in its discipline and community structure bore witness before the rest of society to the moral possibilities of a Christian life and polity. In their economic and social ties, they offer a glimpse of an alternative community under the Word of God. By doing so, they provide a critical standard by which the world can measure itself. Rather than forsaking the world, as H. R. Niebuhr suggests in his famous typology,[51] they serve the world by disclosing new possibilities. The radical position can be presented as not so much a straight rejection of secular political rule as the adoption of an independent standpoint that provides a perspective from which to offer critical discrimination upon a broad range of cultural forms. It offers not withdrawal but criticism both positive and negative.[52]

[50] Schleitheim Articles (1527) in Baylor (ed.), *The Radical Reformation*, 172–80.
[51] H. Richard Niebuhr, *Christ and Culture* (New York: Harper, 1951).
[52] This position is developed by Yoder, 'How H. Richard Niebuhr Reasoned', 31–90.

It is not hard to see why this model holds attractions for Christian ethics today. The growing dissociation of church from contemporary civil society brings into sharper focus the possibilities of anabaptist ecclesiology. Doubts about the prospects for national churches in an age of secularism and pluralism occasion a search for alternative models. In recalling these sixteenth-century examples from the left wing of the Reformation, we are taken back to the situation of the church prior to Constantine. The features of early church life resonate with the conditions on the left wing of the Reformation and in many quarters today. These include a lack of interest in mastering the world, a willingness to subordinate to the church one's loyalty to other communities, the renunciation of violence, and the readiness to suffer in the cause of Christ. The moral seriousness of this radical Christianity is one of its most compelling features. Of the six characteristics by which Menno Simons claimed the church to be known, four are explicitly ethical.[53] In addition to the purity of doctrine and a scriptural administration of the sacraments, we find obedience to the Word of God, brotherly and sisterly love, a bold confession of God and Christ, and a readiness to embrace suffering for the sake of the Word.

The dechristianisation of society today gives weight to the more counter-cultural ecclesiologies of the radical reformation. For the moment, we should note the historical similarities, the contemporary appeal and the genuine possibilities it provides. The social space is available within which a greater measure of independence from civil society and established religion can be achieved. This is evidenced *inter alia* by the growth in independent churches and the charismatic movement, and by the rise in the number of weddings outside the established and Roman Catholic sectors. There is a renewed questioning of the practice of infant baptism, a criticism of the moral laxity and tokenism of the religious establishment, and a return to the themes of discipleship and obedience that one finds in the radicals. Implicit in this is a tendency to question the Lutheran doctrine of justification by faith alone. The timing is ironic given the recent agreement of the Roman Catholic Church and the Lutheran World Federation on this very subject. Against this, one now hears echoes of

---

[53] See George, *The Theology of the Reformers*, 287. These are discussed by Hans-Jürgen Goertz, *The Anabaptists* (London: Routledge, 1996), 96.

Balthasar Hubmaier's exhortation to good works in the time allotted us: 'The most pious and godly Christians must also confess that they are unsaved until their death. May God help us to make something of our lives.'[54]

CONCLUSION

This rapid tour of historical approaches is not intended to induce a single, normative doctrine of the state. The variety of contexts and approaches militates against this, even if recurrent themes can be detected in the early church, the medieval and the Reformation periods. However, several conclusions can be tentatively advanced on the basis of this reading of the theological tradition.

The theory of church and state is largely a medieval phenomenon in which the relationship between two dominant institutions was set out. It belongs to a context in which Christianity has become established as the majority religion in late antiquity. The need to differentiate and relate the roles of political and ecclesiastical rulers necessitated a theoretical account. Nonetheless, we find extensive theological consideration of the civil realm at earlier times. Here, however, reflection is less focused on the state, as a single, quasi-metaphysical entity. Instead what we have are discussions of a range of social and civic phenomena including that of imperial rule.

Within the early church, it is clear that both church and state are to be set within and subordinated to a theological vision of the divine rule in history and its eschatological outcome. In anticipating this and bearing witness to it through baptism into the church, Christian theologians expressed a sense of 'alien citizenship'. While in later contexts that are less marked by persecution and hostility this might be better termed 'subordinated citizenship', it is clear that this literature provides an important sense of dissonance and a critical standard by which existing socio-political realities can be measured. There are powerful reminders of this ineluctable dissonance in both the monastic movement and the radical Reformation.

The development of a concept of the common good, partly under the influence of Aristotle together with the emergence of a strong sense of *communitas* in the second half of the Middle Ages, is apparent. This

---

[54] Baylor, *The Radical Reformation*, 184.

is significant for a social theology that perceives the rule of God and the hope of the world not merely in ecclesial forms. And reinforced by the Reformed commitment to social transformation, this discerns the possibility, indeed the imperative, of a Christian contribution to the secular realm. The capacity of this realm to exercise more than a negative function of restraint suggests that the dominion of God can be exercised there in quite positive ways. Significantly, even in the more negative characterisations of political society in Augustine and Luther this is recognised. Our neighbours are not merely those within the church. God's command to love them directs us inevitably to social and political forms. Moreover, the *bonum commune* may enable us again to recognise that a political theology is not to be exhausted by an account of the legitimate function of the church in relation to the state.

Nevertheless, the fitful recognition of liberty of conscience and religious tolerance in the Lutheran Reformation draws attention to the need for accommodating a greater degree of religious diversity than was advocated during the Middle Ages. With the gradual breakdown of the organic unity of church and society, this becomes a pressing issue in the early modern period.

CHAPTER THREE

Crises of liberalism

If history is our guide, there is no enduring connection between becoming modern and valuing personal autonomy.

(John Gray)[1]

POLITICAL LIBERALISM

The Peace of Westphalia, which ended thirty years of European warfare in 1648, is said to have re-embraced the principle 'cuius regio, eius religio', by which the religion of the governed should be that of their territorial ruler.[2] So Europe, exhausted by wars in which, according to some estimates,[3] half of its population was killed, settled for being religiously diverse. Roman Catholic, Lutheran and Reformed states remained and coexisted. In this particular arena of international conflict, the critical ingredient of religion was largely removed.[4] The Westphalian settlement, however, though recognising religious diversity across the continent, did not end the argument about diversity within states. By the middle of the seventeenth century claims for religious liberty were increasingly being advanced by individuals and groups. These recalled arguments already rehearsed by Renaissance

---

[1] *Two Faces of Liberalism* (Oxford: Polity Press, 2000), 98.

[2] The expression derives from the earlier peace treaty at Augsburg in 1555; dissenting subjects were permitted to emigrate. Although the rule excepted the Imperial Free Cities in which both Lutheran and Catholic groups were permitted freedom of worship, this appears to have operated in only eight cities. See Geoffrey Parker (ed.), *The Thirty Years War* (London: Routledge, 1984), 19.

[3] E.g. Ronald G. Asch, *The Thirty Years War: the Holy Roman Empire and Europe 1618–48* (Basingstoke: Macmillan, 1997), 185.

[4] 'The abatement of this major destabilizing influence in European politics was one of the greatest achievements of the Thirty Years' War'; Parker (ed.), *The Thirty Years War*, 219.

humanists and reformers a century earlier. Now they were presented with greater clarity and cogency, especially amongst dissenters in England.

During this early modern period developments of a position (or set of related positions) now known as political liberalism appear in Europe. According to a standard interpretation of the matter, liberalism emerged from the realisation that a basis for public life had to be found that was relatively independent of religious loyalty. To put the point most minimally, people of differing faith commitments had to find a way of living together without recourse to violence. Debilitated by war, both international and civil, a growing number of citizens recognised that neither force nor reason would produce religious uniformity. The only alternative to further bloodshed was to organise a polity on principles that could be affirmed by different faith communities. In the seventeenth century, of course, this diversity often extended not much further than rival groups within Protestantism, yet it began the journey to some of the standard claims that are made for political liberalism today.

Political liberalism typically includes public recognition of the following three broad claims: the equality of all citizens under the law; the freedom of each to pursue the goods of his or her own choosing while not interfering unduly with another's freedom; and the neutrality of the state with respect to the particular preferences of its citizens, including religion. These claims are asserted on varying grounds, some positive and others negative. What emerges is a set of positions displaying various family resemblances.

For Thomas Hobbes, a system of monarchical government is advocated on the basis that each individual will suffer far greater woe under the conditions of anarchy. By submitting to the sovereign, each citizen may pursue within limits the goals of his or her choosing. In advocating the equality of each person and the necessity of individual consent to government, Hobbes in some ways prefigures more modern features of liberalism. His political treatise *Leviathan* (for some of us a first philosophical textbook) offers a sombre account of life at the time of the English civil war. It advocates strong government, but on a basis that asserts the priority of the individual and his or her interests.[5]

---

[5] Thomas Hobbes, *Leviathan* (1651), ed. Richard Tuck (Cambridge: Cambridge University Press, 1996). For a brief historical and philosophical overview of political liberalism see John Gray, *Liberalism*, 2nd edition (Buckingham: Open University Press, 1995).

Hobbes' early modern concern was to establish a basis upon which government of a religiously diverse and politically splintered society could be formed. His motivation was not so much to promote the later ideals of autonomy, self-expression and pluralism, as to prevent the potential for grave harm (actual in Hobbes' own time) where rival traditions each seek a political hegemony.

On a more positive basis, John Locke, who himself suffered religious persecution, offers a model of civil society as an association of free citizens, equal under the rule of law, pursuing their own ends but always with respect for each other's natural rights. This account of natural rights is derived from Locke's theism, and is expressive of the divine nature from which all natural law and right derives. In particular, we have rights to liberty and property albeit with reference to God's claim upon us.[6] Other related versions of liberalism emerge in France, Germany and Scotland during the eighteenth-century Enlightenment. These too vary in the grounds offered for liberal theory, but several standard features begin to emerge and can be noted as follows. These might be read as specifications of the three broad principles outlined above. (i) The stress on the equality and freedom of each citizen entails a prioritising of the individual over the community. (ii) Individual equality and freedom are typically maintained through a system of law, although differences of opinion on the ordering of freedom and equality influence the types of law that are enacted. (iii) Government is by consent of the people. (iv) There is a recognition of the importance of possession of property and freedom to engage in economic activity without undue state interference. This is perceived as vital to prevent collective or state control. Hence political liberalism has historically existed in close relationship with economic liberalism. (v) The state will tend to tolerate religious differences and lifestyle choices that do not interfere with the liberty and equality of other citizens. To this extent, it adopts a position of neutrality with respect to competing traditions. (vi) There is a growing tendency to rank the 'right' over the 'good' since, as noted above, a liberal society embraces a diversity of lifestyle ideals and world-views. Respect for individual rights here takes precedence, at least in principle, over public recognition of what constitutes the good life. Whether

---

[6] John Locke, *Second Treatise on Civil Government* (c. 1681) in *Political Writings* (Harmondsworth: Penguin, 1993), 261–387.

or not these claims were successfully embodied in European societies in the eighteenth and nineteenth centuries, it is clear that they derive their rationale from the fundamental assumptions of liberal political theory.

In other important respects, however, differences of outlook can be detected amongst political liberals. For some, it is a strategy of perfectionism by which individuals and societies can attain a greater measure of self-realisation than has hitherto been historically achieved. A belief in progress and indefinite improvement informs the political philosophy of Condorcet and Diderot. One can also detect this progressivism in writers at the end of the nineteenth century. While it is easy to mock the naiveté of their historical optimism, the expectation of indefinite economic growth and rising levels of prosperity continue to be widely assumed today in western societies. This assumption may also manifest itself in the quasi-imperialist conviction that if other societies are offered some exposure to the political and economic standards of the West, they will inevitably display a preference for these.[7] For others such as Hume, liberal government is more akin to a system for checking the worst excesses of human nature. This urbane account is consistent with the view that while societies may undergo periods of improvement these can be followed by times of regression. Social progress, while possible, is neither inevitable nor indefinitely probable.

Classical liberalism tends to assign a minimalist role to the state – this was apparent through much of the nineteenth century – whereas revisionary liberalism advocates a more proactive role to government in delivering those social goods that are necessary for the attainment of liberal ideals. These may include the introduction of a minimum wage, development of employment laws, health and welfare provision, subsidy of the arts, and redistribution of wealth through progressive taxation. This shift to revisionary liberalism is apparent in much of John Stuart Mill's work. In retrospect, it may have become necessary with the drive towards universal adult suffrage and the enfranchisement of larger sectors of the population. But the tendency to promote

---

[7] This is not dissimilar to the assumption of some secularisation theorists that progression to a less religious and more secular condition is an inevitable outcome of social advance. As pluralism is embraced so religious choices are relegated to a quasi-aesthetic status of lifestyle preference.

equality at the expense of individual liberty and to extend significantly the role of the state have been criticised by twentieth-century theorists seeking a return to something more akin to classical liberalism.[8]

One of the most problematic features of political liberalism from the Enlightenment onwards is its set of universalist assumptions. It tends to presuppose that a liberal polity represents an advance on all early forms so that every society should eventually progress to this condition. This is closely related to a further assumption about justification. The grounds on which liberal society is constructed are universally recognisable and binding upon all rational individuals. This is most apparent in Kant's claims about the moral knowledge available to all autonomous agents simply by virtue of their rationality, although it is present also in other theorists. Ironically, exponents of political liberalism, in espousing this form of universalism, offer rival moral theories none of which have proved capable of commanding a consensus.[9] Political liberalism has been undergirded by different meta-ethical systems ranging from the pragmatism of Hume's account, through Kantian deontology to J. S. Mill's utilitarianism. This failure of any meta-ethic to command the field exposes a fundamental weakness – there is no commonly agreed moral basis from which liberalism can be derived. Hence the universalist assumption that has so often animated political liberalism has now become deeply problematic.

The most distinguished exponent of political liberalism in recent times is the American philosopher John Rawls. Contemporary discussions of the subject often take their cue from his work. In Rawls' later writings, the principles of political liberalism cannot be demonstrated on metaphysical grounds.[10] Yet they do represent something approaching a consensus in many societies today and may be considered in good working order. As such they provide a sound basis for the regulation of society and the conduct of political debate. Anyone advancing a political measure or programme should be able and

[8] E.g. F. A. Hayek, *Constitution of Liberty* (New York: Legal Classics Library, 1999); Robert Nozick, *Anarchy, State and Utopia* (Oxford: Blackwell, 1975).

[9] This is explored in Alasdair MacIntyre's seminal study, *After Virtue* (London: Duckworth, 1981). I have sought to discuss these issues more fully in *Community, Liberalism and Christian Ethics* (Cambridge: Cambridge University Press, 1998).

[10] 'Justice as Fairness: Political Not Metaphysical', *Collected Papers* (Cambridge, MA: Harvard University Press, 1999), 388–414.

willing to justify this on the basis of reasons accessible to most other citizens within a liberal society. Thus a proposal which is based on an appeal to an authoritative text or ecclesiastical institution cannot be propounded unless this is capable of being justified also by reference to publicly recognised principles of freedom, equality and justice. This is not intended to prevent political disagreement; its effect is rather to determine the appropriate language within which debate can take place. It remains possible for those espousing political liberalism to differ sharply over a range of issues such as the control of the economy, progressive taxation, the provision of health care and social welfare, state subsidy for the arts, and censorship of the media, though whether recourse to the principles of liberty outlined by Rawls can resolve these issues remains questionable. Sustained discussion of Rawlsian liberalism suggests that much policy making must inevitably repose upon particular, thick traditions of justice that presuppose agreements beyond those recognised by the terms of Rawls' own theory.[11]

This endemic weakness of political liberalism is further illustrated by the phenomenon of globalisation. At a time when capitalism has spread its influence throughout the world, there has been a resurgence of local, national and religious identities. This calls into question the extent to which economic and political liberalism form an organic unity. Thus, in Southeast Asia, market economies have flourished but on different cultural soil from that of western societies. Here economic growth has not generally coincided with the rise of western political and cultural forms. Notwithstanding its material prosperity, Japanese society remains very different from that of western Europe or North America. Moreover, the emergence of much greater lifestyle diversity within western societies through migration, communication, technology, and heightened prosperity (often enabled by the practice of political liberalism itself) has created a higher degree of moral and religious pluralism. The 'ordeal of value pluralism', to use John Gray's expression, also tends to defeat forms of post-Enlightenment liberalism with their universalist assumptions.

---

[11] E.g. H. L. A. Hart, 'Rawls on Liberty and Its Priority', *Essays in Jurisprudence and Philosophy* (Oxford: Oxford University Press, 1983), 223–47.

These problems may also be worsened by the diminished role of the nation state in many parts of the world. The project of political liberalism tends to assume the capacity of the state to legislate, control and organise society in such a way as to command the allegiance of (almost) all citizens. Yet the fragility of the nation state in the Balkans, in the former USSR and in parts of Africa again suggests that western models may no longer provide a universal prescription for social harmony and cohesion. The importance of developing programmes, institutions and forms of government along lines other than the nation state indicates the need for a greater diversity of models.

Difficulties with Enlightenment forms of political liberalism have led some thinkers to return to early modern strategies for pacifying society. Rather than seeking to construct society around a moral consensus, attention has turned to thinkers such as Hobbes whose overriding concern was peaceful coexistence. Moral differences are no longer presented as a temporary phase in the evolution of a liberal polity. Since these are fundamental, enduring and irresolvable, the task is to find ways of living peacefully that can accommodate diversity. Such approaches take 'value pluralism' as an ineradicable feature of modern societies and seek to find a *modus vivendi* that respects this.[12] What emerges is not so much a wholesale dismissal of the liberal programme as a way of accommodating some of its basic features within a different ethical framework. The importance of securing a peaceful, morally diverse society is affirmed but not on the assumption that this is to be achieved through promoting a universal ethical code to which everyone subscribes. Again this is not to reject the claim that every settled society must have minimal standards of political legitimacy, enforceable by law, to which each subculture and group subscribes. But it is to deny the stronger claim that these standards can be derived from a single universal moral theory affirmed by all rational persons.

While the foregoing is indebted to John Gray's recent retrieval of this early modern approach, it is not clear that his own position requires the assumption of 'moral irrealism'.[13] Indeed it must

---

[12] E.g. Isaiah Berlin, *Four Essays on Liberty* (London: Oxford University Press, 1969); Gray, *Two Faces of Liberalism*.
[13] Gray, *Two Faces of Liberalism*, 64.

surely suffer from it. That there are different, incommensurable value schemes incapable of resolution may simply be a fact of life. But this does not require the further assumption that there are no moral truths. Nor does it commit one to denying the possibilities of achieving a greater measure of agreement through conversation, or even moral conversion to a different way of life. Indeed to commit oneself to a position of moral irrealism has the unintended consequence of overriding moral pluralism since it denies what is central to much moral vision, particularly amongst the religions of the world – the sense of being constrained by what is the case independently of one's perceiving it. To this extent, the denial of moral realism undermines the notion of vocation that often animates ethical commitment. A further problem for modern western societies, not adequately acknowledged here, is not so much moral conflict as the absence of any strong moral commitment on the part of its citizens. The *anomie* of much modern life is as much a problem for the health of liberal societies as is value pluralism. Moreover a non-realist construal of value pluralism may also miss the importance and necessity of moral change and transformation. It is through conversation and civil interaction with others of alternative moral persuasion that our own views sometimes shift, develop and change. At other times, our own views are clarified and disagreements become more focused. The maintenance of institutions and practices that permit this is vital for a morally diverse society.

THE FIRST AMENDMENT

The terms of the debate over Rawls' political philosophy reflect the influence of the American constitutional tradition. According to the First Amendment to the constitution in the US Bill of Rights ratified by all the confederating states in 1791,

Congress shall make no law respecting an establishment of religion or prohibiting the free exercise thereof; or abridging the freedom of speech, or of the press, or the right of the people peaceably to assemble, and to petition the Government for a redress of grievances.[14]

---

[14] The full text of the constitution and amendments is reproduced in John R. Vile, *A Companion to the United States Constitution and Its Amendments* (Westport: Praeger, 1997), 243–54.

Before examining recent interpretations of the First Amendment, it is worth exploring its setting in the thought of James Madison, who drafted the amendments that eventually made their way into the Bill of Rights. Madison's thinking was partly influenced by his correspondence with Jefferson and the fear of anti-federalists that a single national government would prove oppressive in its exercise of power. For Madison, we have both a right and a duty to render to God such worship as we believe acceptable. This is a sacred matter for the conscience of each individual person that cannot be infringed by persons or groups representing a majority party. The freedom and equality of all citizens under God means that the state cannot display any preference for one form of religion. This argument has been summarised by Ronald Thiemann in the following terms: 'The establishment of religion denies the freedom of some and the equality of all, and thereby denies essential freedom of conscience. Genuine freedom implies pluralism; pluralism demands equality; and equality cannot be maintained under an ecclesiastical establishment.'[15] The emphasis on liberty of conscience is supplemented by an argument against factionalism. The tendency, inherent in human societies, for factions to form and act in an oppressive manner must be arrested. This is to be achieved by a system in which representation is diffuse and diverse, in other words a system of checks and balances. Factionalism is especially liable to arise from the zeal surrounding religious matters and must therefore be resisted by the strict no establishment principle. Religious majorities cannot persecute or disadvantage minorities. The republic is therefore legally bound to uphold individual liberty and equality in religion, in large part through attention to the dangers of factionalism.

It is a further feature of Madison's thinking that the republic can only uphold individual liberties by promoting public virtue and the common good. A commitment to public well-being is necessary if citizens are to be bound together in the commonwealth, and this is not merely an aggregate of private individual goods. Madison is clear that there must be virtue in the people if freedom and happiness are to be secured. But how is such virtue to be realised? Here Madison's

---

[15] Ronald Thiemann, *Religion in Public Life: a Dilemma for Democracy* (Washington, DC: Georgetown University Press, 1996), 21. In what follows I owe much to Thiemann's discussion.

thought seems to be that it would come through the emergence of virtuous persons as civic leaders. These would set a standard which others would follow.[16] With the benefit of hindsight, this reasoning now appears somewhat circular, if not naive. Where are virtuous leaders most likely to originate, if not in a society that tends to produce such people? If the state is to be served by those who are virtuous, then there will need to be civic traditions which promote the dignity of public service, an understanding of the common good, and a belief in the honour of political office. The high ideals of liberty and equality thus require for their security thick traditions of moral enquiry, communities and traditions that articulate these and transmit them across the generations.

This problem has historically been solved, at least in part, by the manner in which Christianity has functioned at the cultural level as the established religion of Americans. In 1789, the same year in which the Bill of Rights was approved, Congress also appointed a chaplain and passed a resolution calling on the first President to call a national day of thanksgiving. Since then, every president, except Jefferson, has issued a Thanksgiving Day proclamation urging citizens 'to give thanks to the Creator for the manifold gifts of freedom and prosperity'.[17] For two centuries, American society has been marked by the political disestablishment of religion and the cultural establishment of a Christianity that gradually became more ecumenical and in more recent times formed alliances with Judaism. This has sometimes resulted in the championing of something called the Judaeo-Christian tradition. At the cultural level, Christian theism has often functioned as a civil religion making using of the rhetoric of creation, covenant, providence and destiny. So, for example, in *Marsh v. Chambers* (1983) the Supreme Court upheld the legitimacy of prayers by a publicly funded chaplain in the state of Nebraska on the grounds that such prayers had a long history, including that of the First Congress, and

---

[16] By the delegation of power to elected representatives Madison assumes that it will be possible 'to refine and enlarge the public views by passing them through the medium of a chosen body of citizens, whose wisdom may best discern the true interest of their country and whose patriotism and love of justice will be least likely to sacrifice it to temporary or partial considerations'; The Federalist, No. 10, in James Madison, Alexander Hamilton and John Jay, *The Federalist Papers*, ed. Isaac Kramnick (Harmondsworth, Penguin, 1987), 126.

[17] Thiemann, *Religion in Public Life*, 30.

that they do not threaten those not wishing to participate as they would in a more restrictive school setting.[18]

Whatever the historical benefits of this arrangement, it is clear that it no longer works in the manner envisaged in the late eighteenth century. A much greater degree of pluralism now characterises American society. The churches in the USA, though stronger than their European counterparts, cannot claim to command the support of an overwhelming majority. Other voices, many of them explicitly secular, are now heard, while suspicion will habitually surround any coalition of religious interests that campaigns for some new public measure. Much controversy now surrounds the Supreme Court's interpretation of the First Amendment. The so-called 'Lemon Test', following *Lemon v. Kurtzmann* (1971), sets out three criteria for judging whether laws relating to religion are constitutional. These must (i) have a clear non-religious purpose; (ii) have a primary intended effect that neither promotes nor curbs religion; and (iii) avoid 'excessive entanglement between church and state'.[19] The application of these criteria has at different times prevented prayers in public schools and permitted state exemption of church property from taxation. The confusion has been catalogued in the following way:

The Court has held that the state may reimburse parents for the costs of public bus services to take students to and from nonpublic schools, but it may not pay for buses to take students on field trips. The state may furnish textbooks, but not other educational materials such as maps or film projectors. Publicly funded remedial teaching off the school premises is allowed, but remedial teaching on the school premises is not. The state may reimburse a sectarian school for administering state-created tests, but it may not fund tests created by school's own teachers. Finally, the state may fund a wide variety of institutions and activities indirectly through tax subsidies that it may not fund directly.[20]

One of the primary difficulties with interpreting the crucial clause in the First Amendment resides in whether it requires state non-involvement or impartiality. Jefferson spoke of the First Amendment as creating a high wall of separation between church and state. Nonetheless, this widely used metaphor may be somewhat loaded. It

---

[18] Vile, *A Companion to the United States Constitution*, 130.   [19] Ibid., 129.
[20] 'Note: Developments in the Law: Church and State', *Harvard Law Review* 100 (1987), 1677, quoted by Thiemann, *Religion in Public Life*, 44.

suggests a principled non-involvement of government on all matters of a religious nature, whereas in its original historical context the First Amendment may only have implied that no single ecclesial body was to become established. Chief Justice William Rehnquist thus argued that the image of the wall of separation was misleading; the First Amendment is violated only by the establishment of a national religion not by government benefits or preference for religion rather than irreligion.[21] On a strong non-involvement reading, the state would remain apart from any religious cause or organisation. It could not allow use of public funds for any religious function. Yet on an impartiality reading, it would be required not to be uninvolved but simply to treat all religious groups fairly by showing no preference for any one. This could then be combined with state provision for religious causes provided that this was extendable to all parties.

It is clear, however, that the strong non-involvement reading is suggested by recent philosophies of political liberalism which prioritise rights of freedom and equality over particular and competing conceptions of the good. It is these which must be secured by the state without displaying any preference for one conception of the good over others. This position draws much strength, for example in the writings of Ronald Dworkin, from the observation that there is at present little prospect of widespread agreement about the ends of human life and those social goods that are to be sought. The fear of totalitarian imposition of a particular conception of the good gives impetus to the liberal stress upon the plurality of human goals and the need to organise society as far as possible on the basis of procedures of freedom and equality.[22] This argument for state neutrality with respect to the diversity of goods, however, is not based on sheer scepticism. It is grounded in convictions about the priority of rights, the principles of justice, and human equality and freedom. At its roots is the conviction that it is better for people, other things being equal, to pursue their own way of life than to have one thrust upon them. In this respect, it affirms the value of individual autonomy.

[21] See Vile, *A Companion to the United States Constitution*, 129–30.
[22] In his recent work, Dworkin argues for a balancing of 'dependent' and 'detached' conceptions of democracy to achieve procedures and outcomes consistent with principles of equality and liberty; *Sovereign Virtue: the Theory and Practice of Equality* (Cambridge, MA: Harvard University Press, 2000).

State neutrality is thus a notion that rests upon claims about human freedom. In practice, however, every state faces decisions which favour some competing conceptions of the good over others. As Susan Mendus points out, to have unrestricted Sunday trading is to favour the atheist or non-Christian over the Christian. On the other hand, to have laws limiting Sunday trading and employment practices is to favour a Christian conception of the good over some other.[23] Other examples relating to laws governing marriage and divorce, the promotion of minority languages, the public funding of religious schools, abortion, and the extraction of stem cells from embryos all reveal the manner in which particular views of human nature, of flourishing and of the ends of life typically inform public decision-making. The end result is often produced by an amalgam of particular perspectives, or some occasional consensus based on custom and established practice, rather than an overriding account of what is implied by the principles of liberty and equality.

The embeddedness of decisions in particular world-views and attendant moral conceptions of the good life leads to one of the most recurrent criticisms of liberalism. This has been described as its doctrine of the unencumbered self.[24] By prioritising the right over substantive and conflicting notions of the good, liberalism posits an individual whose autonomy is its supreme and inalienable right. The individual must remain free and untrammelled. Such commitment to the priority of the autonomous self reflects the Kantian roots of much political liberalism and its modern variant in the work of Rawls and others. It presents the individual as already valuing its autonomy prior to any other substantive moral commitments. In doing so, it denudes the self of the necessary resources for moral reasoning and decision-making. The individual of political liberalism is thus deracinated. She or he is no longer situated in a community or tradition of moral enquiry in terms of which judgements can be understood and practised. The shared goods and ends of human life are no longer built into the liberal individual's initial moral situation. These can be selected and endorsed by an act of freedom, but for the unencumbered self it is hard to see on what basis reasons favouring one

---

[23] Susan Mendus, *Toleration and the Limits of Liberalism* (London: Macmillan, 1989), 84.
[24] See Michael Sandel, *Liberalism and Its Critics* (Oxford: Blackwell, 1984).

decision over another could be offered. This philosophical criticism finds some support in social analysis which suggests that citizens of western societies are increasingly atomised, lonely and detached from those communities which once sustained the habits, thought patterns and practice of their ancestors.[25] Guignon and Hiley point to the manner in which psychotherapists encounter in their patients not so much the oppressive anxieties but symptoms which reveal a rootlessness, aimlessness and lack of any overriding moral or spiritual purpose.[26]

This criticism of the liberal doctrine of the self is also accompanied by complaints that appeals to particular visions of the good in public debate are frequently bracketed out or rejected as illegitimate by virtue of their inaccessibility to all participants in the debate. Someone who wishes to advocate, for example, redistribution of wealth, nuclear disarmament or a curtailing of the right to abortion should do so on grounds that are accessible to all members of a liberal society. Only those reasons must be advanced that are public, that is, have a rational claim upon all or at least most members of a society. Yet this restriction, it is claimed, excludes from the debate those whose political commitments are grounded in theological convictions about what the Bible or the church teaches. Those reasons that weigh most heavily with groups within society are declared invalid by virtue of their provincialism. This had led to complaints, most notably within American society, that a culture of disbelief has been created. The significance of religious claims is restricted to the private sphere. Where they intrude upon public debate they are often castigated as fanatical, bigoted or medieval (whatever that may mean). The effect of liberalism in this respect is not to include competing conceptions of the good within a varied, patchwork society; it is to create a narrowing of considerations and traditions which can legitimately be expressed in public debate. This thesis has been popularised by Stephen Carter in his book *The Culture of Disbelief*. He argues that while the original intention of the First Amendment was to keep the state out of religion, its current effect is the converse one of keeping religion out of public life. Whereas Madison was concerned about the civil coercion

---

[25] See Putnam, *Bowling Alone*.
[26] Guignon and Hiley, 'Biting the Bullet: Rorty on Private and Public Morality', 339–64.

of religion, now the preoccupation of the American courts is to remove religion from public life altogether. The effect, he claims, has been to create a new establishment, 'the establishment of religion as a hobby, trivial and unimportant for serious people, not to be mentioned in serious discourse. And nothing could be further from the constitutional, historical or philosophical truth.'[27]

This problem becomes most acute in the case of those communities whose practices and convictions reject the priority attached to the autonomous self. Susan Mendus considers the example of a Muslim community committed to schools which teach young girls the importance not of autonomy and choice, but of obedience and piety. How does this play in a liberal society? Is it to be tolerated or denied in the name of freedom? It is at this juncture that the paternalism inherent in political liberalism becomes most apparent. Joseph Raz, for instance, argues that under specified conditions groups must be brought humanely but, if necessary, coerced by law to a point where they can perceive the value of those social arrangements that promote autonomy.[28] In criticising similar moves, Gray argues that these depend upon what he calls Mill's Wager.[29] Any individual who has tasted the autonomy and range of choices made available in a liberal polity will opt for this form of life rather than an alternative.[30] On account of this latent paternalism within secular liberalism, leaders of religious minorities within the United Kingdom are somewhat supportive of the establishment of the Church of England. The latter is

---

[27] Stephen Carter, *The Culture of Disbelief* (New York: Basic Books, 1993), 115.

[28] 'So long as they are viable communities offering acceptable prospects to their members, including their young, they should be allowed to continue in their ways. But many of them are not self-sustaining. Often it is clear that they cannot be expected to survive for long as an isolated group in a modern society . . . In such cases assimilationist policies may be the only humane course, even if implemented by force of law'; Joseph Raz, *The Morality of Freedom* (Oxford: Oxford University Press, 1986), 424.

[29] John Gray, *Mill on Liberty: a Defence* (London: Routledge & Kegan Paul, 1983), 70ff.

[30] Peter Berger makes a similar point in his criticism of the secularisation thesis: 'A minority of sociologists of religion have been trying to salvage the old secularization theory by what I would call the last-ditch thesis: Modernization does secularize, and movements like the Islamic and Evangelical ones represent last-ditch defenses by religion that cannot last; eventually, secularity will triumph – or, to put it less respectfully, eventually Iranian mullahs, Pentecostal preachers, and Tibetan lamas will all think and act like professors of literature at American universities. I find this thesis singularly unpersuasive'; 'The Desecularization of the World: a Global Overview', in Peter Berger (ed.), *The Desecularization of the World: Resurgent Religion and Global Politics* (Grand Rapids: Eerdmans, 1999), 12.

preferable to the prospects of a resurgent secular liberalism that seems to deny religious convictions access to public debate.

RECOGNITION AND COMPROMISE

Recent discussion of political liberalism has pointed to the manner in which its espousal of state neutrality can discriminate in practice against those citizens whose identity is tied to a minority grouping. In adopting a 'blind' approach to communal affiliation, the laws of a liberal state can unwittingly display a bias against subcultures that deviate from the prevailing ethos of the society. A concealed political hegemony is thus exposed. This issue has been addressed, for example, in discussion of native American Indians, the francophone culture of Quebec, and Muslim communities in western Europe.[31] The survival of these communities, and hence the identity of their members, may depend upon differential treatment by legislative bodies that recognise their particular status. Non-recognition in this context may be regarded as a form of oppression in which the particular cultural identity of some citizens is either ignored or constructed in a demeaning fashion. The Salman Rushdie affair provides one dramatic illustration of how the liberal right to free speech can clash with the self-esteem of a religious minority. The result is an aggrieved sense that the maintenance of Islamic identity is a matter of indifference (or even worse) to a western polity that is an outgrowth of Christian society.[32]

In similar vein, feminists have also argued that political liberalism can function in a way that disregards the status and identity of women by imposing upon all citizens a set of masked patriarchal assumptions. Despite its concern with the equality of individual citizens, liberalism has often assumed that attitudes of benevolence regulate the life of each household. Yet the family is not marked by a harmony of interests amongst its members; women's hunger, domestic violence, marital rape and unequal access to education all too frequently

---

[31] For a discussion of this issue see Charles Taylor, 'The Politics of Recognition', in Amy Gutman (ed.), *Multiculturalism* (Princeton: Princeton University Press, 1994), 25–73.
[32] See Malise Ruthven, *A Satanic Affair: Salman Rushdie and the Rage of Islam* (London: Chatto & Windus, 1990).

characterise household relations in societies across the world.[33] This criticism reflects a wider feminist unease with the abstractionism of much liberal thought – it fails to attend to the context of those institutions which deprive women of equality. Another example of this is the way in which, despite equal-opportunities legislation, the career paths of many professions tend to impede the progress of women who devote a significant proportion of their time to raising children.

In the politics of recognition, preferential treatment may be accorded to minority groups in acknowledgement of the importance of maintaining their communal identity. This must be seen against the ideal of a multicultural society in which a measure of pluralism is valued above a more monochrome polity. So the promotion of a fragile Gaelic culture in Scotland takes place through the funding of schools in which Gaelic is the medium of instruction. Another instance would be state funding for religious schools that seek to develop the distinctive ethos and values of a particular faith tradition. Other measures have been developed around the world to protect the culture of threatened minority ethnic and religious groups, some of whom suffered grievously under western colonial rule. While such measures sit uneasily with the individualism of much political liberalism, greater sense can be made of them in terms of the arguments pursued above. Liberalism is better perceived as a project for securing the peaceful coexistence and prosperity of different groups and subcultures, since individual moral identity is inextricably tied to community, tradition and belief system.

Understood in this way, a pluralist society is inevitably one in which peaceful coexistence is purchased at the price of compromise. Substantive disputes cannot be resolved by laws instantiating universal principles of liberty and equality. As the criticism of Rawlsian liberalism demonstrates, such laws must embody particular conceptions of the good rather than merely procedural principles. And in a diverse, democratic society these laws will inevitably reflect a compromise that has been worked out between conflicting arguments and points of view. (This is not to pretend that laws may not often reflect the imposed will of the most powerful faction.) Compromise is a notion fraught with moral danger yet its necessity governs the life of every

[33] See Martha Nussbaum, *Sex and Social Justice* (Oxford: Oxford University Press, 1999), 65.

home, institution and society. It is moreover a moral necessity, if we perceive the alternatives to be oppression or violence.

A morally legitimate and socially constructive account of compromise can be offered by contrasting it with two closely related alternatives. In one of these, agreement is reached by a trade-off between interests on the model of bartering. In the same way as the price of a house or car is determined by a process of haggling between the interested parties, so a moral dispute might be resolved by striking the best available deal. A second alternative is to follow the 'path of least resistance' by accepting whatever settlement will be most likely to maintain peace. These options have been described as trading and trimming[34] and are to be distinguished from a process of negotiation leading to a moral compromise in which conflicting principles are each partially satisfied. On some issues, of course, the achievement of a compromise while retaining one's moral integrity is impossible. A dispute about slavery, infanticide, or paedophilia cannot be resolved by compromise since such an outcome would effectively concede the breach of a principle held by one side as inviolable. This is rightly parodied by G. K. Chesterton: 'Whatever the merits of torturing innocent children to death, and no doubt there is much to be said on both sides, I am sure we all agree that it should be done with sterilised instruments.'[35]

Yet on a range of issues compromise is necessary. This is established by a process of negotiation in which each retains something of what was sought and finds his or her deepest moral principles satisfied in some measure. The Good Friday Agreement in Northern Ireland initiated a peace process that has since made significant progress. It was achieved neither through surrender of all principles nor through a barter-style arrangement between the most powerful factions. Set out by the governments of Ireland and the United Kingdom and brokered by Senator Mitchell with the support of Clinton, principles cherished by both sides were upheld to produce an agreement that gave each side something that really mattered, while also enabling them to live, albeit uncomfortably, with what had been conceded to

---

[34] Richard Bellamy and Martin Hollis, 'Consensus, Neutrality and Compromise', in Richard Bellamy and Martin Hollis (eds.), *Pluralism and Liberal Neutrality* (London: Frank Cass, 1999), 54–78.

[35] Quoted by Bellamy and Hollis, ibid., 62.

the other. These included the democratic consent of those living in Ulster as necessary for radical constitutional change, a commitment by all parties to the cessation of terrorist activity, the development of cross-border political institutions, reform of the Royal Ulster Constabulary, and, after an appropriate interval, early release of prisoners convicted of terrorist offences. Despite persistent problems and outstanding issues, genuine progress has been achieved.

A less contentious example might be Sunday trading. The dispute between those who favour complete deregulation and those who wish to form a society in which the fourth commandment is recognised can be resolved by legitimate compromise. Here essential services, limited opening hours for selected retails outlets, and forms of entertainment might be permitted on the grounds that by no means everyone recognised the validity of the fourth commandment. It could be agreed that not all economic activity and leisure pursuits should be prevented one day each week by a single religious outlook. On the other hand, legislation might ensure that no one could be discriminated against for refusing on religious grounds to work on a Sunday (or on any other holy day), while a broad consensus might support the view that a day of rest free from regular employment was generally good for most people.

A much tougher example is that of abortion. At first sight, there can be no compromise between pro-life and pro-choice advocates, and for those adopting these positions this is probably true. Current legislation in most western countries, for example, must appear an unsatisfactory compromise between competing factions. On the other hand, discussion about the moral status of an embryo, together with consideration of hard cases involving rape, incest and juvenile pregnancy, may lead a majority to the compromise position that while abortion is to be generally avoided, there may be some circumstances in which it is permissible or where some latitude should be extended to individual choice. The compromise is not dishonourable, especially if in the process of negotiation a greater appreciation of one side for the other emerges. Yet there lurks danger in regarding this as a settled resolution. What begins as a legitimate compromise can slowly become an exercise in trading or trimming. This in effect is what has happened in the United Kingdom with the 1967 Abortion Act, originally defended as a measure for dealing with a limited number of hard cases, now effectively legalising a regime of abortion on demand. The moderate church consensus that supported this legislation has generally failed either to perceive this or to address the issue.

The inability of political liberalism to adopt a position of sheer neutrality with respect to rival conceptions of the good necessitates forms of democratic politics that enable broad access to public decision-making bodies. Institutions, organisations and movements within civil society require to be fostered. Without them, negotiated compromises are much harder to secure. In this respect, the political representation of group identity is dependent upon the health of civil society. It is at this level that the churches in interaction with other groups increasingly need to function. Democracy can operate in a multicultural polity less through recourse to the law courts (although there are signs that this is the prevailing trend) than through the reasoning, conversation and arguments of groups of citizens who seek mutually acceptable solutions. There are doubtless dangers here – these include the risk of a 'Balkanisation' in which society is divided into subgroups with debate dominated by well-organised units functioning in a hierarchical manner – and a risk of idealising the political process.[36] Nevertheless, for a plurality of groups and rival moral conceptions to coexist within a democratic system something along those lines will be required.

Some of the most searching moral dilemmas arise where the communal traditions of a religion clash with liberal principles. Is the imposition of liberalism at this point merely an act of (western) cultural hegemony? Or are there moral imperatives that can override practices central to an established religious culture? This problem may be less acute in western societies that have been characterised historically by a close alliance of church and state, yet problems arise even here for religious minorities. Is animal slaughter to be tolerated according to the practices of Islam and Judaism, or are these to be trumped by secular appeal to animal rights? Similar issues can emerge with respect to female circumcision, child marriages, inheritance rights, the wearing of headscarves, and the entitlement of divorced women. Again there is often a need for discernment and compromise, matched by a sense

---

[36] The distinction between liberal democracy and democratic liberalism is explored in this context by Richard Bellamy, *Liberalism and Pluralism: Towards a Politics of Compromise* (London: Routledge, 1999), 91ff.

of where religions need to be tested and confronted. Here several observations are apposite. Religious thought and practice have sometimes benefited from the challenges posed by secular convictions. At times, assumptions that seemed to be deeply embedded within a faith tradition prove difficult to justify in the face of criticism. In discarding them, the tradition evolves and comes to a position whereby it recognises that, despite the length of their tenure, these assumptions were neither consistent with nor demanded by the core commitments of the religion. Something like this process has resulted in a shift of moral positions within the Christian churches, although one should not assume that every change is a mark of inevitable progress. In this respect, religions are not static, monolithic institutions incapable of moral change or disagreement.

In exploring the sensitive issue of clashes between established religious practice and human rights within contemporary India, Martha Nussbaum has appealed to the notion of central human capabilities, each of which ought to be satisfied in any conception of a worthwhile life.[37] This notion is presented as not so much the upshot of a liberal account of the self as marking out an area of consensus or common ground occupied by differing conceptions of the good life. For Nussbaum, the importance of each person's capabilities reposes upon the Kantian principle of each person as an end. However, this moral basis might be expressed in terms of a different set of metaphysical convictions.[38] Her list of central functional capabilities includes bodily health and integrity, emotional development, and the capacity for forms of affiliation. These might be expressed or enumerated differently according to the emphases of some particular vision of life, yet the approach provides a moral check by which religious practices can be assessed. In many cases, the capabilities will conflict. The need for religious freedom and self-expression may clash with other capacities relating to bodily health or emotional development. Nonetheless, by balancing these capabilities while considering what is essential for the flourishing of a given religious tradition one may judge that a serious threat to human capacities is posed. A delicate weighing of arguments

---

[37] *Women and Human Development: the Capabilities Approach* (Cambridge: Cambridge University Press, 2000).
[38] For a similar insistence upon equality and persons as ends-in-themselves but from a theological perspective see Duncan Forrester, *On Human Worth* (London: SCM, 2001).

is required and Nussbaum, for example, reaches the conclusion that where polygamy is a deeply ingrained feature of a religious tradition it should be permitted, at least on a temporary basis. Some tragic choices may be inevitable, yet when considering female genital mutilation[39] or the forcible return of a woman to her marital home,[40] she argues on the other side for the necessity of challenging traditional cultural beliefs and practice.

This confrontation of traditional religious practice and modern ethical standards is not unidirectional. We should not assume that it is a matter of religious systems being measured in Kantian style by moral principles that are clearly intuited on independent grounds. The challenge works both ways with the widely accepted mores of a pluralist society being measured and tested by the insights of long-standing religious traditions. The blindspots, prejudices and distortions of modern social life might equally well be exposed from the perspective of a religious community with its patterns of service, witness and devotion. For example, if opinion polls are to be believed, the temptation to affirm voluntary euthanasia on grounds of autonomy seems almost irresistible for many. Yet we may find ourselves having to reconsider this through the testimony of a faith tradition that perceives life as a precious gift, that recognises human motivation never to be simple and pure, and that has an honourable record of caring for those at life's end.

CONCLUSION

The diversity and incompatibility of values, lifestyles and practices exhibited by different social groups cannot be accommodated on a classical liberal model which attaches a primary significance to the autonomous individual. The historical antecedents and philosophical commitments of this position reveal it to be only one amongst several options. Liberalism remains a worthy and necessary strategy for enabling the coexistence of rival perspectives, creeds and lifestyle. But, as a unitary politico-ethical theory to which everyone can be expected to subscribe, it has ceased to be credible.

---

[39] 'Judging Other Cultures: the Case of Genital Mutilation', *Sex and Social Justice*, 118–29.
[40] *Women and Human Development*, 222.

Nonetheless, despite its intellectual subsidence, liberalism has contributed to a social order in which a greater measure of freedom of expression has been attained. In this respect at least, it compares favourably with the late Middle Ages, the Reformation and the early modern period. Without commitment to a philosophy of political liberalism, one can discern in liberal society arrangements that are ineluctable in our current situation. These typically include freedom of worship, association and political action, and more recently a commitment to the equality of the sexes. What is significant in this context is that these are endorsed by a range of groups not through allegiance to a liberal moral philosophy but on the basis of a variety of thick commitments which represent different traditions and communities. This endorsement of civil liberties takes place on grounds that often reflect the particular arguments of early modernity rather than philosophies of the Enlightenment.

What is the significance of the foregoing for theology today? A commitment to some of the features of liberal society may be secured upon distinctive theological arguments for religious tolerance. These are predicated upon assumptions about faith, freedom and divine action, to which I shall turn in the following chapter. Furthermore, as we have already seen, the commitment to the welfare not only of the church but to one's neighbour creates an obligation to promote the well-being of society. This is rooted in biblical demands for the dominion of God to be expressed in every sphere of human activity, in the medieval notion of the common good that is sought by all political societies, and in the Reformed ideal of a godly society. Since our social life is perceived here as an arena for the service and work of God, a theologically grounded political commitment will be predicated upon particular faith-based assumptions. These cannot be bracketed out, although they may be expected to clash, intersect, or converge with commitments articulated on other grounds.

For these reasons, the church finds itself constrained to speak and to act in the public realm on the basis of its beliefs and practices. Without assuming a shared foundation of theory, it can form alliances and make common cause with other voices and convictions from differing ideological perspectives. This is reinforced by the acknowledgement that the membership of the church usually finds itself positioned in other communities and institutions, some of whose insights are inevitably internalised into the life of the Christian community. Civil society comprises a range of overlapping communities and groups which interact and influence one another in complex ways. Without reference to such influence it would be hard to understand changes in the last fifty years or so, in Christian attitudes to the welfare state, contraception, democracy, women's rights and remarriage of divorced persons.

Furthermore, in the absence of a common moral theory that unites all citizens and provides a basis for resolving all disagreement, institutions like churches and universities assume greater importance. The arts also have a significant contribution to make to the moral character of society. They provide the context for ongoing conversation about which social goods are to be sought and how these are to be prioritised. Only through the facility of civil debate can we avoid a situation in which disagreement results inevitably in recourse to the law courts or to *force majeure*. Our current task is not to identify a single moral framework acceptable to all citizens, but instead to promote what common moral ground we share through ongoing debate. This need not necessitate the abandonment of distinctively theological convictions.

Arguments for social justice in the civil rights movement in the USA and in the anti-apartheid movement in South Africa were persuasively advanced by those such as Martin Luther King who appealed explicitly to the language of the Bible and whose political convictions were rooted on religious soil. Yet their ability to connect with other discourses and movements resulted in a measure of political success. Their achievement resided in the power of scriptural images to mobilise resistance and change, yet it required also some fusion of these images with the language of human rights and justice. A constructive political theology need not surrender to a secular philosophy, but it does require the skills to engage in conversation with it and other discourses. A multilingual moral fluency has characterised some of the leading moral exemplars of our day, revealing the capacity of a moral stance based on a thick religious tradition to resonate with a wide global audience. In the work of Desmond Tutu and Aung San Suu Kyi, to cite two different examples, we can recognise and be moved by an authentic commitment to justice irrespective of whether we are Christian or Buddhist.[41]

We may still fear that the forsaking of a unitary moral framework within our current social context will prove divisive. Yet this fear should be allowed to mask neither the divisions that currently do exist, nor the prospect that common cause can be found.

The agreement arrived at need not be agreement based on principles rich enough to settle all substantial political issues whatsoever. Sufficient if it be agreement on the matter at hand. It need not be agreement based on principles shared by all alike. Sufficient if all, each on his or her own principles, come to agreement on the matter at hand. It need not be agreement for all time. Sufficient if it be agreement for today and tomorrow. It need not be agreement that one can reasonably expect of all human beings whatsoever. Sufficient if it be agreement among us. It need not even be agreement among each and everyone of us. Sufficient if it be the fairly-gained and fairly-executed agreement of the majority of us.[42]

---

[41] The international significance of virtuous individuals is explored by Peter J. Paris, 'Moral Exemplars in Global Community', in Max L. Stackhouse and Don S. Browning (eds.), *God and Globalization*, vol: II: *The Spirit and the Modern Authorities* (Harrisburg: Trinity Press International, 2001), 191–219.

[42] Nicholas Wolterstorff, 'Why We Should Reject What Liberalism Tells Us about Speaking and Acting in Public for Religious Reasons', in Paul Weithman (ed.), *Religion and Contemporary Liberalism* (Notre Dame: University of Notre Dame Press, 1997), 181.

CHAPTER FOUR

The theological case for toleration

> We need to understand how people are *inter*dependent as well
> as *in*dependent.
>
> (Susan Mendus)[1]

DEFICITS OF TOLERANCE

The growth of toleration in the early modern period took place on religious soil. Theological arguments for the recognition of liberty, dissent and diversity were advanced by groups threatened by different ecclesiastical establishments. But if the defence was theological, so also was the prosecution. While political, economic and social considerations interlocked, there took place a series of disputes and conversations that were fundamentally theological in nature. Against the world-view of the magisterial Reformers and their medieval predecessors, exponents of toleration, appealing to the New Testament, sought to mobilise earlier themes that had been latent in the tradition.

The early modern case for religious tolerance can best be approached by considering the arguments for intolerance and the ways in which these were gradually overcome. Within the Reformed tradition, for example, the ideal of a united godly society generated problems for dissidents. The stress upon church order, discipline, and a society under the Word of God, a distinguishing feature of Reformed church life, is apparent in the work of Bucer, Calvin, Knox and others. In Scotland, *The First Book of Discipline* (1560)[2] is often

---

[1] *Toleration and the Limits of Liberalism*, 67.
[2] Cameron (ed.), *The First Book of Discipline*. It is worth recalling that the programme outlined here, following a Levitical model, also advocated capital punishment for those convicted of adultery. In adopting this position, Knox followed Calvin and Bucer; ibid., 165–6.

hailed for its commitment to ideals of comprehensive education and poor relief. The struggle to reform and reorganise embraced not so much the gathered congregation as the whole of civil society.[3] In part, this explains why the practice of baptising infants continued into the magisterial Reformation; by virtue of birth, one became a member of the godly commonwealth. Yet a less attractive feature of the effort to fashion such a society was the difficulty in accommodating legitimate diversity. In aspiring to create not merely a church but a civil polity according to the Word of God, the social position of anyone confessing a different faith was inevitably threatened. In Scotland, for example, ideals of religious tolerance commanded acceptance rather later than in England and in other parts of Europe. In the middle of the seventeenth century, leading Scottish divines wrote treatises against claims for freedom of conscience.[4] Holding these to be detrimental to the moral and spiritual identity of a covenanting society, they continued to cite Old Testament precedents for compulsion and discipline in matters of religion. By doing so, they maintained the old Augustinian tradition of compelling them to enter. Although compulsory measures tended to be regarded as remedial rather than retributive, the most reprehensible act of civil enforcement of religious orthodoxy was the execution for heresy in 1697 of Thomas Aikenhead, an Edinburgh divinity student.[5]

The problem of religious intolerance was not of course confined to the Reformed tradition. Although Calvin's treatment of Servetus now provides the most notorious example of the infringement of religious liberty in the Reformation, it is by no means egregious. Similar problems attended Catholic social thought with its related tradition of the common good. If the *bonum commune* was to be secured by general adherence to the Catholic faith, then it could be

---

[3] For a discussion of religious tolerance in Scotland see James K. Cameron, 'Scottish Calvinism and the Principle of Intolerance', in B. A. Gerrish (ed.), *Reformatio Perennis: Essays on Calvin and the Reformation in Honour of Ford Lewis Battles* (Pittsburgh: Pickwick Press, 1981), 113–28. Cameron concludes that Scottish church life was actually more intolerant in the late seventeenth century than at the time of the Reformation.

[4] E.g. Samuel Rutherford, *A Free Disputation against Pretended Liberty of Conscience* (London, 1649); George Gillespie, *Whole Severity Reconciled with Christian Liberty* (London, 1645). Cf. W. Campbell, 'The Scottish Westminster Commissioners and Toleration', *Records of the Scottish Church History Society* 9 (1947), 1–18.

[5] For a recent overview of the Aikenhead case see Arthur Herman, *The Scottish Enlightenment* (London: Fourth Estate, 2002), 2–7.

argued that political rulers had a duty to promote such adherence if necessary by force. Gregory XVI, for example, resisted liberty of opinion and the separation of church from state. The Catholic faith is true and ought to be believed, he maintained. Only in this way is the common good promoted.[6] In the writing of Thomas Aquinas we have already noted arguments for the suppression of heresy, and also in Augustine the insistence that Donatists should be compelled to enter the church. It is not accidental, one suspects, that the Reformed and Roman Catholic theological traditions historically had the greatest difficulty, at least in the Christian West, with accommodating ideals of religious tolerance.

A survey of the history of arguments for tolerance reveals that these first emerged in the sixteenth and seventeenth centuries and were often defended on theological grounds.[7] By contrast, more modern convictions regarding tolerance have been promulgated on the basis of secular assumptions about human autonomy, spontaneity, rights and state neutrality. Following the argument of the previous chapter, the claim will be advanced that a theology of toleration is better served by attention to arguments from the early modern period than by secular claims that are often corrosive of our deepest convictions. What emerges will be an account of tolerance which in some respects demands more but in other respects may be less tolerant than secular ideals.[8]

THE LIMITS OF TOLERANCE

Before discussing further the historical arguments for and against tolerance, it may be worth offering some conceptual analysis. Tolerance is a curious virtue in that it suggests that we ought to accept beliefs and activities of which we disapprove. We only tolerate those things

---

[6] These problems are analysed from the perspective of Vatican II by David Hollenbach, *Justice, Peace, and Human Rights: American Catholic Social Ethics in a Pluralistic World* (New York: Crossroad, 1990), 101–7.

[7] Early modern arguments for tolerance were anticipated in some measure by Jewish and Christian writers of antiquity. In opposing coercive measures, Josephus, Tertullian and Lactantius could each appeal to the voluntary nature of religion. Cf. Peter Garnsey, 'Religious Toleration in Classical Antiquity', in W. J. Shiels (ed.), *Persecution and Toleration* (Oxford: Blackwell, 1984), 1–27.

[8] I am indebted here to the argument of Susan Mendus, *Toleration and the Limits of Liberalism*.

which we dislike or deplore. So I may be said to tolerate smoking in restaurants, the ringing of mobile phones in lectures, and the music played by teenage children. There are several reasons for this attitude of tolerance. These include a pragmatic recognition that 'you cannot win them all'; the realisation that friendship, family life, and social institutions can only flourish where there is a tolerance of other people's habits and beliefs (or at least, most of them); and the hope that we may learn from those who are different while they in turn will tolerate our own idiosyncrasies, defects and opinions. In these respects, the attitude of tolerance often functions negatively and borders on the patronising and the indifferent, while the reasons advanced to justify it display some variety

Despite this negative construction of tolerance, we have to reckon with the shift that has taken place in the meaning of the term. 'To tolerate', considered verbally, still connotes the negative idea of 'putting up with', whereas the substantive term 'tolerance' has become a central modern virtue. In its first article, the 1995 UNESCO Declaration of the Principles of Tolerance outlines this more positive construction of the term.

Tolerance is respect, acceptance and appreciation of the rich diversity of our world's cultures, our forms of expression and ways of being human. It is fostered by knowledge, openness, communication and freedom of thought, conscience and belief. Tolerance is harmony in difference. It is not only a moral duty, it is also a political and legal requirement. Tolerance, the virtue that makes peace possible, contributes to the replacement of the culture of war by a culture of peace.[9]

This semantic tension between 'to tolerate' and 'tolerance' itself suggests some ambivalence, and may conceal a range of reasons for valuing tolerance, not all of which are plausible let alone compatible. Nonetheless, it is embedded in our moral discourse and for reasons outlined below is necessary for the religiously diverse societies of modernity.

The standard liberal arguments for tolerance can be found in J. S. Mill's famous essay *On Liberty* (1859). Here Mill appeals to the autonomous self which can flourish only where it is left free to make

[9] The text of the UNESCO 'Declaration of the Principles of Tolerance' can be found at www.unesco.org/tolerance/declaeng.htm.

its own choices, form its beliefs and adopt whatever lifestyle it judges most authentic. To secure the conditions under which persons can thus flourish it is necessary that the state not infringe individual liberties and, in so far as possible, maintain a position of neutrality with respect to the beliefs, actions and lifestyle options of its citizens. Mill's account of tolerance, moreover, is a protest against social customs that stifle innovation, spontaneity and eccentricity, a protest evident in his relationship with Harriet Taylor, whose own convictions permeate much in his writings. The possibility of adopting different lifestyle options is vital to the free development of personality and the moral health of society. In defending liberty, Mill perceives it not merely to be a device for accommodating diversity but as necessary to the achievement of self-fulfilment. Autonomy is not merely a prior condition enabling different lifestyles, but is itself to be prized as internal to the good life. 'If a person possesses any tolerable amount of common sense and experience, his own mode of laying out his existence is the best, not because it is the best in itself, but because it is his own mode.'[10] This account of tolerance is one that many citizens today almost intuitively hold. Freedom to make our own lifestyle choices is a right, and we should therefore tolerate the choices that others make. We live and let live. So attempts to criticise the particular choices of others will often meet the charge that these are judgemental and intolerant. On this account, moreover, a diverse society is not merely to be tolerated but is positively to be encouraged. Where there is a wider range of cultural alternatives, the scope for the exercise of autonomy is correspondingly extended. Since it enhances our freedom, a patchwork society, in which there is a plurality of lifestyle choices, is to be preferred.

Despite its attractions, this justification of toleration has been subjected to some formidable criticisms. Its account of the unencumbered self, detached from commitments and traditions, is illusory. This was explored in the previous chapter in the discussion of political liberalism. The choices we make are inevitably shaped by our upbringing, education and social context. There is no possibility of judging competing alternatives from some Archimedean point of unattached

---

[10] John Stuart Mill, *On Liberty*, ed. David Bromwich and George Kateb (New Haven: Yale University Press, 2003), 131.

simplicity. It is customary to complain in this context that where such attitudes are adopted with respect to religion the result is not impartiality so much as sheer indifference.[11] Religion is reduced to one consumer product amongst others. It is available in different forms for selection and use, but there is no overriding imperative from the perspective of the neutral observer to make any particular choice. Thus David Tracy remarks that religion 'is a private consumer product that some people seem to need. Its former social role was poisonous. Its present privatization is harmless enough to wish it well from a civilized distance.'[12]

Other cultural commentators complain that the exaltation of liberal ideals of tolerance breeds subjectivism and relativism. This is the theme of Allan Bloom's best-selling work *The Closing of the American Mind*. Bloom deplores the attitude of today's educated youth, an attitude he detects in his students. Everyone has his or her own values. These are to be tolerated and there can be no argument about which are right and which are wrong. This high level of tolerance, Bloom argues, leads to a narrowing of moral and intellectual possibilities. There are no standards which define the self and so provide opportunities for notions such as vocation, honour and heroism. The result is a mindset that produces apathy and scepticism in ethical debate.[13] What at first sight appears to be a positive moral appreciation of diversity slips into an attitude of bland indifference. This is confirmed by some statistical evidence, at least from American society. According to a recent survey, 67 per cent of citizens agreed that morality was 'a personal matter and society should not force everyone to follow one standard'.[14]

This difficulty is compounded by the impracticality of the unencumbered state. No polity can remain neutral in respect of the goods

---

[11] See Kieran Flannigan, 'Theological Pluralism, Religious Pluralism and Unbelief', in Ian Hamnett (ed.), *Religious Pluralism and Unbelief: Studies Critical and Comparative* (London: Routledge, 1990), 81–113.

[12] *The Analogical Imagination* (London: SCM, 1981), 13.

[13] Charles Taylor, however, argues that Bloom ignores a genuine ideal of sincerity in criticising its debased forms in modern culture. In part, I share this argument by attempting to return to early modern ideals of tolerance to produce a viable alternative to more modern notions of autonomy. See Charles Taylor, *The Ethics of Authenticity* (Cambridge, MA: Harvard University Press, 1991).

[14] Cited by David Hollenbach, *The Common Good and Christian Ethics* (Cambridge: Cambridge University Press, 2002), 25.

it values and promotes through the passing of laws. This is true on a range of measures including broadcasting, sex education, pornography, Sunday trading, advertising standards, asylum seekers and abortion. Decisions are made not on the thin basis of securing freedom and maintaining state impartiality. These have their place, but thicker notions of the good are necessary to the formation of substantive policies in each of these fields. The problem of urban poverty, for example, cannot be addressed merely through a strategy of tolerance. It requires a shared set of social goals together with some political agreement about the measures most likely to achieve these.[15] On a more pessimistic reading, Alasdair MacIntyre argues that decisions in the modern liberal state reflect not so much a consensus as the interests of those with the power to adjudicate. This itself is a function of the wider distribution of political, social and economic power.[16] In light of these problems, a theology of toleration may fare better by taking its bearings from early modern arguments emerging from the religious disputes of the Reformation than from more recent liberal ideology.

Considered as a guiding principle for moral action, the mandate of tolerance is inadequate. We cannot simply live and let live. This must inevitably lead to a neglect of those common goods that are necessary for human well-being. These are not to be assessed as instrumental commodities, necessary for each of us as individuals to do our own thing. The sociality of human life necessitates a commitment to common goods that are 'non-rivalrous in consumption'. The nature of these goods (e.g. public parks, libraries and museums) does not entail consumption by one individual at the expense of another. Our identity as individuals is not defined prior to or apart from our relationship to other persons. This is argued *inter alia* in the work of the philosopher John Macmurray who claims that the 'I' of the western, egocentric tradition must be deconstructed. The individual only comes to self-consciousness and freedom through agency within the

---

[15] This is argued persuasively by David Hollenbach: 'Toleration alone will not overcome class divisions and the despair they engender among the poor . . . This means that the dominant middle-class morality writ small, with its preference for the quiet virtues, is an inadequate cultural resource for addressing the plight of American cities'; ibid., 40.

[16] E.g. 'Toleration and the Goods of Conflict', in Susan Mendus (ed.), *The Politics of Toleration: Tolerance and Intolerance in Modern Life* (Edinburgh: Edinburgh University Press, 1999), 141.

public world and a network of relationships beginning in infancy with our primary carers. There is no 'I' without a 'you' and no self without the other. The freedom and love we seek can only be realised in relations of friendship, and these in turn require membership of properly ordered communities and societies. '[I]t is the sharing of a common life which constitutes individual personality. We become persons in community, in virtue of our relation to others. Human life is *inherently* a common life.'[17]

Furthermore, it is worth noting in this context that education in the ways of tolerance is itself dependent on institutions, customs and forms of moral training that enable us to respect and become sensitive of difference. Despite appearances, the virtue of toleration is not intuited as obviously right without reference to our social conditioning. I have sometimes met students who speak, usually in dismissive terms, of grandparents who were brainwashed to think and believe dogmas that they have now discarded two generations later. Yet the thought seldom occurs that our own assumptions and convictions may similarly derive from patterns of upbringing, the education system, exposure to the media and peer-group pressures. The modern stress on tolerance requires explanation in terms of a particular institutional setting. Tolerance reposes upon cultivated ways of living together rather than indifferently existing apart. In modern society, our habits of tolerance require the moral nurture and reasoning that are developed from the nursery onwards. These are embedded within the school syllabus, in the patterns of work and play that are encouraged, and in the moral vocabulary that is taught to children.[18]

THE EARLY MODERN CASE

The standard whiggish interpretation of the history of religious toleration is that it was articulated by Renaissance humanists, lost sight of by the first generation of magisterial Reformers, but steadily recovered by later writers throughout the early modern period. As an

---

[17] John Macmurray, *Conditions of Freedom* (Canada: Ryerson Press, 1949), 37. For a summary of Macmurray's account of community see Frank G. Kirkpatrick, *The Ethics of Community* (Oxford: Blackwell, 2001), 65–79.

[18] The claim that tolerance itself is socially generated is argued by Hollenbach, following Charles Taylor, in *The Common Good and Christian Ethics*, 72.

account of religious practice, this has been challenged in recent historiography.[19] Tolerance was patchy in the sixteenth and seventeenth centuries. There are some surprising examples of toleration to be registered from times when latitude might be least expected. But one has also to debit widespread persecution of marginal groups and individuals well into the seventeenth century. Heiko Obermann has remarked that it is at the margins of society that tolerance is best measured.[20] While a desire for peaceful coexistence emerges within Christianity – particularly after the Thirty Years' War – there remains, for example, evidence of intensified persecution of those accused of witchcraft.

Nonetheless, whatever the difficulties with a schematic reading of the rise of religious toleration, we find some clear landmarks in the history of ideas. In the writings of Erasmus and other Renaissance humanists, arguments are encountered which, although muted in the magisterial Reformers, became crucial in the growing demand for toleration in later centuries. These can be enumerated as follows.

1. Reference to the example of Christ and the apostolic church reveals that there was no attempt to coerce men and women to join the early Christian community or to embrace its doctrines. The way of persuasion was pursued by Christ. At the centre of the Christian religion is the search for peace and concord. Locke would later speak of the holiness of conversation found in Christ and his disciples.[21]

2. A distinction between the moral essence of the Christian faith and some of its inessential dogmatic claims must be maintained. The upshot of this is that where ethical unanimity can be established it is unnecessary and futile to argue about more obscure issues on which certainty cannot be attained: 'You will not be damned if you do not know whether the Spirit proceeding from the Father and the Son has one or two beginnings, but you will not escape

---

[19] E.g. Ole Peter Grell and Bob Scribner (eds.), *Tolerance and Intolerance in the European Reformation* (Cambridge: Cambridge University Press, 1996). For a recent 'post-revisionist' account of the growth of religious toleration in England see John Coffey, *Persecution and Toleration in Protestant England 1558–1689* (Harlow: Longman, 2000).

[20] 'The Travail of Tolerance: Containing Chaos in Early Modern Europe', in Grell and Scribner (eds.), *Tolerance and Intolerance in the European Reformation*, 29.

[21] 'A Letter Concering Toleration' (1685), in *Political Writings* (London: Penguin, 1993), 393.

damnation, if you do not cultivate the fruits of the Spirit.'[22] (This alternative condition for salvation remains somewhat daunting.)

3. The coercion of belief is futile and even counterproductive of genuine piety. Thus Erasmus criticised the intervention of political rulers to resolve dogmatic disputes and to impose orthodoxy: 'That which is forced cannot be sincere, and that which is not voluntary cannot please Christ.'[23]

We might note that stress is not yet on the positive value of religious diversity. We are far from the modern pluralist ideal of the beauty of a patchwork society comprising different cultures, religions and lifestyle options. There are indeed illiberal strains in Erasmian thinking. If we cannot achieve certainty on dogmatic matters, then we must have recourse to the traditions of the church. If moral rather than dogmatic conformity is what matters, then the civil ruler may have a duty to suppress anarchy and disorder. This appears to have constituted his response to Anabaptist rejection of the authority of the civil magistrate. So Bainton concludes that on the issue of toleration Erasmus was a bell calling others to church while himself remaining in the steeple.[24]

In Calvin's Geneva, as in other societies, all citizens were subject to both civil and ecclesiastical law. The Consistory comprised ministers and elders, the latter group including prominent members of Genevan society nominated by the magistracy. It was intended to meet weekly with the purpose of enforcing ecclesiastical discipline in the entire community. Its remit was extensive and it developed a reputation for being unnecessarily inquisitorial and prying.[25] The partnership between the civil and religious here envisaged represented a Reformed commitment to social transformation.[26] This ideal of social transformation is one which characterised Reformed churches at other times

---

[22] From Erasmus' preface to Hilary as cited by Roland Bainton in his edition of Sebastian Castellio, *Concerning Heretics* (New York: Columbia University Press, 1935), 33.

[23] Ibid., 34.

[24] Ibid., 42. The limits of toleration in Erasmus' thinking can be located at that point where religious, social and political concerns converge. Where a theological error manifests itself in sedition then civil suppression is justifiable. Cf. A. G. Dickens and Whitney R. D. Jones, *Erasmus the Reformer* (London: Methuen, 1994), 271.

[25] See the discussion in F. Wendel, *Calvin* (London: Collins, 1963), 69ff.

[26] This is less evident in Lutheranism which was dominated by the doctrine of the two kingdoms. As we have seen, however, the two-kingdoms doctrine was interpreted in different ways, not all of which were radically different from Reformed views.

and places, although from the early modern period onwards there arose a perceived need for a greater distancing of the state from the church, and for a stronger account of religious liberty.[27] The earlier organic unity of church and civil society thus declined as a greater measure of religious and cultural diversity came to be accommodated.

The Geneva of Calvin's heyday is frequently criticised for producing a cramped social order with an imposed uniformity, an invasion of privacy and an overbearing moral censoriousness. His treatment of Servetus is symptomatic of the impossibility of religious dissent or nonconformity in this world. Yet the Reformed ideal of social transformation with its stress on comprehensive education and the relief of poverty is animated by the same theological impulse. While this desire for a godly commonwealth has occasioned much praise, this has not always been accompanied by the recognition that the deficits of the Reformed *polis* arise from a common source. If we desire transformation yet with a greater measure of toleration some theological adjustments will be necessary to accommodate both aspirations within the Reformed tradition. This problem is inadequately addressed in the literature. In extolling the social and political commitment of their tradition, Reformed writers have paid too little attention to its potential for illiberal consequences.

In examining Calvin's writings and ministry, we can gain some further understanding as to why tolerance and religious diversity were not live options. Later notions of state neutrality and religious pluralism are neither possible nor desirable. Intolerance was justified on a variety of grounds.

1. There is the argument for the maintenance of religious purity within a community. For the sake of this great good, those who deviate from the path of true religion must be suppressed or rooted out. According to the magisterial Reformers and confessions of their churches, this is a responsibility of civil rulers. The spiritual health of a community requires the disciplining and even forceful exclusion of heretics.

2. There is also an argument that it is for the good of heretics themselves that they be suppressed. If they are risking the fate of eternal

---

[27] See David Little, 'Reformed Faith and Religious Liberty', in Donald McKim (ed.), *Major Themes in the Reformed Tradition* (Grand Rapids: Eerdmans, 1984), 196–213.

damnation, it is better that they be subjected to some temporal discipline and punishment in order to avert a much greater eschatological evil. (How this squares with the doctrine of election is not entirely clear.) There are several theological assumptions here concerning matters such as the relation of this life to the next, divine retribution, the significance of right belief, and the nature of hell as eternal torment. However, with some or all of these arguments in place, a plausible case can be presented. If the most important goal in life is to secure a favourable destiny for one's soul, then it cannot greatly matter how this is achieved. By remaining outside the faith, one is condemned to burn through all eternity. To escape from this through burning of the temporal body is greatly to be preferred, especially if this is the only avoidance strategy available. By enforcing the faith, therefore, the interests of those coerced are in the long run fulfilled.[28]

3. A third argument and the one which really held sway with Calvin was the maintenance of divine honour. The first commandment must be upheld. Blasphemy can never be tolerated for this is an offence against God of the most serious and vile nature. Thus Servetus is not merely offering one theological opinion amongst others. He has denied the being of God and has therefore placed himself in a position in which he must be punished for the sake of restitution. For if we require restitution for crimes committed against human persons, how much more must we demand restitution of those who deny the divine persons?[29]

4. There may also be a fourth argument that is not often recognised in Calvin. It can be detected at the close of the *Institutes*.[30] Religion is a universal human phenomenon. All people are religious, and every society must have a theological identity. Therefore in organising the life of a people the civil ruler has no alternative but to make some decisions about which religion is to be promoted amongst his or her people for the glory of God and the well-being of society. The idea of state neutrality is still a long way off. It is not possible

---

[28] Cf. Preston King, *Toleration* (London: Allen & Unwin, 1976), 76–7.

[29] Calvin's defence of his role in the Servetus affair is found in 'Defensio Orthodoxae Fidei De Sacra Trinitate contra Prodigiosos Errores Michaelis Serveti Hispani', *Calvini Opera*, vol. VIII, 452–643.

[30] *Institutes*, IV.20.

to conceive of a society which does not favour one form of religion over another. Once again we encounter the principle 'cuius regio, eius religio'.

The case for greater toleration emerges historically not so much from a welcome embrace of diversity as through the refutation of arguments for intolerance. Here the work of Sebastian Castellio deserves attention.[31] A contemporary and one time colleague in Geneva, Castellio found himself at odds with Calvin over the interpretation of the Song of Songs, the treatment of Servetus and the doctrine of election. He penned his pseudonymous defence for religious tolerance in reaction to the burning of Servetus and in concern at the civil wars raging in France. His work is an ingenious selection from the writings of humanists and reformers in support of tolerance.

Castellio argues that conversion is a voluntary matter. Christ does not force people to follow him. Not only is this a violation of another person's soul, it is a pointless exercise since religious belief cannot be coerced in this way. Here emerges something like the positive value of liberty of conscience. Castellio suggests that the murder of a heretic is a greater evil than heresy itself. The freedom of the individual is a good, particularly where religious faith is concerned, and to violate that freedom by the taking of life is a greater evil than the failure to exercise freedom in correct judgement. As we shall see, this humanitarian argument, if valid, may require some revision of the earlier theological assumptions noted above.

An important subsidiary reason advanced by Castellio is that in practice many of the differences between Huguenots and Catholics are not so striking and not matters on which Scripture pronounces. In any case, these are issues on which certainty eludes us. This recalls Erasmus' earlier stress on the insignificance of dogmatic disputes in distinction from the importance of good practice. The blend of arguments in his preface written for the Duke of Württemburg is worth noting. It anticipates strategies that were to be pursued by thinkers in the following centuries, particularly in Locke's 'A Letter Concerning Toleration' (1685), which has become a *locus classicus* in the field. The teaching of Christ bids us to be merciful and forgiving. We are to consider the beam that is in our own eye before attending to the

---

[31] I am indebted here to an unpublished paper by Michael Langford.

mote in our neighbour's. Heresy is not to be condoned, but we must beware of convicting others who will in the long run turn out to be vindicated, as Christ and his disciples were. Even when discipline is appropriate, moreover, it should not be excessive.

The essence of the Christian religion, Castellio proposes, is belief in God, Father, Son and Spirit, and approval of the commandments of true religion as set out in Scripture.[32] A distinction is made between the uncertainties of doctrinal points of difference and the widely acknowledged principles of true conduct. 'In the matter of conduct, if you ask a Jew, Turk, Christian, or anyone else, what he thinks of a brigand or a traitor, all will reply with one accord that brigands and traitors are evil and should be put to death.'[33] Yet on matters of right belief there is widespread difference between Jew, Turk and Christian even though all agree that there is one God. Amongst Christians there are many disagreements on points of doctrine. No one position is self-evidently true: 'Great controversies and debates occur as to baptism, the Lord's Supper, the invocation of the saints, justification, free will, and other obscure questions, so that Catholics, Lutherans, Zwinglians, Anabaptists, monks, and others condemn and persecute one another more cruelly than the Turks do the Christians.'[34] There then follows a plea for peaceful toleration of one's theological opponents. Together, through forbearance and kindness, we may hope to arrive at the truth. Divided, we deny the name of Christ before the world: 'Who would wish to be a Christian, when he saw that those who confessed the name of Christ were destroyed by Christians themselves with fire, water, and the sword without mercy and more cruelly treated than brigands and murderers?'[35]

This case for peaceful coexistence in pursuit of the truth can be sustained by a theology of the Word and Spirit. The truth is discerned through the patient hearing of God's Word and the guidance of the Spirit, but there is also a need to listen to the testimony of other Christians in the community of faith even when (or perhaps above all when) their opinions are diametrically opposed to one's own. This requires tolerance, humility and the proper conditions for respectful conversation. Worth recalling in this context is the oft-cited comment

---

[32] Castellio, *Concerning Heretics*, ed. Bainton, 130.
[33] Ibid., 131.   [34] Ibid., 132.   [35] Ibid., 133.

attributed to John Robinson, a Puritan divine and exponent of religious tolerance: 'The Lord hath yet more light and truth to break forth from His Word.' Similarly, John Milton's argument for religious freedom in the *Areopagitica* is based on the assumption that a forum for free speech, dialogue and conversation is necessary if the truth is finally to emerge. The practice of conversation rather than mutual anathematising is advocated for the sake of the truth and the welfare of all parties.

The argument against intolerance proceeds on the basis that it is irrational to attempt to alter by force a person's most fundamental convictions. Outward behaviour and insincere speech can be coerced but our deepest allegiances cannot be eradicated in this way. Indeed they may only be reinforced. This leads to the valuing of liberty of conscience. We have a personal responsibility for our faith, a responsibility that cannot be transferred to the state or even the church. Hence in the slipstream of arguments against intolerance there is an enhanced claim for the sanctity of individual conscience. So we find Roger Williams in Rhode Island in the 1630s promoting a religiously diverse society on the conviction that the only authentic faith is voluntary and grounded in the conscience of the individual.[36] And from his exile in the Low Countries in 1685, John Locke argues for an England that is more tolerant:

It appears not that God has ever given any such authority to one man over another as to compel anyone to his religion . . . Whatever profession we make, to whatever outward worship we conform, if we are not fully satisfied in our own mind that the one is true, and the other well pleasing unto God, such profession and such practice, far from being any furtherance, are indeed great obstacles to our salvation.[37]

Arguments for the irrationality of intolerance and the sanctity of the individual conscience were not presented in isolation from those wider cultural factors that shaped greater latitude of opinion.[38] Expansion of world trade had brought closer contacts with and a more

---

[36] When the Westminster Confession was exported to the USA, its chapter on the civil magistrate had to be rewritten. Drafted by John Witherspoon, the new chapter sought to put greater distance between church and state.

[37] 'Letter Concerning Toleration', 394.

[38] In what follows I am indebted to Christopher Hill, 'Tolerance in Seventeenth-Century England: Theory and Practice', in Mendus (ed.), *The Politics of Toleration*, 38ff.

informed awareness of other civilisations and religion. These had achieved cultural excellence independently of Christianity. By the early Enlightenment of the late seventeenth century, attention had shifted from establishing orthodox Christian belief by coercion, to demonstrating its rational superiority. Reason rather than force became the means of vindicating the faith. International trading, moreover, made tolerance an economic necessity, with some European cities reaping the economic benefits of providing a home for dissenters.[39] The broadening of intellectual horizons saw greater scholarly interest in other religions. The single state church in England came finally to coexist with traditions of dissent that it could not overcome. At the same time, the dissenters could not control the state without perpetual strife and damage to those socio-economic groups in which they were chiefly represented.[40] Finally, abandonment of specific eschatological hopes combined with the declining belief in hell achieved what Hobbes had thought was essential for civil peace. The demise of the prospect of eternal rewards and punishments for earthly loyalties helped to pacify society. Hill points out that when John Mason attracted large crowds at Water Stratford in 1694 he was not prosecuted for proclaiming the imminent end of the world.[41] He was advised to take his medicine. A gradual shift towards civility, moral improvement and a less clearly differentiated theism would become even more apparent in the theological writers of the eighteenth century.

In assessing the growth of toleration in early modern England, John Coffey notes the inherently theological nature of the arguments. By studying the example of the early church, exponents of toleration concluded that religious repression and coercion could not be justified. The hero in the story was not Erasmus of Rotterdam but the New Testament itself.[42] For early modern writers, the case for tolerance was based on a cluster of related arguments – the example of Christ and his first followers, the legitimate limits of state power, the irrationality of coercion, the sanctity of each person's faith commitment, the need

---

[39] See Ole Peter Grell 'Introduction' to Grell and Scribner (eds.), *Tolerance and Intolerance in the European Reformation*, 7ff.

[40] Hill, 'Tolerance in Seventeenth-Century England', 41.   [41] Ibid.

[42] Coffey, *Persecution and Toleration in Protestant England*, 211. This remark is derived from A. G. Dickens.

for peace and social cohesion, and the promotion of conversation amongst those who differ for the sake of a greater approximation to God's truth.

We should note that the case for tolerance was initiated by those on the underside of historical processes. It was not at first a grudging concession by those in charge. Instead it was demanded by groups who were persecuted, disempowered and endangered. Anti-Trinitarians, Quakers, Independents, Arminians, Baptists, Socinians, Ranters, Jews and recusant Catholics were all threatened, marginalised or excluded in different contexts in the seventeenth century. Toleration was initially the argument of the dissenting rather than the condescending gift of the ruling. The argument, moreover, retains its validity even when more modern claims for autonomy are increasingly suspect. At a time when liberalism is increasingly under attack, we need to be reminded of the preceding theological case for toleration. This is recognised by secular thinkers for whom a pragmatic 'liberalism of fear' is most plausible. So Bernard Williams writes, 'The case of toleration is, unsurprisingly, a central one for distinguishing between a strongly moralized conception of liberalism as based on ideals of individual autonomy, and a more sceptical, historically alert, politically direct conception of it as the best hope for humanly acceptable legitimate government under modern conditions.'[43]

A fuller account of the implications of tolerance requires us to recognise not merely individual preferences, but the significance of group identity and solidarity. Society is not an aggregate of private consumers who make their own choices. It comprises a variety of groups, communities and traditions with their different and sometimes competing loyalties. It is these that shape our identity and influence the choices we make. If the goal of tolerance is not simply the protection and extending of individual choices but rather the promotion of the common good, this may result in policies which are in different ways more and less tolerant. Christian theology with its traditions of the godly society, the common good, and the nation under the kingly rule of Yahweh should be able to articulate these aspirations. In this context, it is necessary to stress the importance of securing freedom of worship and association, while also articulating

---

[43] 'Toleration, a Political or Moral Question?', in Paul Ricoeur (ed.), *Tolerance between Intolerance and the Intolerable* (Providence, RI: Berghahn, 1996), 47.

those neighbourly bonds that unite individuals and groups within society. This is illustrated by those early Christians who, in arguing for religious freedom, were able to appeal to the wider social contribution of the church.

It has already been argued that for individuals to belong to a wider community they require not merely tolerance but something more akin to recognition, acknowledgement or respect. This was noted by Hegel when he argued that for persons to achieve self-consciousness it is necessary that their identity be affirmed by other self-conscious subjects. What is true for persons is also true for communities and nations. Something richer and more positive than tolerance is sought. In the context of a modern society comprising many solidarities and identities, this may require more tolerance for the different practices, customs and beliefs of subgroups. The insistence that all fit a paradigm of autonomous choice can fail to comprehend the manner in which it is group identity that shapes individual desires and preferences. What tolerance requires is not simply an available menu of choices but recognition of the outlook, sensitivities and practices of the subculture. In this respect, something more than mere tolerance is demanded. Indeed, within some social settings, strategies of tolerance themselves can be perceived as oppressive and threatening. For example, in India a Hindu nationalism that sets out grounds for tolerating the presence of other religions may actually be suspected of quite significant forms of discrimination. Mere toleration in this sense is not equivalent to full recognition through the freedom to practice and participate in public life. It is a concession granted within an otherwise restrictive polity.

Inevitably, the comprehension of differing convictions in a single society must create points of tension and conflict. Yet here we can return to the early modern desire for public space within which groups are accorded respect and provided an occasion for civil conversation. Thick communities of discourse must find ways of articulating for their members moral standards that can be assented to by all (or most) members of the wider civil society. These will typically require a capacity for self-criticism, and a readiness to empathise with traditions other than one's own.

Despite this, in other contexts a stronger sense of the common good may result in a restriction of choice, an awareness that there are places where tolerance is overstretched. If communities find their self-esteem eroded in the public domain by attitudes and practices of free individuals there arises a *prima facie* case for intolerance. It is at this sensitive juncture that issues relating to censorship in the media and the advertising industry arise. An outlook which has some sense of the need to maintain the common good by supporting differing solidarities may find itself on occasion less tolerant when standards of public decency and self-respect are violated. It is hardly coincidental that the most troubled critics of the graphic portrayal of sex and violence in entertainment and commerce are parents struggling to socialise their children into a different form of life. Here tolerance, even if conceded, will often be grudging. If we still tolerate smoking in public places, justification will be offered less on grounds of respect, difference and the need to learn, and more through a recognition that coercion is too problematic and counterproductive. More fundamentally, every moral tradition will find itself on occasion unable to tolerate violations of the most rudimentary standards. Its commitment to tolerance will be situated within boundaries outside of which lie intolerable beliefs and practices. Ricoeur deplores in this connection the disguised return to practices of slavery, extreme forms of inequality, and manifestations of racism.[44]

In advocating tolerance, theology is not left unchanged. Arguments for freedom of conscience in matters of faith, freedom of worship, and respect for other religions signal a shift from some of the nostrums of medieval and Reformation Christianity. These require revision for a theology of tolerance to take proper shape. For example, there needs to be the recognition that God is active in other faiths and social movements, and that therefore the choices of others are to be affirmed on account of the goods that these realise for individuals, communities and the world. Without this assumption, a theology of tolerance will not stretch far enough. It is no coincidence that Vatican II is able to attach a high value to freedom of conscience in religion while also affirming the values realised in other faiths, and that Reformed theologies today have generally abandoned the grievous assumption

---

[44] 'The Erosion of Tolerance and the Resistance of the Intolerable', in Paul Ricoeur (ed.), *Tolerance between Intolerance and the Intolerable*, 198.

that those practising other religions cannot belong to the company of God's elect.[45]

Michael Walzer has recently suggested that the arguments for the virtue of toleration can be located on a spectrum of views running through five possible positions.[46] The first reflects the origins of religious toleration in the sixteenth and seventeenth centuries and is simply a resigned acceptance of peace for the sake of peace. A second possible attitude is passive, relaxed and benign indifference to difference. 'It takes all kinds to make a world.' A third approach is the principled recognition of the rights of others to express themselves in particular ways, even if we do not much like what they do. Fourth, we can adopt an attitude of curiosity or respect; a willingness to listen and learn, conscious that we do not ourselves hold all the answers. Finally, there is the possibility of an enthusiastic endorsement of difference; this represents the wonderful diversity of human culture and extends human choice in a way that promotes greater self-expression.

If the foregoing is correct, a theology of tolerance can affirm at least three of these, and probably four. Religious diversity can be tolerated for the sake of peace. It can be welcomed for the positive contribution it makes to the self-understanding and witness of the Christian community and to the peace and prosperity of civil society. It does not require a bland reduction of all theological claims or the promotion of high levels of religious indifference. But it does necessitate a commitment to the salvation of the world and the action of God in Christ *extra muros ecclesiae*. Furthermore, a properly placed humility will acknowledge that in the history of the church the beliefs and practices of one generation are neither complete nor immune to revision by the next. Through exposure to alternative ways of life, competing convictions, and other communities, we can hope to learn and advance in our own beliefs and practice. At the

---

[45] In twentieth-century Reformed thought, Barth's christocentric theory of universal election together with his account of 'secular parables of the Word of God' offers one influential revision of earlier exclusivism. For a discussion of this see George Hunsinger, *How to Read Karl Barth* (Oxford: Oxford University Press, 1991), 234–80. For an application to interfaith dialogue see David Lochhead, *The Dialogical Imperative* (London: SCM, 1988).

[46] *On Toleration* (New Haven: Yale University Press, 1997), 10ff.

same time, the theological underpinning of this proposal means that some forms of diversity remain problematic. The first commandment, the lordship of Christ, and the eschatological expectation of the divine dominion all suggest the unity of the human race under God. A theology of tolerance that recognises the partial unity that can be achieved through the suppression of intolerance, the promotion of mutual respect and a commitment to civil conversation can anticipate something of the promised reign of God.

Nevertheless, an account of toleration that is indifferent to division, separation and conflicts over human goods cannot be supported. For this reason, the practice of tolerance must sometimes fall short of Walzer's fifth stage. In any case, the affirmation of tolerance simply on grounds of autonomy will lead, as we have seen, to indifference and forms of relativism. Walzer's fifth type may thus suggest a sixth into which it slides – indifference and moral scepticism. In effect, this is the argument of Ricoeur who points out in support of this thesis that contemporary preoccupation with security and health are all that remain when the public domain has been evacuated of strong convictions. His remedy for tolerance is a much stronger sense of what we regard as intolerable.[47]

CONCLUSION

The claim of this chapter is that the necessary virtue of tolerance is not to be established on a modern philosophy of autonomy, but with reference to the practical concerns of early modern writers preoccupied with religious divisions. Tolerance is not so much one value but a set of attitudes and practices that may be adopted for different reasons.

The range of considerations that spawned attitudes of tolerance needs to be recalled in the face of the indifference and scepticism, often induced by the standard moves of political liberalism. The need for peaceful coexistence, the irrationality of state coercion, the freedom of the act of faith, and the prospect of civil conversation with others unlike ourselves from whom we have a good deal to learn – all create

---

[47] Ricoeur, 'The Erosion of Tolerance and the Resistance of the Intolerable', 196.

the space within which modern societies can flourish. Some changes of theological tack may be required here. Consequently, the story of modern theology is bound more closely to the gradual rise of pluralist societies from early modernity onwards than is sometimes recognised in the textbooks.

CHAPTER FIVE

Moral formation: the church's contribution

> Moralities are like languages. We are born into them and we must learn them if we are to communicate and have relationships with others. Like languages, moralities embody ancient and living social processes. We do not invent them by our individual choices. Instead, by learning them we take our part in a particular tradition which long preceded us and which will continue long after we are no longer here.
>
> (Jonathan Sacks)[1]

CHRISTIAN IDENTITY IN CRISIS

In his aforementioned study, Callum Brown claims that since the 1960s the changes that have taken place in British culture constitute a transition from a Christian to a post-Christian society. Instead of perceiving the slow decline of several centuries as the tide of religion ebbs, he describes a sudden draining away of church affiliation, practice, and Christian construction of social identity.[2] Brown's thesis has been challenged in various ways: changes in British society since the 1960s may be attributable to causal factors already embedded in its history from at least the nineteenth century; early periods of twentieth-century history, especially the aftermath of the First World War, reveal widespread disaffection and crises of confidence for institutional Christianity; and, in any case, many of the social changes that he perceives as signs of dissociation may themselves have been promoted by the churches. But, notwithstanding these caveats, it is difficult to contest the claim that the traditional markers of Christian identity have been in rapid decline during the past generation.

---

[1] *Faith in the Future* (London: Darton, Longman & Todd, 1995), 66.
[2] Callum Brown, *The Death of Christian Britain*.

We can find much anecdotal and statistical evidence to support this. At a trivial level one encounters astonishingly high levels of biblical illiteracy – students who now have to look up the table of contents in the Bible to find the book of Genesis, or the contestant on the quiz show who has to defer to the audience when asked the name of the garden inhabited by Adam and Eve. Statistics for regular church attendance in the United Kingdom reveal that only 7 per cent of the population worship on most Sundays, and even this figure conceals the extent to which a younger generation is almost entirely absent. The demand for baptisms and church weddings is down, with an increasing number of couples cohabiting and raising children. What is striking is not the conscious rejection of the Christian ideal of marriage but the sheer incomprehension when confronted with this notion. Christine McMullen documents research amongst young couples as to why they opted not to marry.[3] Predictably the responses reveal a sea change in popular opinion – a wedding is too expensive, parents get in the way, you can have sex and cohabit without the hassle, the formality of the marriage contract removes the romance from the relationship, freedom and equality are compromised by the institution. Set in historical context, these responses reveal a sudden departure from earlier ideals shaped by church teaching and practice. So much is this so, that the expression 'living in sin' has become archaic and quaint. Even the funeral service, the rite of passage that seemed most stubbornly resistant to change, has started to alter. Increasingly custom-designed, services now reflect the tastes and interests of the deceased and mourners. These are becoming less recognisable as traditional acts of Christian worship.

Other indicators of the social significance of the churches reveal steady decline. The pronouncements of church leaders are accorded fewer column inches and less broadcasting time, while the influence of church opinion on government policy is not readily perceptible. The Church of Scotland has adopted a policy of opposition to the possession of nuclear missiles on Trident submarines, and their deployment at Faslane on the west coast. Though robustly argued and consistently maintained, this opposition has not met with any obvious measure of success. There was widespread ecclesiastical resistance to the

[3] Christine McMullen, 'Cohabitation and Marriage', *Crucible*, January–March 2001, 42–53.

establishment of the National Lottery in the 1990s, yet this has been spectacularly ineffective, the lottery becoming a national institution in the space of a few years. In October 2003, the Church of Scotland received two nominations for its moderatorial office. Both nominees were female, thus guaranteeing a woman moderator for the first time in the church's history. Yet the *Scotsman* newspaper relegated this story to an inside page, on a morning lacking any major national or international news.[4] Even Christmas, a festival universally celebrated in the West, is now marked by self-conscious attempts to dechristianise its expression. There is no point in bewailing this scenario, and little prospect of a return to a position of social establishment. Yet this change of cultural location must be faced.

One of the paradoxes in this situation of sharp decline is that it has contributed to a greater self-confidence amongst Christian theologians and ethicists. Several factors are probably at work here. There is a sense of liberation in the realisation that the church no longer speaks for society, exercising a central role in promoting consensus and achieving social stability. This frees the representatives of the community to speak on distinctively Christian grounds, to fulfil the fundamental task of bearing witness to the faith, and to set aside the burden of being the state's major partner within civil society. A second factor at work in recent theological ethics derives from contemporary moral and ideological fragmentation. The relative demise of Christian consciousness has not coincided with the establishment of an alternative moral viewpoint. Our moral condition has been described as lacking coherence. What we have to hand are relics of older traditions but no longer sustained by the world-view, practices and social support which once gave these plausibility. This moral fragmentation can be viewed with varying degrees of concern. Most famously, perhaps, in the closing stages of *After Virtue* Alasdair MacIntyre announces the collapse of our wider political civilisation. What is required is not the shoring up of the old *imperium*. Instead we need to promote local forms of community and civility which can be sustained throughout the new dark age that is already upon us.

---

[4] A spokesperson for the church suggested that the two nominations were welcome for the astonishing reason that it was time the church caught up with modern society. If this has become the basis for ecclesiastical decision-making, one can now look forward to commissioners of the General Assembly smoking pot.

This time, he claims, the difference is that the barbarians are not threatening invasion from beyond our gates – they are already in government.[5] By contrast, Jeffrey Stout in *Ethics after Babel*, surveying the same symptoms, finds the diagnosis unduly pessimistic. We can survive on moral fragments through a process of *bricolage*; that is, selecting and blending from different moral traditions in ways that civilise and unite us morally. And, he maintains, we have sufficient in common to provide the cohesion that will offset the process of fragmentation. This is illustrated by reference to the moral platitudes of the nursery where infants are taught friendship towards strangers, truthfulness, cooperation, and the negotiation of problems without recourse to violence.[6] Of course, the environment of the school playground sometimes reveals a harsher world of intimidation, bullying and exclusion. Yet the problems of socialising children should not occlude the moral agreement that can be found amongst persons of different religions, outlooks and lifestyles.

Whatever one's verdict on ethical fragmentation, it provides those who inhabit communities like the church with an opportunity to rediscover the ways in which their practices, beliefs, rituals and communal life animate a moral viewpoint. In the absence of any overriding moral framework in secular society, the practitioners and theorists of Christian ethics are not without hope. This argument, of course, rests on the assumption, defended in earlier chapters, that secular liberalism or something like it cannot provide a coherent moral framework. It must itself be seen as another tradition lacking consensual support and being subject to a range of objections. Or perhaps it must be perceived from this perspective as a moral viewpoint which at a crucial juncture is parasitic upon older and thicker assumptions about human nature, the goals of human life, and social justice. Either way, analyses of current moral pluralism suggest that the decline of mainstream Christianity in our culture is matched by some loss of confidence in rival systems, most notably Marxism and neo-liberalism.

The situation in which we find ourselves may also have a further positive aspect for theological ethics. The eclipse of Christianity in our social landscape creates a curiosity and interest which may have

---

[5] MacIntyre, *After Virtue*, 263.
[6] Jeffrey Stout, *Ethics after Babel* (Cambridge, MA: Clarke, 1988), 214.

previously been lacking. The familiarity which breeds contempt is gone, or at least is on its way. There is a greater interest in theological matters amongst the practitioners of other disciplines than was the case a generation ago, particularly in philosophy, the natural sciences and the health sciences. And despite the exodus of a younger generation from the mainstream churches there are more students taking courses in theology and religious studies than ever before.

CONGREGATIONAL NURTURE

In this context, Stanley Hauerwas has called upon Christians to make hay while the sun is shining. We should give up seeking to be the dominant moral force in society – this leads only to corruption in any case. The demise of Christendom instead presents an opportunity to keep the faith in new and exciting ways. The mission of the church is to be located first in the adequacy and faithfulness of its witness to Christ, and only secondarily in the task of the numerical enlargement of the community. In other words, our core business is neither the takeover of the world nor the maximising of church membership. It is in providing an authentic moral voice in a world too often compromised and confused. Above all, this ethical witness will take pacifist form and so testify against the endemic violence of our personal, social and political existence.

The project of articulating the distinctive ethical witness of Christians and the formative role of their communities has attracted the interest of biblical scholars, historians and theologians. Our current situation of a post-Christendom church is one that is compared with the New Testament, the first four centuries and minority groups within the Reformation. In pleading for a more countercultural form of Christianity, one can thus draw upon resources from other periods of ecclesiastical history.[7]

Recent attempts to articulate the countercultural nature of Christianity draw on the work of the German Confessing Church in the 1930s and theologians such as Barth and Bonhoeffer who were associated with the movement. In his early work on *The Cost of*

---

[7] A recent example of this multidisciplinary interest in Christian ethical formation is William P. Brown (ed.), *Character & Scripture: Moral Formation, Community and Biblical Interpretation* (Grand Rapids: Eerdmans, 2002).

Discipleship, Bonhoeffer had already launched an assault on the cultural imprisonment of Christianity. His expression 'cheap grace' derided the nominal church membership that accompanied social status: 'We justified the world, and condemned as heretics those who tried to follow Christ. The result was that a nation became Christian and Lutheran, but at the cost of true discipleship . . . the call to follow Jesus in the narrow way was hardly ever heard.'[8] Bonhoeffer's own attempt to cultivate a Christian piety at once both ecclesial and worldly is well documented. The discipline of prayer, confession, worship and study was not in the interests of a narrow sectarianism. It was oriented towards a world created by God and redeemed by Christ. He would later write of the secularity of faith and of the need to participate in the sufferings of God in the world.

In the context of Bonhoeffer's martyrdom this is deeply moving and impressive. But does it survive as more than rhetoric or pious hope when applied to the contemporary situation? Within the recent writings of Hauerwas it is linked to good effect with criticisms of liberalism, a preference for virtue ethics, and a stress on the significance of narrative for the moral life. The outcome is an ethic which stresses the importance not of moral autonomy but of character formation within the Christian community in faithfulness to the story of Jesus. Virtues such as those of peacemaking, patience, and hopefulness are given due weight, and attention is devoted to the moral differences that they make on a range of issues. The result is the advocacy of church opposition to abortion on demand, legalised euthanasia, and nuclear weapons. This is coupled with support for lifelong marriage, gay friendship, vegetarianism and church schools. Hauerwas' approach to Christian ethics is enormously influential, perhaps surprisingly so within the established churches of the United Kingdom.

Strongly countercultural approaches to Christian moral formation of course face an array of criticisms. There is the oft-repeated charge of sectarianism, which is usually false or meaningless. If it implies a retreat into a social subgroup which is deliberately detached from the wider host culture, it misrepresents the position. There is much to be learned from this culture and in any case the scope of Christian witness

---

[8] *The Cost of Discipleship* (London: SCM, 1948). For a discussion of Bonhoeffer's understanding of the relationship of church to world see Keith Clements, 'Community in the Ethics of Dietrich Bonhoeffer', *Studies in Christian Ethics* 10 (1997), 16–31.

is not the church but secular society. The church is here positioned towards the world; it exists not to withdraw people from the surrounding society but to transform it. Hence it is not detachment that is advocated but a more dialectical form of engagement. Descriptions of so-called sect churches, for example in Troeltsch and H. Richard Niebuhr, tend to overlook the point that a selective, critical appraisal of society is called for on distinctively Christian grounds.

Ernst Troeltsch contrasts the sect-type with the church-type form of Christian organisation.[9] Whereas the church-type accepts the prevailing social order, tends towards universality and seeks to dominate the masses, the sect-type organises itself into small groups, eschews secular domination, and tends to shun state and civil society. It operates on a principle of detachment from the world. Although Troeltsch acknowledges the sect's connection with the essential claims of Christianity, his typology does not adequately capture the possibility offered by Hauerwas. A subgroup may seek to distance itself from the prevailing culture in order to make a distinctive contribution to its self-understanding and to provide agents better equipped to contribute to its well-being. The mission of the church is directed towards the world. Hauerwas' vital claim is that this mission is most effectively enabled by a strategy of becoming an authentic church rather than seeking assimilation into the world. Indeed in so far as his writings provide a sustained attack on the disjunction of private and public realms in political liberalism they may be perceived as an attack on some modern forms of sectarianism or compartmentalisation.[10]

A second type of criticism is that this model of the church as a community of distinctive moral formation nowhere resembles the empirical church. Much of the moral division and fragmentedness of contemporary society is internalised within the church. Its members can read the *Telegraph*, the *Guardian* or the *New York Times*, and they can disagree politically and ethically in much the same way as other readers of these broadsheets. It would be difficult, moreover,

---

[9] *The Social Teaching of the Christian Churches*, trans. Olive Wyon (Louisville: Westminster/ John Knox, 1992), vol. I, 331ff.

[10] I have addressed some of these issues in *Community, Liberalism and Christian Ethics*, 48–79. For further discussion of this issue see the comments of Nigel Biggar, 'Social Withdrawal: Is Stanley Hauerwas Sectarian?', in Mark Thiessen and Samuel Wells (eds.), *Faithfulness and Fortitude: In Conversation with the Theological Ethics of Stanley Hauerwas* (Edinburgh: T. & T. Clark, 2000), 141–60.

to claim that the consensus within western Protestantism about the ordination of women and the value of artificial contraception has not been, in part, determined by the influence of secular assumptions about equality and freedom. On some moral issues we have more in common with our contemporaries outside the church than our ancestors within it. In any case, it has been pointed out that much of the ethical teaching of the New Testament displays significant similarities to pagan teaching about morality. Most of the virtues and vices can be found in other traditions. Much of Paul's ethical exhortation would be familiar to those outside the church. Marital fidelity, love of one's neighbour, maintaining peaceful relations with others, and seeking the welfare of society would all be recognisable moral claims to a pagan audience.[11] Today the children of the church are often influenced as much or more by the media as by the ecclesial community, and unless they are deprived of television, web access, and magazines and have the strength to resist massive peer-group pressure, they will struggle to develop a distinctive Christian identity of the kind that is desired. It is doubtful whether this problem can be entirely overcome.

But in response to it, legitimate appeal is made to the local congregation and to the surprising ways in which women, men and children succeed by divine grace in maintaining their faith in ways that are authentic and deeply moving. There is here something of a postmodern shift of attention from the national face of the institution to its local and particular expression in the lives of people. The frequent emphasis upon the examples of the saints and upon the need to absorb their stories reveals a catholic element in Hauerwas and other recent Protestant writing. The church, as Karl Rahner argues, must present 'in a historically tangible manner the victory of God's grace'.[12] The remembering and recitation of the stories of other Christian lives is a part of our formation. This embraces not only those who command public attention but our first-hand encounter with the 'ordinary saints' often hidden within every congregation. 'Good communities are known by their saints. By naming these ordinary but theologically

---

[11] E.g. Wayne Meeks, *The Origins of Christian Morality* (New Haven: Yale University Press, 1993).

[12] 'The Church of the Saints', *Theological Investigations*, vol. III (London: Darton, Longman and Todd, 1967), 97.

and morally impressive people, we discover resources that we did not know we had.'[13]

The recital of stories of how the faith has been lived out with striking success has generally been an important feature of spiritual formation. These memories provide an awareness of possibilities that can shape and direct our lives. Averil Cameron points to the significance of the practice of storytelling in the rhetoric of Christianity, and of its function in shaping ancient culture.[14] The primary story is that of Jesus, yet the logic of the resurrection requires that his story, although unrepeatable, transform and reconfigure the lives of his followers. As risen and ascended, he is known and made present through the work of the Spirit in the church. The slogans of *sola gratia* and *simul iustus et peccator* should not be used in ways that are inconsistent with this moral claim.

We return again to the thought that Christian allegiance must make some empirical difference to the way we are. There is an almost seamless shift in the New Testament from description of the work of Christ to its effects in the lives of the community. Spiritual gifts, changed lives, and ethical effort are the outcomes of divine grace as it is received and understood. In this respect, it demands not only theological formulation but empirical description. Robin Gill in a recent study, *Churchgoing and Christian Ethics*, has taken this with sufficient seriousness to ask whether and how far church membership makes a difference to the way we live. He notes the way in which in a given society the moral differences between churchgoers and others are relative, and the extent to which church communities often reflect the standard moral disagreements of their society. His conclusion, however, is that church attendance from an early age determines in some measure how we think and act. This is illustrated by surveying the differences between two groups of non-churchgoers, those who were brought up in the church as children and those who were not. The former group displayed significant differences in moral belief and

---

[13] Stanley Hauerwas, *In Good Company* (Indiana: University of Notre Dame Press, 1995), 57. I would also want to argue that the church can in its moral pronouncements, at least sometimes, offer a position which without commanding the universal support of its members, can reflect a consensus amongst those who have talked, listened, prayed and wrestled with the issues. The maintenance of settled positions on nuclear weapons, third-world debt and universal health care provide examples of this.

[14] *Christianity and the Rhetoric of Empire* (Berkeley: University of California Press, 1991), 89ff.

practice. Moreover, in surveying those who continued to practise their faith, Gill notes the formative role of worship through communal singing, praying, listening and sacramental participation.[15]

This leads to a third and related objection to claims for Christian ethical distinctiveness. Christians do not have a monopoly on moral perception or virtuous behaviour. Inspiring examples of justice, courage and forgiveness are found in other places. The instances of Gandhi, Mandela and Aung San Suu Kyi offer compelling evidence of moral insight and heroism from a diversity of traditions and religions. These are to be acknowledged by the followers of Christ as shining examples of divine grace at work in other places. A point long recognised by Christian moralists,[16] this prevents any ring-fencing of good works around the community of faith.

Nevertheless, one can acknowledge that there is no clear hiatus between Christian and non-Christian moral perception without abandoning the importance of ecclesial moral formation. The context in which the moral life is set by Christian faith makes for a difference. It belongs to a life of praise, gratitude and service of God. Set within a fellowship and related by Word and sacrament to Christ and his people throughout the ages, it testifies to the importance of forgiveness, reconciliation, support and mutual encouragement. In this context, intense significance is attached to forgiveness, humility and love of one's neighbour. One does not need to claim that these are absent or lack exponents outside the faith in order to recognise the ethical difference that being brought into the circle of faith must make. If we consider not only moral perception but also commitment, seriousness, motivation and perseverance, then belonging to the church can plausibly be presented as determining moral identity.

SOURCES OF FORMATION

An opportunity to consider traditional forms of character formation has been provided by recent appraisals of virtue ethics. As opposed to utilitarianism or Kantian deontology, the tradition of virtue ethics

---

[15] *Churchgoing and Christian Ethics* (Cambridge: Cambridge University Press, 1999).
[16] Hauerwas seems open to the moral witness of other faith communities. His remarks on Judaism and Islam confirm this. The target of his criticism is secular liberalism and its corrosive effects.

understands moral conduct in light of those dispositions that shape forms of character and community. Through the formation of habits and the development of regular patterns of perception our moral conduct is determined. As a result of this emphasis, one can better view the ethical significance of particular forms of community, nurture, education and devotional practice. For too long this was obscured by theories of moral development that understood the aim of nurture to be release from external authority in favour of individual moral intuition, autonomy and spontaneity.[17] Within the western Christian tradition, moral formation relied upon the use of key texts, particularly the Apostles' Creed, the Lord's Prayer and the Ten Commandments. These were used for training in the faith through much of the Middle Ages, and reappeared later in the catechisms of the Reformation. Today there are welcome signs of this tradition's retrieval.[18] Written at the end of his life, the testimony of Comenius (1592–1670) remains instructive:

If anyone asks about my theology, then like the dying Thomas Aquinas (and I will shortly die), I will take a Bible and with my lips and in my heart I will say: 'I believe what is written in this book.' And if someone asks about my confession of faith, I will name the Apostles' Creed, for none is so short, so simple, so pithy, none brings the decisive things so excellently together, and none cuts so briefly across all controversies and points of conflict. If anyone asks about my formula of prayer, I will name the Lord's Prayer, for the prayer of the only-begotten Son, who came forth from the Father, is the best key to open the heart of the Father. If anyone asks about the standard by which I live, the answer lies in the Ten Commandments, for what is pleasing to God no one can tell us better than God Himself.[19]

In summarising the faith, the creed provides a set of doctrinal standards not for passive intellectual assent but for shaping one's

---

[17] With Charles Pinches, Hauerwas argues for the significance of obedience in the Christian life. This can avoid standard criticisms of authoritarianism, fanaticism and infantilism by its connections with other virtues such as wisdom and temperance. Stanley Hauerwas and Charles Pinches, *Christians among the Virtues: Theological Conversations with Ancient and Modern Ethics* (Notre Dame: University of Notre Dame Press, 1997), 129–47.

[18] Much of Jan Milic Lochman's theology appeared as discussion of these three classical texts, e.g. *The Faith We Confess: Towards an Ecumenical Dogmatics* (Edinburgh: T. & T. Clark, 1984), *The Lord's Prayer* (Grand Rapids: Eerdmans, 1990), and *Signposts to Freedom: The Ten Commandments and Christian Ethics* (Minneapolis: Augsburg, 1982).

[19] Jan Amos Comenius, *Unum necessarium*, x, 9. Quoted by Lochman, *The Faith We Confess*, 3–4.

world-view so as to structure belief, practice and hope. Its use in worship, sometimes within the sung Latin Mass, directed hearers to the way in which it was offered in the praise and service of God. Situating the believer within the faith of the Catholic church across space and time, the creed could also function as a story within which the individual found his or her bearings. The reference to God as creator recalls the unity of the two testaments and the drama of creation and redemption. More extensive, the second article positions the gospel account of Jesus at the centre of this drama and leads forward into an account of the ongoing action of the Holy Spirit in the church and to the hope of life everlasting. There are elements in the creed that, if not absent, are too implicit: the failure to mention Israel; the lack of reference to the life of Jesus between his birth and passion; the mission of the church; and the social dimension of eschatological hope. Yet its use as an instrument of education and nurture continues by virtue of its doxological function, its summary nature and the bond it establishes with the church across the ages. In naming God as Father, Son and Spirit, the creed, as it is repeated and assimilated, shapes consciousness of nature, history, self and others.

Recent scholarship on the decalogue draws attention less to its deontological appearance and more to its setting within the history of God's dealings with Israel.[20] The commandments are offered to organise and prosper the relationship of God to the community. Their context is that of covenant faithfulness; the fruits of that faithfulness are realised within a peaceful, ordered and holy society. Patrick Miller writes of the ways in which the commandments (Exodus 20:1–21; Deuteronomy 5:1–21) create 'a good neighbourhood' through enabling love of God and of the other person.[21] These relations are not to be disturbed by idolatry, the lust for power and sex, or consumerist envy. Respect for the divine command promotes the covenant that God has initiated and in doing so it orders the human community that is thereby elected. Upon the establishment of this covenant,

---

[20] E.g. Stanley Hauerwas, *Sanctify Them in the Truth: Holiness Exemplified* (Edinburgh: T. & T. Clark, 1998), 37–60.

[21] Patrick D. Miller, 'The Good Neighborhood: Identity and Community through the Commandments', in William P. Brown (ed.), *Character and Scripture*, 55–72. Miller is careful to point out that this neighbourhood is not a middle-class, suburban enclave but one in which otherness is accommodated and valued.

neither God nor Israel can be thought of except in relation to one
another. This does not exclude the possibility of God having other
stories and people to befriend, but it does imply that this God is
always to be thought of as the God of Israel.

The setting of the decalogue, its proximity to the Shema
(Deuteronomy 6:4–9), and the theme of the first commandment all
point to the way in which the moral life of the community takes the
form of obedience to God. This is not to be interpreted as submission
to an alien authority since the covenant is initiated by sheer divine love
for the people. Nonetheless, the seriousness, durability and force of
the commandments derive from the simple call to obedience. Given
for human well-being, the decalogue requires commitment, repeated
stress and attention. Furthermore, the Hebrew Bible generally regards
the law of God to be not so much a tiresome burden as a source of
pleasure, worthy of constant recitation and reflection. Its capacity to
shape human desire is evident, for example, in the claim of Psalm 1
that the delight of the just and godly person is in the divine law.

Reflecting many of these Hebrew themes, the Lord's Prayer also
reflects important features of the life and ministry of Jesus. Its opening
possessive recalls that it is the faith of the community and not merely
the individual that is being expressed. The invocation of God's reign
suggests a universalising of the good neighbourhood; Jesus' prayer is
that the whole created order will become the divine commonwealth.
Its expression of eschatological hope is of significance for understanding the character of earthly forces and powers. Asking for one's daily
bread is a reminder not only of our material needs but also of the
precariousness of life and the futility of seeking long-term security
through the amassing of possessions. The divine forgiveness of sins
brings the obligation to offer and seek the forgiveness of others. In
praying that we be spared impossible temptation and delivered from
evil, there is a recognition of the need for divine grace in the moral
life, and also a way of maintaining commitment and desire to serve
God above all else. It acknowledges the possibility that even the most
sanctified can stumble, and so reveals the daily but lifelong struggles
of discipleship.

Taken together these classical texts of Christian devotion reveal
the integration of prayer, nurture, and character formation in the
church. The attention to thought and desire is significant for moral

commitment in a range of ways: articulating the source of moral motivation; the seriousness and vocation of ethical practice; the importance of commitment and perseverance across a lifetime; and, not least, the prospect of forgiveness, repentance and renewal in the inevitable event of failure. All these features of the moral life are necessarily conditioned by the doxological and educational practices of the church. Such practices can only be described in terms that are irreducibly ethical. We should not focus exclusively here on the distinctive content of Christian ethical claims – the strengthening of commitment, motivation and vocation are also vital to the moral life. The capacity of the faith community to sustain these should not be overlooked: 'Let us not grow weary in doing what is right' (Galatians 6:9).

This ecclesial formation does not happen in isolation from other influences. What takes place in our homes and schools will be as significant as the training we receive in the church, while of course the power of the modern media is not to be underestimated. The need to connect moral formation in the church with other communities lends weight to the case for faith-related schools, especially in those circumstances where, as their church affiliation is exposed, children experience negative pressures and a resultant loss of self-esteem.[22] There is also a danger in overstating the impact of what actually takes place inside the churches – this is especially true of some recent theological writing on the significance of the eucharist. External influences are of course internalised in disputes about the correct interpretation of Scripture and tradition, for example in relation to gay relationships. But the case for an ecclesial contribution to moral formation remains.

COUNTERCULTURAL PRACTICES

The extent to which the early Christians required to be socialised into a new world of meaning[23] alerts us to the difficulties facing the

---

[22] A recent study conducted by the Medical Research Council in Glasgow suggests that, unlike Roman Catholic children attending denominational schools, Protestant children attending 'secular' schools are singled out as 'odd' and 'geeky'. Reported in *Sunday Times* (Scottish edition), 19 October 2003, 15.

[23] I am thinking here of the first Christian communities as described in Wayne Meeks, *The Moral World of the First Christians* (London: SPCK, 1986).

practice of Christian living in our own cultural context. The reshaping of perception, desire, and will is constantly at odds with the signals and paradigms which bombard us from the mass media. The easy availability of a range of entertainment forms threatens regular practices such as prayer, contemplation, the study of Scripture, and public worship. The monotonous eroticism of the advertising industry leaves us in what John Macmurray once described as a condition of chronic exasperation.[24] The unmasking of the sordid flaws of our cultural heroes and politicians induces a deep cynicism about human nature. The possibilities of regeneration and steady spiritual progress are neglected as boring, if not illusory. As if in an interminable soap opera, all human life is reduced to a random series of episodes in which we desperately seek pleasure by lurching from one goal to the next. The closer walk with God, the calm and steady frame – these images seem increasingly remote. Perhaps hardest of all to combat are the peer-group pressures applied to teenagers. Here the twin goals of the successful life are material wealth and sexual adventure.

The countercultural nature of the Christian life can be illustrated by reference to the following two historical examples – Thomas Aquinas on the passions, and Karl Barth on the sabbath.[25] Both reveal the way in which socialisation into the habits and practices of the church makes a difference. Aquinas' treatise occupies a significant place at the beginning of the second part of the *Summa Theologiae*. A passion, he argues, is what draws us towards some thing or course of action. This is constituted by a bodily transmutation that determines the soul. 'Passion strictly so called cannot therefore be experienced by the soul except in the sense that the whole person, the matter–soul composite, undergoes it.'[26] To be in a passion is to undergo bodily changes such as clenching, rapid heartbeat, hurried breathing, perspiration, shaking or weeping. This typically prompts us to a particular course of action. The end, or other, to which we are drawn is set in view and becomes the source of attraction through the functioning of our passions. The good of the object creates a corresponding good in the subjective

---

[24] *Reason and Emotion* (London: Faber & Faber, 1935), 139.
[25] In what follows, I have drawn from earlier material published in 'Reclaiming the Doctrine of Sanctification', *Interpretation* 53 (1999), 380–90.
[26] *Summa Theologiae*, 1a2ae, 22.1.

inclination. This is designated as love (*amor*) which itself is considered a passion.[27] The final passion that organises all others in the human being is the love of God. The enjoyment of God is the one delight (*delectatio*) surpassing all others. Thus Thomas quotes Psalm 16:11: 'You show me the path of life. In your presence there is fullness of joy; in your hand are pleasures forevermore.'[28]

The attention devoted to the passions reveals the integration of desire and reason in Thomas' moral psychology. It is a mistake to assume that first we have moral perception, and thereafter it becomes the task of the will to subject the passions to this understanding. The relationship is more complex in accordance with his Aristotelian understanding of body and soul. What is most rational is most delightful. An animal experiences physical delight in attaining its goal. A rational creature such as an angel or a human being finds true delight in union with its final goal. Our narrow human delights, however, must be shaped and expanded by that goal itself. In other words, we must be shaped by the love of God to find our delight in God and the divine purpose for creation. The location of the treatise on the passions reveals their importance for an ethic of sanctification. It is only as our passions become trained and directed towards God that we become holy. Our passions 'resonate' with our reason;[29] they contribute to prompt action, and are a sign of the will's intensity.

What is curiously modern about this approach is its eschewal of more cognitive, intellectualist approaches to human action. Ethical or spiritual perception does not precede emotional response. The way we perceive the world is largely bound up with the regular ways in which our bodies react to stimuli. Experimentation in neurophysiology reveals that habitual reactions to stimuli have a definite biochemical character. Each passion has a particular bodily signature involving biochemical and neurophysiological changes. This reveals not only that the whole organism is involved in the process of perception and evaluation, but also that the body is capable of rational response to stimuli prior to the appropriate signals reaching the visual cortex of

---

[27] *Summa Theologiae*, 1a2ae, 26.3.   [28] *Summa Theologiae*, 1a2ae, 34.3.
[29] This is the translation of 'redundantiae' suggested by Simon Harak, *Virtuous Passions: the Formation of Christian Character* (New York: Paulist Press, 1993), 79. Cf. *Summa Theologiae*, 1a2ae, 23.3.

the brain.[30] Thus our minds are shaped in some measure for good or ill by our habitual desires and bodily dispositions. In the course of time, body and mind together can be configured to perceive and feel in particular ways through repeated interaction with a person, an activity or state of affairs. This repeated interaction with 'the other' tends to reconfigure the whole self, body and mind together. We thereby become physically disposed towards continuance of that interaction.

Those who have sought to overcome an addiction are painfully aware of this. In part, every programme of action will require of the participant the exercise of mind over body. But the aim will eventually be a retraining of the body to orient its desires and responses to a different set of ends. 'Habit reversal' will be a condition and criterion of success. To achieve this, a regular regime will be followed that will refocus the thinking of the participant, expose recurrent feelings and actions of which one is barely conscious, and prescribe regular exercises and patterns of behaviour for the training of the body in new habits.[31]

For a doctrine of sanctification this is highly significant. As Harak claims, 'we must give our embodied self new and healthier interactions, and *time* to allow those new interactions to reconfigure us corporeally, if we ever want our passions to change'.[32] The discipline of regular spiritual exercise can now be seen as a way in which the self is changed through steady interaction with the divine 'other'. Through the directing of one's attention to objects worthy of desire we learn to think, feel and react in appropriate ways.[33] All this takes time.

This reference to 'time' recalls traditional wisdom about the need for regular rest, worship and attention to God. By placing his discussion of the sabbath day in the context of his ethics, Karl Barth draws attention to the way in which it shapes the Christian life of

---

[30] This is explored by Harak, *Virtuous Passions*, 7–26.

[31] In a recent programme of habit reversal for the relief of chronic eczema, a strategy with an accompanying set of exercises is recommended that is not unlike some of the techniques required for the so-called spiritual disciplines; Sue Armstrong-Brown, *The Eczema Solution* (London: Vermilion, 2002).

[32] *Virtuous Passions*, 17.

[33] Harak develops this with reference to the Ignatian spiritual exercises with their focus on the passion of Christ; *Virtuous Passions*, 99–121.

obedience to God. The fourth commandment, he notes, speaks about a limiting of our work in order to reflect on God and to participate in the salvation that has come and is still to be expected.[34] In observing this commandment, human beings find their freedom not merely in rest but in beholding the work of God and acknowledging God's grace towards them. In celebrating the day of Christ's resurrection as the sabbath, the church, Barth claims, was acting according to the sense of the Old Testament commandment. In the resurrection – the Lord's Day – it recognised the fulfilment of the covenant which was established in creation.[35] The sabbath commandment points to all the others by drawing attention away from human work to the divine work and what it entails for us. The holiness of the day of rest is a reminder of the God who makes us holy: 'I gave them my sabbaths, as a sign between me and them, so that they might know that I the Lord sanctify them' (Ezekiel 20:12).

As a day of rest, the sabbath resonates with physical and psychological needs yet, according to Barth, it is marked by an aimlessness without the divine service of the congregation: 'To observe the holy day means also to keep oneself free for participation in the praise and worship and witness and proclamation of God in His congregation, in common thanksgiving and intercession. And the blessing and profit of the holy day definitely depend also on this positive use of its freedom.'[36] Barth notes further that one of the contributions of Jewish celebrations of the sabbath is to remind us of the joyous character of this day. In our own time, it is perhaps significant that it is the Chief Rabbi, Jonathan Sacks, rather than any Christian leader, who has argued most persuasively for the sabbath. He draws attention to the social equality, restfulness and harmony of the holy day, and reminds readers of the need to respect the time it affords. It is by

[34] *Church Dogmatics*, ed. and trans. G. W. Bromiley and T. F. Torrance, 4 vols. (Edinburgh: T. & T. Clark, 1956–75), III/4, 50ff. Further discussion of the sabbath can be found in *Church Dogmatics* III/1, 213–28.

[35] Thus while not continuing the Jewish sabbath on the seventh day, an analogical relation emerged by which the Lord's Day recognised in the fourth commandment the significance of a weekly rest, its celebration of redemption, the worship of God, and the anticipation of the fulfilment of creation. This analogical relationship is carefully explored by Andrew Lincoln, 'From Sabbath to Lord's Day: a Biblical and Theological Perspective', in D. A. Carson (ed.), *From Sabbath to Lord's Day* (Grand Rapids: Zondervan, 1982), 343–412.

[36] Ibid., 62.

submitting to the rhythm of the day of rest, by abstaining consciously from the frenetic efforts that characterise other days, that the presence and command of God are learned:

> It was not Christians alone who benefited from Sunday, but everyone, believer or non-believer. For in the most concrete and tangible way it communicated certain messages within a normative framework of shared meanings: that consumption is not everything, that there are things valuable which cannot be bought, that work is only part of our lives, that the world is not ours to manipulate as we wish, and that there is a universe of worth outside individual recreation and exchange. The Sabbath was and is an ongoing tutorial in freedom, equality, human dignity and the independent integrity of the environment as a creation whose guardians and trustees we are, and its privatisation meant that these values lost one of their most powerful embodiments in public, as opposed to private, life. That is why a Jew – or a Hindu or an atheist – might well have felt that private gain was outweighed by public loss. Sunday was an example of the common good.[37]

There is little prospect of a return in civil society to Sunday as it was a generation ago, and it is probably futile to argue for this. Nonetheless, there needs to be an ecclesial recognition that the time spent week by week in rest, worship and fellowship sets a pattern upon one's life and its dominant passions. It is a constant reminder of the limits of one's work, of one's dependence upon grace, of a future that is prayed for and expected, and of the equality of persons in need of divine love. As the Lord's Day it remains a vital gift for hearing, speaking, singing and celebrating the faith of the church. It subordinates the ends of political (in its narrower sense) and economic activity. Moreover, through regular rest and recreation, participants, particularly in urban settings, are better able to connect with the natural world and to esteem it as God's good creation.

The translation of these insights into a practical theology of Sundays is an urgent task, although there are few signs of this being undertaken. Without this, it will be increasingly hard to encourage a spirituality focused on the way of Christ and practised in the community of faith. The death of Christian Britain, to use Brown's expression, is most apparent on a Sunday morning. If civil society

---

[37] Jonathan Sacks, *The Politics of Hope* (London: Jonathan Cape, 1997), 202.

cannot be expected to return to earlier practice, the church must find its own ways of practising the sabbath rest as it strives to make a genuine contribution to our moral formation.[38]

In this setting, what finally separates the Christian faith from every other is neither its particular set of virtues nor its doctrines but only the irreplaceable centrality of Jesus for faith and life. What Lindbeck calls 'christological maximalism' demands the classical doctrines of the Trinity and the incarnation (or something like them) for its expression, yet it is the crucified and resurrected Christ who is absolute rather than any doctrinal deposit. Maximal importance had to be attached to Jesus without infringing Jewish monotheism, hence incarnation and Trinity were mutually supportive doctrines.[39] This creates a tension within the argument. The processes of moral formation, as described above, repose upon strong claims about the identity and action of Jesus in the church. However, the commitment to religious tolerance and to the promotion of a legitimate diversity in civil society depends upon the conviction that the church may learn from other religious and secular groups with their own particular insights. Does this relativise religious truth claims, thus breeding a moral provincialism or indifferentism? Significantly, some secularisation theories hold that when modern societies benignly accept religious pluralism, religious commitment will undergo inevitable decline; there is less at stake and therefore less to command the primary allegiance of the believer.

Some resolution of this tension can be achieved in several ways.[40] By pressing a commitment to the finality of Jesus one is released from maintaining either the absolute nature of Christian dogma or the necessity of the church for salvation. The redeeming work of Jesus may be effective in extra-ecclesial ways, and one can acknowledge

---

[38] The role of theological aesthetics has historically been neglected in this context. John de Gruchy argues that churches might more readily promote transformation by connecting with the world of the arts; *Christianity, Art and Transformation: Theological Aesthetics in the Struggle for Justice* (Cambridge: Cambridge University Press, 2001).

[39] 'This . . . follows from the central Christian conviction that Jesus Christ is the highest possible clue (though an often dim and ambiguous one to creaturely and sinful eyes) within the space-time world of human experience to God'; George Lindbeck, *The Nature of Doctrine* (London: SPCK, 1984), 94.

[40] In part, I am indebted here to Rowan Williams, *On Christian Theology* (Oxford: Blackwell, 2000), 93–106.

that Christian faith is consistent with the revision and development of doctrine. A faith that stresses the centrality of Christ's crucifixion is committed also to a strategy of service rather than domination, and to itself being constantly judged and exposed by its own highest standards. Furthermore, in proclaiming the truth of Jesus, the church is not thereby committed to possessing all truth. The validity of its witness is compatible with the assumption that there is much to learn from other sources, traditions and faiths. Indeed, understanding of its own central theme may be deepened, rather than forsaken, by entering into patient conversation with other communities and ethical viewpoints. Since the Holocaust, this process of engagement has taken place with Judaism. Although Judaism stands in a unique and historically particular relationship to Christianity, a similar process of mutual clarification and partial convergence is beginning to take place with other faiths.

Despite these theological distinctions, the maintenance of the name of Jesus as above all other names is bound to provoke suspicion of any institution making that claim. The church will be judged by how successfully it fulfils the dominical role of service. In a pluralist context, this will require the service of other religions, whether minority or majority, through seeking the welfare of their communities. Here the interpretation of distinctive Christian claims will largely depend on faithful practice.[41]

CONCLUSION

Moral formation in the church is not exclusively preoccupied with the particular ethical insights of the Christian faith. Much of the time, these insights will be shared with others in the overlap of moral traditions and the wisdom they generate. Yet the grounds for moral action, commitment, and persistence will be determined by the specific character of Scripture together with the devotional and educational practices of the church. In a post-Christian setting, these will clash much of the time with forces inside secular society. For the sake of moral

---

[41] This is one outcome of George Lindbeck's argument in 'The Gospel's Uniqueness: Election and Untranslatability', *The Church in a Postliberal Age* (London: SCM, 2002), 223–52.

formation, therefore, countercultural passions, activities and groups will require to be kept in good working order. This will generate not merely an ethical orientation that is in part distinctive to the life of the church; it may also provide an antidote to the amoralism – noted in the previous chapter – that can be highly tolerant while indifferent to the common good.

CHAPTER SIX

Modern social theology: Barmen and Vatican II

> After the Christian faith had adjusted itself to the present
> world . . . the expectation of a complete world-renewal could
> only be introduced into Christianity from outside through the
> pressure of intolerable conditions.
>
> (Ernst Troeltsch)[1]

The historical survey of theologies of the state in the second chapter
argued for the contemporary relevance of several themes: the separate though related functions under divine providence of church and
state; the promotion of the common good by both ecclesial and civil
bodies; the necessary interaction of the church with the institutions
of civil society; the derivation of political authority from God and its
necessary acknowledgement by the consent of those living under its
jurisdiction; the dignity of political office; and the recurring injunction to seek the welfare of the city and to offer it critical support. In
what follows, I shall explore the reception of these themes in two of
the most significant twentieth-century texts in the field – the *Barmen
Declaration* and *Gaudium et Spes*.

BARMEN IN HISTORICAL PERSPECTIVE

The *Barmen Declaration* is the most significant political document
in twentieth-century Protestant theology. Composed largely by Karl
Barth and two Lutheran pastors, Hans Asmussen and Thomas Breit,
it was adopted in May 1934 by 138 delegates (including only one
woman) from twenty-five state and provincial churches in Germany

---

[1] *The Social Teaching of the Christian Churches*, trans. Olive Wyon (Louisville: Westminster
John Knox Press, 1992), vol. II, 817. The German edition was published in 1912.

who attended a synod at the Reformed Church of Barmen-Gemarke.[2] It provided formal, confessional opposition to the infiltration of National Socialist ideology in the life of the church, and became a focal point of subsequent church resistance to Hitler. The Confessing Church thus arose. A loosely affiliated group of Christians through-out the German church, it was united by opposition to aspects of the Hitler regime and subscription to the *Barmen Declaration*. Since the war it has been adopted formally as a confessional statement by evangelical churches in Germany, the Reformed Church in the Netherlands, and the Presbyterian Church of the USA.

The evangelical content of Barmen is familiar to anyone acquainted with the theology of Karl Barth. Although Swiss, he taught in Germany from the 1920s until he was removed from his post in Bonn for refusing the oath of loyalty to the Führer.[3] The political context was the attempt of the Hitler regime to coopt the German churches into the service of the state and its ideology. To this end, there was a drive towards a single national Protestant church with the appoint-ment of Reich Bishop Müller in 1933. Barth's opposition to natural theology in the 1930s was set in opposition to accounts of blood, soil and race which appealed to sources outside Scripture as authoritative for church life and political conduct. The theology of the German Christians was marked by a disjunction of Old and New Testaments, the minimalising or outright denial of Jesus' Jewish identity, a hero-ism based on the crucifixion as a noble sacrifice, preservation of racial purity and hostility to Jews, Marxists and Freemasons. Attempts to conjoin the symbols of the swastika and the cross were perceived to compromise the Reformation principles of *sola Scriptura* and *solus Christus*, while also infringing the traditional separation of civil and ecclesiastical powers. Although the bizarre theology of the German Christians was effectively overcome by a storm of protest following

---

[2] For a commentary on the confession and an account of the synod in its wider context see Klaus Scholder, *The Churches and the Third Reich*, vol. II (London: SCM, 1988), 122–71. The German church struggle is also discussed by Arthur C. Cochrane, *The Church's Confession Under Hitler* (Philadelphia: Westminster Press, 1962). The church in Barmen was destroyed by Allied bombers in 1943.

[3] For the narrative of Barth's career at this phase see Eberhard Busch, *Karl Barth* (London: SCM, 1976), 235ff.

the rally in the Berlin Sports Palace in November 1933, the intrusion of national socialist policies into church affairs continued.[4]

With the so-called Aryan paragraph in 1934, the state attempted to exclude from ecclesiastical office those who either by birth or by marriage had Jewish or mixed racial connections. Alongside this, Müller had also issued a decree, known as the 'Muzzling Order', prohibiting discussion from pulpits of the church controversy or any other public criticism of the church government. Any pastor infringing this rule was liable to suspension, dismissal and loss of salary. This interference in church life precipitated a crisis. The Pastors Emergency League had been formed by Niemöller and others in 1933, and several synods met the following year. In May 1934 the final text of the *Barmen Declaration* was agreed. In both form and content the language is essentially that of Barth, though there were compromises with his Lutheran colleagues. He claimed humorously to have seized the initiative at the drafting meeting in Frankfurt some two weeks earlier. After lunch, fortified by strong coffee and Brasil cigars, he prepared the theses while his colleagues enjoyed their three-hour siesta. 'Thus the Lutheran church slept, while the Reformed church stayed awake.'[5]

The text follows a pattern of confession and renunciation, and appeals explicitly to a range of biblical passages. Its first thesis runs:

Jesus Christ as he is attested in Holy Scripture is the one Word of God whom we have to hear and whom we have to trust and obey in life and in death.[6]

The *solus* of the Reformation is maintained in the notion of the 'one Word', while the christocentrism of Barth's theology is also apparent.

---

4 This is discussed by Klaus Scholder who notes the differences between Barth and Niemöller at this juncture. Criticising the emphasis upon political tactics, Barth called for more outright theological protest at the underlying errors of the German Christians and those who continued to enjoy the support of Müller; *The Churches and the Third Reich*, vol. 1 (London: SCM, 1987), 550ff.

5 Busch, *Karl Barth*, 245.

6 The English translation used here is that of Douglas Bax from *Journal of Theology for Southern Africa* 47 (1984), 78–81. It is reproduced in Eberhard Jüngel, *Christ, Justice and Peace: Towards a Theology of the State in Dialogue with the Barmen Declaration* (Edinburgh: T. & T. Clark, 1992), xxi–xxix, and also in Clifford Green (ed.), *Karl Barth: Theologian of Freedom* (Edinburgh: T. & T. Clark, 1989), 148–51. The German original can be found in Gerhard Niemöller, *Die erste Bekenntnissynode der Deutschen Evangelischen Kirche zu Barmen* (Göttingen: Vandenhoeck & Ruprecht, 1959), vol. II, 196–202. The earlier English translation of A. C. Cochrane appears in the *Book of Confessions of the Presbyterian Church of the USA*. It can be found also in Cochrane, *The Church's Confession under Hitler*, 238–42.

Both the authority and content of Scripture are affirmed as the single overriding source and norm of theology. A corresponding disclaimer is then offered:

We reject the false doctrine that the church could and should recognise as a source of its proclamation, beyond and besides this one Word of God, yet other events, powers, historic figures, and truths as God's revelation.

Each of these four terms belongs to the socio-political context of 1930s Germany; 'events' referring to the rise of national socialism; 'powers' to the forces of blood and soil; 'figures' to the personality cult of Hitler; and 'truths' to the ideology of race and fatherland. The fifth thesis of Barmen is its most explicitly political:

'Fear God, honour the King!' (1 Peter 2:17)
Scripture tells us that by divine appointment the State, in this still unredeemed world in which also the Church is situated, has the task of maintaining justice and peace, so far as human discernment and human ability make this possible, by means of the threat and use of force. The Church acknowledges with gratitude and reverence toward God the benefit of this, God's appointment. It draws attention to God's Kingdom, God's commandment and justice, and with these the responsibility of those who rule and those who are ruled. It trusts and obeys the power of the Word, by which God upholds all things.

Barmen here draws upon classical Reformation teaching about the divine appointment of the state. The state has the task of maintaining justice and peace within its borders, if necessary through the use of force. Political authority is by divine appointment and is given for human well-being. However, this authority is to be exercised in light of the divine kingdom (*Reich*). The confession draws attention to the command of God and divine righteousness – the word used for righteousness (*Recht*) is the same as that for justice, thus making explicit the connection. The separation of powers is also adverted to in the following repudiation. Church and state have different commissions that are not to be confused. This is the most explicit criticism of the Aryan paragraph in the confession and the attempt to create a single national church under a department of state.

We reject the false doctrine that beyond its special commission the State should and could become the sole and total order of human life and so fulfil the vocation of the Church as well.

We reject the false doctrine that beyond its special commission the Church should and could take on the nature, tasks and dignity which belong to the State and thus become itself an organ of the State.

The *Barmen Declaration* can be read as combining Lutheran and Reformed themes within the context of the united churches of Germany. In speaking of the separate functions of church and state it recalls the Lutheran two-kingdoms doctrine. The church preaches the gospel, while the state, by the sanction of force, maintains a peaceful civil society in which it can function. In places, this may suggest a separation of spheres and a political quietism for as long as the state respects the domain of the church. The language, however, has to be read in the context of the more Reformed (and Barthian) elements of the confession. There is a criticism here of some constructions of the two-kingdoms doctrine that attempt to keep the church out of politics by restricting its competence to private and ecclesiastical matters, a view perhaps held by a conservative majority in the German churches. Against this construction, the rule of Christ over all spheres of existence is maintained by Barmen. The second thesis states explicitly that in Christ we encounter the divine claim upon our whole life. No segment of political existence, therefore, can be found outside the claim of God as we know this in Jesus. An ethic of obedience in the secular realm is subject to the standards and norms of behaviour that govern the private and ecclesial lives of Christians:

We reject the false doctrine that there could be areas of our life in which we would belong not to Jesus Christ but to other lords, areas in which we would not need justification and sanctification through him.

In the context of the 1930s the reception of Barmen was mixed. While it was enthusiastically welcomed by many,[7] it encountered several forms of criticism. The most immediate attack came from Lutheran quarters. Although the semi-pagan theology of the German Christians had proved an easy target, more subtle criticism based upon the doctrine of the orders of creation and the distinction between gospel and law was forthcoming. Barmen had recognised the division between the powers of church and state, but had said nothing about

---

[7] Scholder reports that in Westphalia alone by 1935 there were 500,000 who held the 'red card' identifying them with the Confessing Church; *The Churches and the Third Reich*, vol. II, 168.

the latter as a divinely ordained, natural order of creation. According to Lutheran critics, it thus failed to offer a sufficiently positive and constructive account of state and civil society under the providence of God. Only by reintroducing the distinction between gospel and law, would it become possible, so the critics claimed, to perceive the orders of society as divinely ordered and disclosed in natural law. The cultural achievements and organisational forms of German society could thus be perceived as fulfilling a divine purpose. Here an organic unity of church and society could be affirmed through the coordination of the respective spheres of gospel and law.

This particular attack on Barmen was led by Werner Elert and Paul Althaus, two distinguished Lutheran scholars who were involved in the production of the so-called 'Ansbach Advice' (*Ansbacher Ratschlag*) later in 1934. The principles of the 'Ansbach Advice' state that the divine law is encountered in the particular forms of family, nation (*Volk*) and race. On this basis, a remarkably positive affirmation of the Hitler regime is proposed: 'In recognition of this, as believing Christians we are grateful to the Lord God, that he has sent our nation (*Volk*), in its need a leader (*Führer*), as a pious and trustworthy ruler, and in the national-socialist state wills to prepare "good government", government with "discipline and honour".'[8] The terms of this misguided criticism shed further light on the content of the *Barmen Declaration*. Its vehement opposition to natural theology, further expressed in the same year by Barth's 'No!' to Emil Brunner, requires to be set in the context of a fusion of Lutheran theology and culture in German society. This was perceived not as an aberration of the 1930s but as deeply entrenched in Protestant theology from at least the early nineteenth century onwards. In his address at the Barmen synod, Hans Asmussen had already made it clear that the protest of the declaration was not narrowly political but was a fundamental theological objection to a phenomenon that had menaced the churches for over two centuries.[9] What was at stake, therefore, was the proper reception of the Reformation tradition itself and its commitment to the first commandment. In the post-1945 context of

[8] The 'Ansbach Advice' is cited in Gerhard Niemöller, *Die erste Bekenntnissynode der Deutschen Evangelischen Kirche zu Barmen*, vol. I, 245. The translation is my own.
[9] Quoted by Klaus Scholder, *A Requiem for Hitler and Other Perspectives on the German Church Struggle* (London: SCM, 1989), 90.

union between Reformed and Lutheran churches in Germany and the modern distrust of civil religion, it is hard to appreciate this historical context. As Scholder remarks, 'The traditional relationship of trust to the state, strikingly expressed in the centuries of the legal institution of church government by the local ruler, gave way to a critical solidarity. That has in fact become an ongoing feature of Protestant church history in the post-war period.'[10]

The charge of Althaus that Barmen represented a liberal doctrine of the state may be surprising given Barth's hostility to forms of theological liberalism.[11] Political liberalism with its espousal of individual rights seeks to detach the state from substantive disagreements about religious truth. The relatively neutral state remains impartial on matters of doctrinal import thus eschewing an organic union of the civil realm with any one ecclesiastical communion. That Barth, a Swiss Reformed theologian, was suspected of favouring such an account of the state reveals the target of much of his invective. The notion that a national culture could be expressive of the distinctive essence of Protestantism was distrusted and submitted to theological criticism. This claim had infected the intellectual bloodstream of Germany since the philosophy of Hegel. Having survived the First World War and the Weimar Republic, it now sought expression in the culture of the 1930s.[12] Yet, according to Barth, it was poison to a faithful evangelical identity. The greater separation of church and state was demanded on confessional grounds that recalled the Christian's fundamental commitment to Jesus Christ as attested in Scripture.

THE RECEPTION OF BARMEN

To the complaint that Barmen offered no positive construction of the state, its exponents could reasonably point again to the fifth thesis.

---

[10] Ibid., 93.

[11] Scholder, *The Churches and the Third Reich*, vol. II, 165. It is worth noting that those theologians identified by Robert P. Ericksen as sympathetic to aspects of the Hitler regime – Althaus, Hirsch and Kittel – were also critics in different ways of Enlightenment ideals; *Theologians under Hitler* (New Haven: Yale University Press, 1985). I owe this insight to Donald MacKinnon.

[12] This is explored by Scholder in his essay on 'Modern German History and Protestant Theology', in *Requiem for Hitler*, 35–60.

According to this, the state has the function of maintaining justice and peace through the use of coercive measures. Yet, by virtue of its later insistence that all support is critical and conditional, Barmen is separated from those Lutherans who espoused a more integrated vision. In this respect, Barmen 5 charts a course between on the one side a strict separation of church and state resulting in quietism, and on the other side a fusion of church and state producing an integrated national or folk (*volkisch*) religion. Its final terms also represent something of a consensus between the Reformed and Lutheran members of the drafting committee. Included were amendments that suggested a stricter Lutheran division of the divinely ordained provinces of church and state.[13]

The preoccupation with national government, understandable at that time, results in a political theology that again is overdetermined by the need to position the church in relation to the state. As a result, the various institutions and forces of civil society are not adequately characterised in theological categories. Reference to the terms of the partnership between church and state diverts attention from the ways, many of them positive, in which the church can interact with systems of education, healthcare, welfare provision, local government, charitable bodies and other faiths. Barmen's reference to the kingdom of God may suggest this, but for the most part this point is largely ignored in its declaration.[14] This proved disastrous with respect to its silence on the plight of the Jews in Germany.

Related to this complaint is the further reproach that Barmen is too insular in its political criticism. Its primary concern is with ecclesiastical purity rather than social justice. 'We have little to learn from any church or prophet who cannot recognize murder until it

---

[13] See Rolf Ahlers, *The Barmen Declaration of 1934: the Archaeology of a Confessional Text* (Lewiston, NY: Edwin Mellen, 1986), 63–6. Barth's original draft had included the following repudiation: 'We reject the error that the state is the only and total ordinance of human life. We reject the error that the church has to be "coordinated" with a particular form of the state.'

[14] Eberhard Jüngel argues that for Barth the term 'state' would have included everything that today is understood as comprising 'society'; *Christ, Justice and Peace*, 41. Against this, it can equally well be argued that the tendency to conflate the terms 'Staat' and 'Bürgergemeinde' leads to a narrowing of perspective, as, for example, in Barth's 1946 essay 'The Christian Community and the Civil Community', *Against the Stream: Shorter Post-War Writings* (London: SCM, 1954), 13–50.

is murder in the cathedral'; so wrote another critic.[15] This remark, however unfair, does reflect an ambiguity in Barmen. Is it a confession of ecclesial freedom from state encroachment, or does it move beyond this to provide a theology of Christian action in the civil realm? This question has occasioned much debate in the years since Barmen, and may even have been a source of disagreement between Barth and Asmussen. One is here reminded of frequent complaints that much of the church's social theology has taken place in contexts that were too provincial. It belonged to the ethos of the senior common room, the seminary, the cathedral precincts and the manse study.[16]

Nevertheless, while internal church affairs may have been too great a preoccupation at Barmen, its theses do provide at least an implicit notion of Christian political responsibility. Much hinges on how one reads the theses together. The claim of God is upon all created reality and not only church life. There is thus no separation of a private religious sphere from a secular public one. The tasks of the state are described in terms of the promotion of justice and peace. These concepts are embedded in Scripture and deeply related to the rule of God over the world. There is no possibility, therefore, that they might be hermetically sealed from theological criticism, as if their content could be adequately determined in other ways.[17]

Barmen has also been subject to the criticism of reintroducing a doctrinal rigidity and dogmatism. In returning to Reformation polemics, it was unsuitable for declaring the faith to a modern audience more accustomed to tolerance, freedom of conscience and latitude of theological opinion. An early Swiss critic had asked, 'Where is the tolerant centre, which abhors the compulsion and exclusiveness of religious conviction while at the same time giving it material support? Where are the masses of workers, the millions who no longer understand this church or theologians or at least the

---

[15] Cited by David Nicholls, *Deity and Domination: Images of God and the State in the Nineteenth and Twentieth Centuries* (London: Routledge, 1989), 112.

[16] E.g. Duncan Forrester, *Beliefs, Values and Policies: Conviction Politics in a Secular Age* (Oxford: Oxford University Press, 1989), 95.

[17] Günter Brakelmann argues that Barmen 5 in its theological description of the state is thoroughly political; 'Barmen V – ein historisch-kritischer Rückblick', *Evangelische Theologie* 45 (1986), 3–20.

theological formulations which are already lurking behind the confessions of faith?'[18] With its clear doctrinal identity, the Confessing Church would later be accused of a narrow conservative reaction to the incursion of more liberal trends in theological thought. It is worth recalling that Bultmann's famous demythologising essay of 1941 was first presented as a lecture to pastors in the Confessing Church, to which he also belonged. The hostile reaction it suffered was described by Bonhoeffer as a 'disgrace'.[19]

To assume that subscription to a particular style of theology was a necessary or sufficient condition for correct political action would be hubris. Barth himself lamented in 1945 the political failures of that time and his lack of more explicit criticism and action. We also need to recall that opponents of the Hitler regime had very different religious identities and that the Confessing Church did not have a monopoly on opposition. At the outset, the only common trait amongst the opposition was an uneasy conscience.

> Having an uneasy conscience was obviously independent of age, confession, estate or political alignment. It bound together the old Bavarian nobleman with the young socialist pastor in the Rhineland, the liberal professor of theology in Hessen with the Berlin Dominican father, the Protestant German Nationalist with the Catholic Centre Party member. These uneasy consciences remained, and remain, underivable, personally as well as socially.[20]

Yet notwithstanding the variety of political opposition in the churches and the dangers of a cramped confessionalism, the *Barmen Declaration* returns in a salutary manner to the centre of Christian faith. Under intense pressure, its confession of the faith of Jesus as recorded in the Bible suddenly re-emerged as the only basis that distinguishes the church's voice from others. As with all really decisive confessional controversies, it is the church's free commitment to Jesus that was at stake. This became a bottom line of theological opposition to forces experienced inside and outside the church.[21] The church thus found

---

[18] Cited by Scholder, *The Churches and the Third Reich*, vol. II, 155.

[19] Eberhard Bethge, *Dietrich Bonhoeffer* (London: Collins, 1970), 616.

[20] Scholder, *The Churches and the Third Reich*, vol. I, 279.

[21] 'Thus despite all the tensions, after Barmen the Confessing Church was sure of its way. There was preaching again in Protestant Germany; there was prayer and singing of a kind

itself in a *status confessionis*, a critical moment when the intrusion of ideological forces from the secular realm threatened to undermine its fundamental character as the people of God and the body of Christ.[22]

Other questions have arisen about the effectiveness of the *Barmen Declaration* in its original setting. Although it combated the ideology of the German Christians, it did not stop the Hitler regime in 1934. Despite their dislike of national socialism, many of its signatories remained loyal to the state, becoming chaplains or combatants in the German army during the Second World War. Since the fiftieth anniversary of the declaration in 1984 further issues have come to the fore. The most painful of these concerns the silence of Barmen on the persecution of the Jews. Its focus, and indeed that of the German church struggle generally, was on the purity of church doctrine, government and administration. This is not surprising given the situation. Hitler had come to power in 1933 and there were widespread support and high hopes for his regime. Yet anti-Semitism was already rife and Barmen makes no mention of the plight of Jewish citizens in German society. This charge has been the subject of discussion, especially following the publication of Daniel Goldhagen's controversial study.[23] Goldhagen argues – mono-causally, according to his critics – that German culture, including its church life, was determined by an eliminationist anti-Semitism and that the Confessing Church was not much better in this regard. Whatever the merits of this thesis, failure adequately to address the problem of anti-Semitism was already admitted by Karl Barth in 1967 upon reading Eberhard Bethge's biography of Dietrich Bonhoeffer. He wrote in a letter to Bethge,

---

which had not been heard for a long time. Confessing communities gathered around the Bible, and for many people their Bible evenings became a decisive landmark'; Scholder, *The Churches and the Third Reich*, vol. II, 169.

[22] In a perceptive discussion of this issue, Dirkie Smit has described a *status confessionis* as when 'a Christian, a group of Christians, a church, or a group of churches are of the opinion that a situation has developed, a moment of truth has dawned, in which nothing less than the gospel itself, their most fundamental confession concerning the Christian gospel itself, is at stake, so that they feel compelled to witness and act over this threat'; 'A *Status Confessionis* in South Africa?', *Journal of Theology for Southern Africa* 47 (1984), 29 (21–46).

[23] *Hitler's Willing Executioners: Ordinary Germans and the Holocaust* (Alfred Knopf, 1996). For critical discussion see Robert R. Shandley (ed.), *Unwilling Germans? The Goldhagen Debate* (Minneapolis: University of Minnesota Press, 1998).

Especially new to me was the fact that in 1933 and in the years following, Bonhoeffer was the first and almost the only one to face and tackle the Jewish question so centrally and energetically. I have long since regarded it as a fault on my part that I did not make this question a decisive issue.[24]

Barmen's silence on this matter is deeply regrettable. Indeed its particular form of christocentrism is suggestive of a supersessionism in which the church succeeds and supplants Israel as the chosen people of God. This is nowhere explicitly stated by Barmen, nor could it have been, given Barth's theology of the Jews.[25] Yet, to some the *Barmen Declaration* has appeared consistent with supersessionism.[26] Particularly regrettable in this context is the absence of any Old Testament citations in the theses – all the leading scriptural references are drawn from the New Testament.[27] Albeit with hindsight, its silence on the

---

[24] Karl Barth, *Letters 1961–68* (Grand Rapids: Eerdmans, 1981), 150. Barth also comments that a text containing a more specific petition would not have commanded support in 1934. It might also be noted, in fairness to Barth, that he was seeking to draw greater attention to this issue *inter alia* by 1935. The Confessing Church 'has fought hard to a certain extent for the freedom and purity of her proclamation, but she has, for instance, remained silent on the action against the Jews, on the amazing treatment of political opponents, on the suppression of the freedom of the press in the new Germany and on so much else against which the Old Testament prophets would certainly have spoken out'; Karl Barth, *The German Church Conflict* (London: Lutterworth, 1965), 45.

[25] Although Barth's account of Israel avoids supersessionism it functions largely as the negative counterpoint to the church. For general discussion of this issue see Katherine Sonderegger, *That Jesus Christ Was Born a Jew: Karl Barth's Doctrine of Israel* (University Park, PA: Pennsylvania State University Press, 1992). For a recent defence of Barth against Goldhagen's criticism see Mark R. Lindsay, *Covenanted Solidarity: the Theological Basis of Karl Barth's Opposition to Nazi Antisemitism and the Holocaust* (New York: Peter Lang, 2001).

[26] This argument is developed in the extreme by the Jewish writer, Pinchas Lapide. In elevating the rabbi of Nazareth to the status of God the Son, Christians have tended to deny his Jewish roots and religion. The test of faith thus becomes not so much his ethical teaching as confession of his divine name. This christomonism, Lapide suggests, tends to isolate Jesus from the Old Testament and is thus too easily appropriated by outright anti-Semitism. '"No Balm in Barmen?" A Jewish Debit Account', *Ecumenical Review* 45 (1984), 423–36. There is a valid response to Lapide along the lines of *abusus non tollit usum*, but one cannot deny that Barmen leaves itself open to these charges and is entrenched in a theological culture that is generally supersessionist.

[27] At its session held in Berlin-Weissensee on 27 April 1950 the Evangelical Church in Germany (EKD) approved the following 'Statement on the Jewish Question': 'We confess that we have become guilty before the God of compassion by our omission and silence and thus share the blame for the terrible crimes committed against the Jews by members of our nation.' Neither the Stuttgart Confession of Guilt in 1945 nor the Darmstadt Statement of the Council of Brothers in 1947 had used the word Jews; http://www.ekd.de/bulletin/22000/2200028/html. Yet one needs to register the failure also of the other western churches to respond adequately to those crimes committed against Jewish peoples.

continuing identity of Jews as the people of God is now seen as a glaring omission.

If Barmen made only a little progress in articulating evangelical opposition to Hitler, it was nonetheless a valid beginning. If it did not say everything, it did say at least something in the most trying of circumstances. It was, after all, the reaction of a group of church leaders, most of whom were thoroughly integrated into the national churches of Germany. Although it is not wholly adequate to the political circumstances of the 1930s, it set down a marker, a minimum of political protest at a time of grave crisis.[28] In 1912 Ernst Troeltsch had claimed, in the remark quoted at the outset of this chapter, that the assimilation of the church to its host society could only be dramatically reversed 'through the pressure of intolerable conditions'. While the Barmen Declaration neither provides an explicit summons to political action nor adequately registers the context in which it was written, it does offer political resistance at a point of intolerable pressure.[29]

In his subsequent writings, Karl Barth developed the teaching of Barmen 5 by describing the ways in which the church and the state, though separate, are coordinated. He uses the language of correspondence and parable. The civil community in its own way can correspond to the kingdom of God by the measure of justice and peace it is able to sustain. He offers the model of two concentric circles. The state is the outer, the church is the inner circle, each of which bears witness in its own way to the kingdom of Jesus Christ.[30] Though they have different presuppositions and tasks, the church and the state may together make common cause in furthering God's kingdom. In the laws and social life of a people one may find parables of God's kingdom. This prospect of a partnership of church and state is appealing. It avoids the quietism of some constructions of the two-kingdoms doctrine, a quietism that has often bedevilled Christian communities in circumstances of social privilege and sectarian isolation. There is recognition of the political character of the Christian life. Moreover,

[28] See Jüngel, *Christ, Justice and Peace*, 58.
[29] I am indebted here to Paul Lehmann, 'Of Faithfulness, Responsibility and the Confessional State of the Church', in Hubert G. Locke (ed.), *The Barmen Confession: Papers from the Seattle Assembly* (Lewiston, NY: Edwin Mellen, 1986), 28.
[30] *Against the Stream*, 32–3.

the prospect of making common cause with those outside the walls of the visible church is also suggested, thus avoiding the implausible claim that only within the church is there authentic ethical perception and activity. Yet this model of two concentric circles – the state as outer, the church as inner – is again too simple and overdetermined by its European context. It implies that the state is the church's dominant social partner. There is no mention of other groups and institutions within civil society. It places the church at the centre of society in a way that seems outmoded at a time of secularisation and growing dissociation. The decentring of the church in Europe since the 1930s requires the development of models which recognise its position in relation to other groups and agencies.

Its limitations notwithstanding, the *Barmen Declaration* has exercised significant influence in other political and theological contexts. Its confrontational mode has made it useful to Christian communities who have found themselves placed under 'intolerable conditions'. In its context, it is a bold and prophetic statement. Its exponents displayed political courage in their day and their witness has provided a standard for subsequent Christian political activity. This is evidenced in its influence upon the World Council of Churches since its formation in 1948. The church world-wide is united by its confession of the Lordship of Christ. It is required to speak in humility of its 'yes' and its 'no', what it affirms and what it denies. This has influenced the WCC's commitment to combat racism, nuclear warfare, and economic injustice and is apparent in the proliferation of confessions that have appeared in churches throughout the world since 1948.[31] In the cold-war era, it provided a model for protest against national-security policies which were predicated upon the threatened use of nuclear weapons. Commenting on Barmen, Eberhard Jüngel argues that we are faced with a similar idolatry today if the destruction of peoples and environments is a condition for the survival of the political state. Its self-perpetuation is placed above the justice of God; so it needs to be resisted on theological grounds.

Within South Africa, the *Barmen Declaration* provided a model for theological protests against apartheid. Both the *Belhar Confession* of the Dutch Reformed Mission Church, written in Afrikaans

[31] See Philip Potter, 'Barmen – An Ecumenical Response', *Ecumenical Review* 45 (1984), 421–3.

in 1982, and the *Kairos Document* of 1985 are strongly reminiscent of Barmen though they display a more heightened consciousness of the socio-political context to which they belong.[32] The pattern of confession and renunciation is much the same. According to Belhar, Christ gathers into the church groups and peoples who have been reconciled with God and one another. The credibility of this message is undermined when 'it is proclaimed in a land which professes to be Christian, but in which the enforced separation of people on a racial basis promotes and perpetuates alienation, hatred and enmity'.[33] Although deeply influenced by Anglican traditions of social thought, Desmond Tutu's sermons and writings also borrow confessional themes from the tradition of Barmen. Indeed its theological themes can arguably be considered more successful in mobilising and articulating resistance than in the German church struggle.[34]

CATHOLIC SOCIAL THOUGHT: *GAUDIUM ET SPES*

Catholic theology owns a long tradition of social thought that has been updated in the twentieth century. Its most important expression is *Gaudium et Spes*, the pastoral constitution of the Second Vatican Council, published in 1965 towards the end of the council. In many ways it is a summative document. It carries the signature of Paul VI but reflects the teaching of two earlier encyclicals of John XXIII, *Mater et Magistra* (1961) and *Pacem in Terris* (1963). Here Catholic social teaching, while maintaining continuity with the past, displays different emphases appropriate to the modern period. Older appeals to a natural law accessible to all rational persons are more muted. There is a keener sense of the pluralism and diversity of the modern world, of multiple cultures and traditions which shape belief and

---

[32] See Nico Horn, 'From Barmen to Belhar and Kairos', in Charles Villa-Vicencio (ed.), *On Reading Karl Barth in South Africa* (Grand Rapids: Eerdmans, 1988), 105–19.

[33] *Belhar Confession*, Section 3.

[34] 'If one examines the theology and language of Black theologians such as Buthelezi, Tutu or Boesak in their struggle against apartheid, it soon becomes apparent that they have been influenced by the confessing tradition of Barmen and the German church struggle. Nowhere has this been more in evidence than in Bishop Tutu's defence of the SACC before the Eloff Commission of Enquiry where he witnessed to the "divine commission of the church" in the South African context'; John W. de Gruchy, 'Barmen: Symbol of Contemporary Liberation?', *Journal of Theology for Southern Africa* 47 (1984), 65.

behaviour. A sense of divine grace not as extrinsic to secular forces but as immanent in the rich variety of human experience and cultural life is also apparent. These twin emphases on human diversity and the direction of divine grace towards the life of the world create an agenda for *Gaudium et Spes*. It seeks 'to mediate the meaning of Christianity to a modern pluralistic and often conflictive society and to appropriate the positive values of this society into the life and thought of the church'.[35]

In search of this aim, the conciliar document is driven back upon a closer examination of the ways in which the church's ethical teaching is set in a specific theological context. Instead of a simple appeal to natural law, consideration is given to creation, christology, ecclesiology and eschatology. A doctrinal determination of ethical norms is noticeable. This is evident in the handling of several themes, recalling the theology of earlier conciliar documents, especially *Lumen Gentium*. The church exists in a positive relationship to the world by virtue of its eschatological expectation. The scope of Christ's salvation is the world – this will be realised in the fullness of the divine kingdom. The church, therefore, has the task not so much of rescuing people from a perishing cosmos as of living as the sign and foretaste of God's greater future. In doing so, it can already recognise the signs of God's spirit in secular culture and can contribute in significant ways to its well-being. This reconfiguration of the church–world relationship in Vatican II is positioned alongside the reinvigoration of themes that are recognisably medieval. The social nature of the human person is affirmed; only in friendship, community and society is our human nature fulfilled.[36] God elects and calls us as a people, and not merely as an aggregate of disconnected individuals. A range of mutual dependencies, group identities and institutional affiliations is required for the development of social ties. As human persons, we are irreducibly political by nature and aspiration, hence the Aristotelian-Thomist notion that political society is necessary to our welfare. This

---

[35] Hollenbach, *Justice, Peace and Human Rights*, 6. For a comprehensive historical account of Catholic social teaching see Rodger Charles, SJ, *Christian Social Witness and Teaching: the Catholic Tradition from Genesis to Centesimus Annus* (Leominster: Gracewing, 1998). A discussion of recent teaching is offered by Charles Curran in *Catholic Social Teaching, 1891–Present: a Historical, Theological and Ethical Analysis* (Washington, DC: Georgetown University Press, 2002).

[36] *Gaudium et Spes*, 25.

is reinforced by appeal to the concept of the common good. Love of self and one's neighbour requires promotion of the common good, 'the sum of those conditions of social life which allow social groups and their individual members relatively thorough and ready access to their fulfilment'.[37] For the promotion of this common good, political authority is necessary. In this respect, it is divinely sanctioned, serves each citizen, and should command support in a variety of ways, including participation in democratic processes.[38]

The dignity of the person is understood by reference to Christ, the second Adam: 'It is therefore through Christ, and in Christ, that light is thrown on the riddle of suffering and death which, apart from his Gospel, overwhelms us.'[39] This christological perspective on the dignity of the human person is one that John Paul II has revisited time and again in his encyclicals.[40] Cardinal Ratzinger has said of this, 'We are probably justified in saying that here for the first time in an official document of the magisterium a new type of completely Christocentric theology appears.'[41] In the command to love our neighbour as ourselves the solidarity of all human persons is expressed. This union of persons one with another is a reflection of the union within the Trinity. The church is a sign of that final communion which God intends for all peoples within the divine kingdom. We are to be redeemed not as individuals but as a holy people. The social mission of the church is therefore an expression of its identity. Avoiding forms of collectivism in which group interests violate fundamental human rights, the concept of the common good is to be expounded alongside the teaching of the sublime dignity of the person. In successive stages, *Gaudium et Spes* speaks of the different communities which are determined by divine providence. These include the family, local forms of community, society, the state, and international organisations which are increasingly necessary to economic justice and world peace. In its awareness of the necessity of local and global community for human welfare *Gaudium et Spes*, like *Pacem in Terris*, anticipates many

---

[37] *Gaudium et Spes*, 26. [38] *Gaudium et Spes*, 75.

[39] *Gaudium et Spes*, 22. The English translation of *Gaudium et Spes* is found in Austin Flannery (ed.), *Vatican II: Conciliar and Post-Conciliar Documents* (Dublin: Dominican Publications, 1975). For a compendium of key texts in modern Catholic social thought see David J. O'Brien and Thomas A. Shannon (eds.), *Catholic Social Thought: the Documentary Heritage* (Maryknoll: Orbis, 1992).

[40] See Hollenbach, *Justice, Peace and Human Rights*, 229. [41] Quoted by Hollenbach, ibid.

contemporary concerns surrounding the phenomenon of 'globalisation'. An unlikely commentator on Catholic social thought, Mikhail Gorbachev has recently remarked that 'in that encyclical (*Pacem in Terris*) there is almost all that worries us today, so much so that I have the impression that that exceptional document was written yesterday'.[42]

The council's teaching invests all cultural endeavour with religious significance. God is to be served and honoured in the daily round, in the arts and sciences, and in the practice of politics.

> When men and women provide for themselves and their families in such a way as to be of service to the community as well, they can rightly look upon their work as a prolongation of the work of the creator, a service to their fellow men, and their personal contribution to the fulfilment in history of the divine plan.[43]

One's daily life is thus imbued with a dignity which rescues it from mere drudgery or aimlessness.[44] Also significant is the articulation of the concept of 'subsidiarity'. Now widely promoted in secular politics, this is the notion that power should rest at the most local level compatible with efficiency. This is not to be interpreted as the downwards delegation of power; instead it is the respecting of the most appropriate lower level: 'It is not a trickle-down theory of power, but an acknowledgement of particular stratified competences at each level of society. It does not impart power; it recognises it wherever it exists.'[45] In support of this, the argument is advanced that a loss of subsidiarity too often results in the debilitating of individuals and local organisations. In this respect, subsidiarity is a notion that seeks to offset both loss of individual identity through the tyranny of large collectives, and also the loss of social integrity through the deracination of individuals.

The concept of the common good is repeatedly stressed in recent Catholic social thought. Yet it remains a contested notion and one

[42] *The Tablet*, 1 November 2003, 25.   [43] Ibid., 34.

[44] Much of the recent interest in Thérèse of Lisieux has arisen from her contribution to understanding the sacredness of the quotidian.

[45] Jack Mahoney, SJ, 'Subsidiarity in the Church', *The Month*, November 1988, 970. Mahoney argues that subsidiarity is an important notion in church as well as secular government, a lesson that is instructive for more than one form of church polity. See also his *The Making of Moral Theology: a Study of the Roman Catholic Tradition* (Oxford: Oxford University Press, 1987), 169–71.

that is viewed with suspicion by neo-liberals and others. Two related objections can be discerned. First, its assumption of a social order that is to be acknowledged and promoted by all citizens ignores the phenomenon of moral diversity, particularly in modern multicultural societies. It was precisely the absence of any agreed substantive conception of the good that prompted early modern arguments for tolerance and later liberal claims for state neutrality and the priority of procedural rights. Second, any attempt to override the individual preferences of citizens by legislating in favour of the common good will result in illiberal measures and particularly in the tendency of majorities within a given society to oppress minority groupings. The formation of stronger group identity is often accompanied by hostility to outsiders and dissidents. National zeal is not infrequently fostered through the identification of a common enemy, real or imaginary.

Gaudium et Spes is clearly sensitive to this danger of a collectivism that overrides the interests of individuals and minority groupings within a society. Its reference to the sum total of conditions that enable the fulfilment of both societies and their individual members reflects the influence of liberal arguments predicated upon individual human rights. Yet the claim remains that as persons we are irreducibly relational and social, and that therefore our highest good is attained only in societies where there is a shared commitment to common ends. Is this sustainable in a pluralist age, or is it the ongoing fantasy of churches that ignore diversity, multiple identity and the conditions that are most likely to promote economic growth?[46] One response may be to note that no society can function without some commitment to the common good. There are some goods that individuals and markets cannot be relied upon to provide. Since each of us depends upon these for our individual fulfilment, it is necessary that together we create a system that guarantees these. Such goods might include the maintenance of an army, clean air and water, and efficient regulation of traffic. These can be guaranteed only by government, whether national or local, and funded through public taxation. Thus there will always be the need for some trade-off between individual

---

[46] The neo-liberal case against substantive notions of the common good is usefully summarised though not endorsed by Raymond Plant in *Politics, Theology and History* (Cambridge: Cambridge University Press, 2001), 196–223.

liberties and state-enforced measures that are perceived to benefit all or most individuals. Debates about national identity cards or the fluoridisation of water typically take place along such lines. Beyond these, arguments for state provision of education, health and transport will now meet counter-claims that these are often more efficiently provided on a private, market-led basis.

The theologically based concept of the common good cannot, however, be reduced to those social conditions that are necessary for each individual to pursue successfully the goals of his or her own choosing. In this respect, these aforementioned public goods are not identical to the common good.[47] If the goals of human life are themselves social in nature, an account of the common good will need to identify those ends that we share and hold only collectively. In any case, the way we function as individuals in families, institutions and communities suggests that much of the time we recognise such shared goods and value these. Our commitment to local causes and organisations only makes sense on the basis that there are goods held in common which are not merely instrumental to the fulfilment of our individual preferences but are ends in themselves. These common goods are constitutive of our well-being. Anyone who has run a sports team, a uniformed organisation, or an interfaith group is aware that the goods that these realise are not divisible into the satisfaction of individual desires. Their shared realisation and ownership are integral features of what makes them valuable. We hold these goods together, or not at all.

A counter-objection might claim that although there are local goods that we hold in common these cannot be promoted on a society-wide basis without infringement of moral diversity and impairment of individual liberties. Yet, in practice every society tends to hold common goods and cannot effectively function otherwise. The rhetoric of politicians, however debased, frequently attempts to foster shared commitments and a social vision that can command the support of most, if not all. This is further illustrated in notions of

[47] This is explicated by John Haldane, drawing upon the notion of Maritain that common goods are in some sense 'communicable' to each member of a society; 'The Individual, the State and the Common Good', in Ellen Frankel Paul, Fred D. Miller Jr and Jeffrey Paul (eds.), *The Communitarian Challenge to Liberalism* (Cambridge: Cambridge University Press, 1996), 59–79.

collective shame, guilt or pride that cannot readily be explicated on an individualist basis. In any case, neo-liberal attempts to 'demoralise' the state and political society on the grounds that notions of the common good inevitably threaten moral diversity are unduly pessimistic of the prospects of moral cohesion and democratic conversation.[48] For example, under the right conditions, some consensus can be built in favour of raising taxation to provide public goods such as efficient transport, parks, museums, health care, education services, welfare provision and international aid. Justification for this is not reducible to the claim that it is in the interests of each individual to secure these measures. Instead it is borne of the recognition that the common good of a society is thereby enriched. Moreover, a concept of the common good that is partially defined by its respect for different groups, loyalties, and identities can position itself against a collectivist spirit that denigrates difference or dissidence.[49]

A further way of articulating this last point is to recall another notion with strong theological antecedents – the concept of covenant.[50] In uniting people through allegiance to shared standards, convictions and goals, a covenant is more than a convenient alliance of individual interests. In Scripture, it is the divine decision to covenant with a people that creates the identity and common good of Israel. Within this covenant, there is a repeated stress upon the obligations owed by the people to the most vulnerable and marginal individuals in their midst. The moral health of the covenant community is thereby measured in part by its treatment of the stranger, the orphan, the widow and the poor. The common good and the recognition of the individual are not really separable or divisible. With its appropriation

---

[48] This is argued, for example, by Raymond Plant: '[T]he neo-liberal underestimates the resources of democratic politics, and I see no reason why, in a democratic society, rough-and-ready principles of distribution could not emerge out of democratic debate and dialogue'; *Politics, Theology and History*, 218.

[49] In assessing recent Catholic social thought, Charles Curran notes that the concept of the common good has developed in three ways in recent teaching. It stresses the dignity of the person, distinguishes the temporal good from our eschatological end, and appreciates the global dimension of political society. In relation to the second of these developments, it has become possible to develop a more positive account of religious freedom; *Catholic Social Teaching*, 156ff.

[50] For an attempt to combine the concepts of covenant and the common good see Eric Mount Jr, *Covenant, Community and the Common Good* (Cleveland: Pilgrim Press, 1999).

of human-rights discourse in describing the common good, Catholic social teaching expresses the same conviction.

In *Gaudium et Spes*, we are offered a rich social theology which some Catholics have complained is their church's best-kept secret. Nonetheless, its effects continue to be apparent in papal encyclicals, the pastoral letters of bishops and the teaching of Catholic social theology more widely. But on reading *Gaudium et Spes* at the beginning of the new millennium, one is struck by its confidence and optimism. Embracing much that is of value in the secular world, it conceives the social mission of the church in partnership with other agencies, groups and religions. It envisions a new order of international cooperation to guarantee human rights, world peace and global justice. While these emphases persist in the encyclicals of John Paul II, one is aware of the presence of more sombre themes. In his 1994 encyclical *Tertio Millennio Adveniente*, the Pope demands repentance for the errors and crimes of the last millennium, for those episodes in its history when the church has departed from the Spirit of Christ and his gospel. In trips to Greece and the Middle East, John Paul has kept faith with this, meeting with Orthodox and Muslim leaders to seek forgiveness for the wrongs incurred by the crusades. The same encyclical calls for renewed commitment to the teachings of Vatican II, 'this great gift of the Spirit to the church',[51] in the new millennium. Yet, again there is a note of reserve which can also be detected in other encyclicals. Tempered by fears of syncretism, the dialogue with other faiths is cautiously continued. The defence of democracy is combined with fears about the oppressive nature of majorities and the spread of moral relativism in western societies. The stress on education and academic integrity has coincided ironically with the disciplining of several leading Catholic theologians (Küng, Schillebeeckx, Balasuriya, Boff and Dupuis) by the Congregation for the Doctrine of the Faith. This irony has not gone unnoticed or unchallenged.

In the aftermath of the defeat of communism, papal attention has shifted to the threat to life within democratic societies, particularly to unborn life. *Evangelium Vitae* declares abortion always to be wrong and claims that any destruction of a human embryo from the moment

---

[51] *Tertio Millennio Adveniente*, 20. (Papal encyclicals can be accessed at www.papalencyclicals.-net.)

of conception is abortion. There is here a further tension in the Pope's teaching. In proclaiming the destruction of an embryo from conception onward to be abortion and wrong, the Pope exercises his teaching authority. Yet in doing so, he implicitly acknowledges that this is a disputed question on which there is a range of views and that it can only be settled for Catholics on papal authority. For non-Catholics other views can reasonably be held and, given the Catholic adherence to freedom of conscience, such persons cannot be bound by the Magisterium and should therefore be tolerated.[52]

In light of this, it is hardly surprising that recent encyclicals have adopted an increasingly countercultural tone. *Veritatis Splendor* appeals to the example of the martyrs of the church who bore witness at the cost of their lives to Christ and his gospel. *Evangelium Vitae* speaks of a culture of death spreading through our societies and calls for the church to emulate Mary, the mother of God: 'The Church's spiritual motherhood is only achieved through the pangs and "the labour" of childbirth (cf. Rev. 12:2), that is to say, in constant tension with the forces of evil which still roam the world and affect human hearts, offering resistance to Christ.'[53] Here the spirit of recent papal teaching is more reminiscent of the crisis theology of Barmen, a point that perhaps explains its enthusiastic reception amongst some Protestant ethicists.[54]

The teaching of *Gaudium et Spes* thus works in different ways in changing situations, and it shows how a distinctive Christian ethical voice can have a significant effect in a secular context. When appropriated in the struggle against apartheid in South Africa, the language of Barmen offered an unashamedly theological response to a political crisis, yet it did so in such a way as to connect with other forms of protest. The influence of church leaders such as Tutu and Boesak thus extended beyond their faith communities to society at large, in a manner not dissimilar to that of Martin Luther King in the civil rights struggle in the 1960s. Catholic social teaching has likewise made a contribution to public debate but on positive theological grounds. In

---

[52] Here I am indebted to Paul Vallely, 'Into the Twenty-First Century: John Paul II and the New Millennium', in Paul Vallely (ed.), *The New Politics: Catholic Social Teaching for the Twenty-First Century* (London: SCM, 1998), 138.

[53] *Evangelium Vitae*, 103.

[54] See the essays in John Wilkins (ed.), *Understanding Veritatis Splendor* (London: SCPK, 1994).

attending to the traditional yet vital notion of the *bonum commune* it has also addressed the social good of public services suffering from chronic underfunding, the importance of political participation at all levels at a time of voter apathy, and the dignity of political office in a culture that is too readily contemptuous of its elected representatives.

CONCLUSION

As the most important political texts of twentieth-century Christianity, the *Barmen Declaration* and *Gaudium et Spes* point to ways in which ethics can be significantly determined by theology, but without requiring a retreat into an ecclesiastical enclave or ceasing to make a positive contribution to the life of the world. The different genres and contexts of these documents reiterate two necessary dimensions of Christian social ethics. These are first the primary loyalty owed to Jesus Christ and thus the need always for a stratified citizenship in which allegiance to the state is secondary, provisional and critical. But, second, there is the recognition that the welfare of the city is nonetheless to be sought since its forms of life are not outside the providence of God or the lordship of Christ. In contributing to the common good of society and the world, the church can make a public contribution on the basis of its own insights and standards. Yet this takes place not by functioning as the state's exclusive partner but in myriad ways relating to the domestic, economic and cultural life of the world.

CHAPTER SEVEN

Church and nation

There is a real risk that, without a realistic re-appraisal of its position, a national-minority Church ends up with the worst of all
worlds – with neither the recognition and influence appropriate
to its national status nor the freedom of action and initiative
indispensable for a minority body.

(David Wright)[1]

THE DECLINE OF NATIONAL CHURCHES

The appearance of national churches is largely a Reformation phenomenon made possible by the political and religious fragmentation
of Europe. The rise of nation states and the emergence of churches
organised within their territorial bounds created the conditions under
which a church could be a marker of national identity in modern
times. Although the partnership of church and state was inherited
from the Middle Ages when religious expression could also be given to
regional identity, after the Reformation it was more forcibly translated
into terms reflecting the particular identity of each nation. This was
true especially of the Lutheran churches in Germany and Scandinavia,
the Church of England, and the Reformed churches in Switzerland,
the Low Countries and Scotland. Catholicism could also become an
expression of national identity in countries such as France and Spain.
Largely for this reason, John Locke refused to extend religious toleration to Catholics since it was assumed that their religious identity
implied a political loyalty to a foreign power.

The populations of Europe are still today mostly conscious of the
church as a national institution. A person may be baptised, married

---

[1] Wright, 'The Kirk: National or Christian?', 37.

and buried through the ministrations of his or her local church. These rites of passage have generally been available to all citizens who have requested them, irrespective of regular attendance or financial contribution. The parish church has been a social landmark for several centuries. It has been supported in different ways throughout Europe – by the income from endowments, the patronage of landowners, church taxes and voluntary contributions of committed members. Members of the clergy have often been identifiable by all their parishioners, particularly in rural areas. They officiate at rites of passage, function as chaplains in schools, hospitals and the armed forces, appear at civic functions and provide pastoral care at moments of individual or collective crisis.

Yet, this consciousness of the church as a national institution is now fading from the minds of many people, particularly the young. There is widespread statistical evidence to support this. A majority (55.8 per cent) of the population of the United Kingdom never attends church while at most about 14.4 per cent attend on a frequent basis.[2] Moreover, the increasingly ecumenical nature of Christianity and the more pluralist setting of modern society mean that chaplaincy appointments are no longer monopolised by one denomination, that civic functions will include a range of Christian and multi-faith representatives, and that fewer people can identify their parish priest or minister. In appointing chaplains, organisations such as universities, hospitals and armed forces increasingly seek an ecumenical and multi-faith representation.

Whether or not we continue to speak of churches as national institutions, it is nonetheless clear that in western Europe, they are no longer the dominant force that they once were. In Scotland until about 1960 there is some evidence to support the view that Presbyterianism was a marker of national identity. The Act of Union in 1707 was negotiated in such a way that a single parliament could be created in London if and only if the existence of the Church of Scotland as

---

[2] These data for 1999/2000 are supplied by European Values Study and cited by Grace Davie, *Europe: the Exceptional Case, Parameters of Faith in the Modern World* (London: Darton, Longman & Todd, 2002), 6. The figures conceal variations across the country. In Northern Ireland church attendance is significantly higher than in England. More recent findings suggest that these figures are overestimated. Weekly attendance at church in the United Kingdom may now be closer to 7 per cent. See Peter Brierley (ed.), *UK Christian Handbook of Religious Trends*, vol. III (London: Christian Research, 2003), 2.23.

national, reformed and presbyterian was guaranteed by the state. For two and half centuries this arrangement held firm. Communicant membership peaked in the mid-1950s when there remained a sense (albeit misplaced) of Scotland as a Presbyterian nation within the union of Great Britain and Northern Ireland. It is not merely coincidental that this was also at a time when the Conservative and Unionist Party held the majority of parliamentary seats in Scotland. In recent times, there has been rapid change, with membership of the Church of Scotland standing at less than 15 per cent of the adult population. Its stretched resources make the territorial ministry of the church, particularly in sparsely populated rural areas, difficult to maintain. In any case, the reinvigoration of the Roman Catholic community from the late nineteenth century reveals that Scotland has not been religiously monolithic for some time. More recently, the return of a parliament to Edinburgh has ended claims that the General Assembly of the national church was the effective mouthpiece of the nation, even if the need for the new parliament to rent temporary premises from the church has done no harm to church finances. In England a similar though not identical story can be told about the decline of the national church. In his 1995 study, Steve Bruce records an Anglican membership of 3 million in 1950 against only half of that number in 1990, a decline from 9.2 per cent of the adult population to 3.9 per cent.[3] One does not need to labour the statistics, since anyone who has attended church regularly over the last thirty to forty years has experienced the phenomenon at first hand. Another writer has stated, 'It is not exaggerated to conclude that between 1960 and 1995 the Church of England as a going concern was effectively reduced to not much more than half its previous size.'[4]

The loss of national status, however, is perceived by some to be a gain. There are two possible reasons for this. The first is that the alliance of the church with nationalism is to be deplored. The catholicity of the church means that state citizenship is neither a necessary nor a sufficient condition for church membership; the church can never be coextensive with the population of a nation state. The alignment of churches with nationalist movements can produce deplorable consequences. In this context, one can cite the Thirty Years' War, the

---

[3] *Religion in Modern Britain* (Oxford: Oxford University Press, 1995), 36.
[4] Cited by Grace Davie, *Religion in Britain since 1945: Believing without Belonging* (Oxford: Blackwell, 1994), 53.

German Christians in the Third Reich, and discrimination against Irish Catholic immigrants in Scotland. Hard questions have been asked about the recent role of the Serbian Orthodox Church in the Balkans, and the support of church Hutu leaders in the massacre of Tutsis in Rwanda. David Martin has addressed the painful question of whether Christianity causes war. Does it inevitably intensify human differences, cultural divisions and civil conflicts, or is it merely one amongst several carriers of identity that inevitably become divisive in times of strife but which can also function in socially constructive ways?[5] A second reason for welcoming the demise of the national church is the greater freedom it lends to missionary endeavour and moral witness. Released from the burden of maintaining national identity, the church can function more authentically as the people of God. Its task of proclaiming Christ is carried out by speaking not for the nation but to the people. We should eschew the trappings of power and status, which in any case do not amount to much nowadays, and engage in the evangelical tasks of the church, catholic and apostolic. So it is argued.

In any case, the concept of a national church may be considered a Eurocentric notion. It describes the particular historical conditions under which the church has functioned since the emergence of nation states in Europe in the early modern period. Yet it makes little sense to minority churches at other times and places. A Christian community in a predominantly Muslim country will not perceive itself to function as a national institution, nor, to take a very different example, would the church in China. In a Muslim society, arguments for a national church would be perceived as threatening and confrontational, whereas in the Chinese setting it would suggest support for state control of the church. What is sought in either situation is peaceful coexistence with a measure of relative independence; the aspiration towards a national church is neither necessary nor desirable.

THE COMMON GOOD AND CIVIL SOCIETY

The theology that has been outlined in the foregoing argument is one whereby the church has a vocation 'to seek the welfare of the city'. The

---

[5] David Martin, *Does Christianity Cause War?* (Oxford: Oxford University Press, 1997).

kingly rule of Yahweh and the lordship of Christ are destined to extend over the nations. In the interim, this carries a Christian responsibility to seek, where possible, the welfare of the nations according to the command of God. The concept of the common good, advocated by Aquinas and resonant with Aristotle's *Politics*, means that it is only by relating to one another in a range of interpersonal and social forms that we are capable of anticipating under earthly conditions the greater communal good that is our eschatological redemption. This notion is also apparent in the Reformed vision of the godly society. Every relationship within the household, the church and the parish can be sanctified by obedience, individual and collective, to the Word of God. There is no realm of life that lies beyond the sovereignty of God and the writ of Scripture.

A communal vision of human welfare, rooted in earlier theological traditions, is evident in the commitment to civil society at the time of the eighteenth-century Scottish Enlightenment. Rather than perceiving society on a contractual basis by which individuals come together to fulfil their various individual needs, thinkers such as Adam Ferguson and Adam Smith recognised the constitutive importance of civil society to human nature. As moral agents, we inevitably find ourselves inhabiting public spaces in which responsibilities, roles, commitments and sentiments are realised. The human self does not function independently of these nor can it be perceived, as in some political theories, as situated prior to these commitments.[6] Furthermore, it was acknowledged by Smith that social identity is not determined by the acquisitive nature of economic activity. The self as an economic agent is already morally shaped by institutions and social forces that are not the product of market-based institutions and principles.

The concept of civil society has enjoyed a reawakening of interest in the last ten to twenty years. This is largely as a result of problems confronting political philosophies of the left and the right.[7] The demise of communist regimes in eastern Europe has exposed the

---

[6] In this regard, much of Hume's moral and political theory can be seen as a subversion of this tradition from within. See Alasdair MacIntyre, *Whose Justice? Which Rationality?* (London: Duckworth, 1988).

[7] See Michael Walzer, 'The Concept of Civil Society', in Michael Walzer (ed.), *Toward a Global Civil Society* (Oxford: Berghahn Books, 1995), 7–28.

need to regenerate the semi-autonomous institutions of civil society. Similar trends can be detected in the more recent history of South Africa, Palestine and Iraq. The tendency of totalitarian government to suppress or control civic bodies derives from their capacity to become a seed-ground for the growth of political opposition. While dissidents flourished within a restricted civil society (often including the churches), there was a need following the end of Soviet hegemony to broaden and reinvigorate those institutions that typically mediate between domestic households and the machinery of the state. So trade unions, political parties, community groups, religious organisations, cultural organisations and other associations became the focus of particular attention after 1989. Similarly, the rebuilding of societies such as Kosova and Iraq is dependent upon the contribution of civil society yet hampered by its degeneration.

Further attention to civil society has arisen from the recent perception that in its provision of welfare services the state needs increasingly to function in partnership with the private sector.[8] Voluntary organisations such as churches and other charitable bodies have a long record of involvement in providing welfare support. Rather than rendering them redundant, government policy now seeks to include them in policy formation and programme initiatives. This inclusion of the voluntary sector may also be seen as another expression of subsidiarity. Its value resides not only in enhancing welfare provision, but also in promoting social capital, facilitating local forms of community, providing fora for debate, and fostering skills of citizenship.

Yet, at the same time, a decline in social capital in western societies has been perceived as the result of the individualism and fragmentation of a market-driven society. The forces of consumerism, both at work and leisure, restrict the capacity and scope for social interaction. In some measure, this may itself explain the decline of national churches and their diminished capacity to command the allegiance of large sectors of society. Other institutions and mass movements have shared a similar fate. These include trade unions, the main political parties and the royal family in the United Kingdom. Related to this criticism is the realisation that economic life cannot function

---

[8] E.g. Margaret Harris and Colin Rochester (eds.), *Voluntary Organisations and Social Policy in Britain: Perspective on Change and Choice* (London: Palgrave, 2001).

well except under stable social conditions. These require the health of households and civic groups organised on a non-market, non-contractual basis. The energy we invest in working for an organisation such as our local school, hospital, housing association, community council or soccer team, not to mention raising children, cannot make sense in market terms. The manner in which we experience success or disappointment, pride or shame is integrally related to our awareness that these are goods shared with others. They define our identity as social persons.

The scope of civil society is difficult to delimit. At one end of a possible spectrum it shades into political and economic life. So party political organisations and trade unions have a clear end in view that relates explicitly to the functioning of the state and the economy. Nonetheless, these will function in other ways through fostering community life, providing networks of support, and developing a sense of collective pride and responsibility in the institutions for which we work. In part, commercial institutions such as small businesses, firms and large corporations will reflect patterns of organisation and behaviour that cannot be understood simply in terms of the constraints of the market.[9] At the other end of the spectrum, the households and family groups to which we belong also shape us as social agents in ways that are enriching though often demanding. These also enable us to enter into a range of ties with others in our immediate neighbourhood and wider locality, and thus to some extent may be perceived also as shading into civil society.

The concept of 'global civil society' has been developed in recent literature to articulate the sense that contemporary problems facing local and international communities can only be addressed by a robust set of global networks. These must transcend nation states while remaining independent of political and economic institutions at the multinational level. In non-governmental organisations, charities, single-issue focus groups, websites, sports governing bodies and myriad voluntary cohorts with a world-wide identity, we see the emergence of a global or transnational civil society. Its development

---

[9] The extent to which global capitalism is linked to a range of dynamics, including religion, is noted by Max Stackhouse in his introduction to *Religion and the Powers of the Common Life*, Max L. Stackhouse with Peter J. Paris (eds.) (Harrisburg, PA; Trinity Press International, 2000), 20.

is necessary to address the economic imbalances of international capitalism, threats to the earth's ecosystem, the problems of terrorism, abuse of human rights and the dangers posed by the proliferation of nuclear weapons. On this scale, civil society is a reminder that we are dealing with something crucial to human survival and well-being. John Keane has characterised it as a 'dynamic non-governmental system of interconnected socio-economic institutions that straddle the whole earth, and that have complex effects that are felt in its four corners . . . These non-governmental institutions and actors tend to pluralise powers and to problematise violence; consequently, their peaceful or "civil" effects are felt everywhere.'[10] Described in this way, it includes Amnesty International, the Red Cross, al Jazeera, Greenpeace, the Global Coral Reef Monitoring Network and FIFA. Each of these groups is governed by shared moral norms that are not reducible to national interest, economic profit or personal gain. As with religions, they occupy social spaces that are protected, albeit in varying degrees, from the pressure of the market.[11]

A varied and healthy civil society may signify the kind of tolerance and recognition that was advocated earlier.[12] Group loyalties and corporate identities can be maintained without coercion or undue political interference. These prevent the disintegration of societies into atomic units with a resultant loss of social capital and cohesion. But this is neither as simple nor as compelling a prospect as it may appear. Walzer points out that in myriad ways civil society reposes upon the state: charities depend upon tax exemption; many local community groups will bring pressure to bear upon the political authorities; educational institutions will mostly require state funding through taxation to survive; and global problems involving multinational companies, environmental threats and refugees will require the exercise of political power and wisdom at the national and international levels. Moreover, the provision of a diversity of groups in civil society with their different allegiances, goals and organisational

[10] John Keane, *Global Civil Society?* (Cambridge: Cambridge University Press, 2003), 8. For further discussion of global civil society in relation to religion see Hollenbach, *The Common Good and Christian Ethics*, 212–44.

[11] This theme is explored in relation to civil society by Jonathan Sacks, *The Dignity of Difference: How to Avoid the Clash of Civilizations* (London: Continuum, 2002).

[12] Here I am indebted to Walzer, 'The Concept of Civil Society'.

structures seems attractive but it remains possible that many citizens will feel no pressure to belong to any of them. This is one difficulty with communitarian schemes. While evidence can be adduced to demonstrate that individuals and society may be enriched by an increase in social capital, this does not provide sufficient motivation to guarantee widespread participation. The temptation to miss the latest meeting of the community council by remaining in front of one's television is not easily dispelled. Something more may be required to mobilise us.

The theological significance of civil society can be approached by way of two further themes that are integrally related to the concept of the common good. These are solidarity and subsidiarity. Solidarity is rooted in the biblical injunction to love one's neighbour as one's self, in Christ's incarnate sharing of our human condition and in the determination of God to gather together a people from the nations. Our end in life is attained not alone, but in solidarity with other persons. There is no 'I' without a 'you', and no fulfilment except in communion with other persons. Subsidiarity also recognises this social dimension of human life. By enabling the most local forms of community that are practically possible, the practice of subsidiarity enhances civic identity and responsibility. It enables us to enter into a range of relationships and to share common goals and goods with other citizens. 'In a democratic society, government does not rule but rather serves the social "body" animated by the activity of these intermediate communities.'[13]

Research suggests that at the local level Christian congregations can make a significant contribution to civil society. In studying four British churches, varying in size, membership, and location, Margaret Harris notes welfare projects ranging from informal befriending and visiting of the sick to larger projects offering ongoing support to vulnerable church members and others in the community.[14] She draws attention to several salient features of this contribution: the predisposition of people of faith towards caring activities; the role of the clergy in matching those in need with others who have a capacity to offer support; the routes that exist from congregations into other

[13] Hollenbach, *The Common Good and Christian Ethics*, 102.
[14] This is summarised in Margaret Harris, 'Civil Society and the Role of UK Churches: an Exploration', *Studies in Christian Ethics* 15 (2002), 45–59.

voluntary bodies and institutions; the capacity to link people of different ages, ethnic groups and backgrounds; and the development of personal and social identity. On the other hand, this contribution should not be overstated or idealised. Congregations are generally less well-equipped to mount large-scale welfare projects, and are less effective at sustaining the care of some of the most vulnerable members of society. In these respects, the more comprehensive role of the state cannot be supplanted by the voluntary sector. Study of the contribution of the churches in the USA indicates a formidable contribution to civil society. In particular, there is a strong (perhaps surprising) link between congregational membership and contribution to political activity. This occurs through generating motivation, equipping individuals with the necessary skills to participate, and providing a range of contacts and networks of recruitment by which political engagement takes place.[15]

In relation to ecclesiology, this confirms the local congregation as the primary form of the body of Christ in the world. As a worshipping community gathered to hear the Word of God and to celebrate the sacraments, the congregation establishes patterns of fellowship, witness and mission to the world. Although its local character cannot exhaust its catholic identity, the congregation is the indispensable setting for the praise of God, the formation of saints, pastoral support of members and outreach into society. Except in sacramental communities sufficiently small and local to nurture members, to mediate a sense of vocation, and to mobilise believers to serve God, Christians cannot live and act together in faith, hope and love. For a national church, this also means that, without sufficiently strong congregational life and local involvement, public pronouncements will sound increasingly hollow, strident or platitudinous. The church's ability to express a judgement in the wider political arena will require broader forms of church government and the appointment of persons skilled in this field.[16] But the capacity to do this effectively will depend upon the health of congregational life.

---

[15] Sidney Verba, Kay Lehman Schlozman and Henry Brady, *Voice and Equality: Civic Voluntarism in American Politics* (Cambridge, MA: Harvard University Press, 1995). This is further discussed by Hollenbach, *The Common Good and Christian Ethics*, 103ff.

[16] Harris notes the relative inability of congregations to press for social change, to inform public policy and to exercise a prophetic role; 'Civil Society and the Role of UK Churches', 52.

Without a deliberate wholesale retreat from society, it is hard to see how any church community can escape the responsibility of contributing to the common good. Through the formation of citizens who contribute responsibly to the peace and justice of their societies, each Christian congregation carries an obligation to promote the *bonum commune*. Where the church is widely represented throughout a civil society, its obligations correspondingly increase. In serving the common good, it seeks to influence, for example, the framing of laws, the constitutional arrangement of its society, the institution of marriage, and the provision of education, health care and social welfare. As a catholic body, it draws attention to wider institutional issues. This will typically take place both in its corporate activity and through the presence of its members in other spheres of civic life. In this respect, a church may properly exercise a public role at both local and national levels in faithfulness to its Scriptures and traditions, even where it has ceased to function as a national or state church in the sense outlined at the beginning of this chapter.

Against this claim for the constructive civic contribution of churches, there stand secular anxieties, such as those of Rawls, Rorty and other liberal theorists, concerning the capacity of religion to promote social cohesion. It is not difficult to find graphic stories of the complicity of religious groups in civil strife; these include the countries of Northern Ireland, Bosnia, India and the Sudan as well as terrorist networks such as Al-Qaeda. While notable counter-examples can be produced, the secular suspicion is that these are merely exceptions that prove the rule. It is argued that the general effect of religious identity is to reinforce difference through the fixing of boundaries that divide citizens. By strengthening group loyalty, this inevitably militates against a commitment to diversity. At times of economic and political pressure, a culture of fear, suspicion and violence can be readily created. Over 90 per cent of wars begin as civil conflicts, with factors of religious, ethnic and national identity contributing to the majority of these.[17]

Following the events of 11 September 2001, the publicity surrounding Samuel Huntington's *Clash of Civilizations* has confirmed this

[17] See R. Scott Appleby, *The Ambivalance of the Sacred: Religion, Violence, and Reconciliation* (New York: Rowman & Littlefield, 2000), 17.

secular sense of religion as a cause of global unrest. Current antagonism between Islam and Christianity is the latest in a series of confrontations extending from the Middle Ages onwards. According to the thesis, its present form is one in which a militant, pre-modern Islam faces liberal forms of western Christianity. This is the fault-line that runs throughout much of global culture as is evident in Africa, Southeast Asia, central Europe and the Middle East.[18] Nonetheless, despite some appearance of plausibility the thesis is overstated in its attempt to produce a meta-narrative of Christian–Muslim antagonism across space and time. Counterexamples range from the influence of Islamic thinkers on scholastic theologians of the Middle Ages, through the experience of churches in the Middle East, to the positive desire of Muslim and Christian groups peacefully to coexist and interact in western urban settings; all these suggest that there is a long and living tradition of *convivencia* as well as episodes of violent conflict.[19]

Against the secular charge that religions tend to provoke civil disputes, examples illustrating significant input to conflict resolution can be offered. The following three cases may briefly indicate both the religious diversity and geographical spread of this contribution.[20] A first example is provided by the work of Bishop Carlos Belo in East Timor. After years of bloodshed and famine following the Indonesian invasion of 1975 when about one third of all islanders were killed, Belo successfully drew attention to the plight of his people. Appointed bishop in 1988, he maintained the focus of the international community on the repression despite the collusion of various governments with the Suharto regime and the ambivalence of Vatican officials. Belo faced personal harassment, isolation and threats to his own life. But his sustained commitment to human rights, democracy and peaceful protest was crucial to maintaining a principled struggle for independence. This was intensified by the award of a Nobel Peace Prize in 1996, and its attendant publicity. Through church growth (after the

---

[18] Samuel P. Huntington, *The Clash of Civilizations and the Remaking of the World Order* (London: Touchstone, 1998).

[19] This is explored by my colleague David Kerr; 'Christianity and Islam: "Clash of Civilizations" or "Community of Reconciliations?" Questions for Christian–Muslim Studies', *Studies in World Christianity* 8 (2002), 81–98.

[20] Here I am indebted to Appleby, *The Ambivalence of the Sacred*, 213ff.

invasion, the Roman Catholic population quadrupled), non-violent protest and the forming of alliances with outside political forces (religious and non-religious), a climate was slowly created in which the position of Indonesia (and its international arms suppliers) became unsustainable. Thus independence was achieved for East Timor.[21]

To cite a second and more familiar example, the contribution of religious agencies is apparent both in the opposition to apartheid in South Africa and in the subsequent struggle to reform civil society. Prominent in mounting effective criticism of the political regime, Desmond Tutu also made a significant contribution in chairing the Truth and Reconciliation Commission (TRC). Moreover, Christian discourse and practice of confession, forgiveness, reconciliation and restoration featured prominently in much of what transpired. This took place alongside the shared convictions of other faiths and the secular contribution of lawyers and health-care professionals. Yet without its spiritual context the work of the TRC could hardly have proceeded. The critical and traumatic nature of the task required times of prayer, recollection and devotion. Tutu himself called upon a range of groups to join in prayer for the commission's work. The emphasis upon confession, forgiveness, amnesty and rehabilitation recalled language shared by several religious traditions, as did the recognition that even the worst perpetrators of violence could not be demonised or dehumanised.[22] Hence the political work of the TRC proceeded along lines that required the mobilisation of a range of theological and spiritual struggles. This has evoked some criticism.[23] The language of reconciliation, together with the hamartiological claim that the dividing line between perpetrator and victim runs through each one of us, generated a moral symmetry that obscured the one-sided nature of oppression. So it was argued. The systematic violence of the apartheid regime could not thus be morally equated with acts of civil resistance. Moreover, according to other critics, the confusion of religious and political language creates a moral utopianism that can be unhelpful to the practical business of politics with its

---

[21] The story of Belo's role is told in Arnold S. Kohen, *From the Place of the Dead: Bishop Belo and the Struggle for East Timor* (Oxford: Lion Books, 1999).

[22] For Tutu's own account see *No Future without Forgiveness* (London: Rider, 1999).

[23] See Charles Villa Vicencio and Wilhelm Verwoerd (eds.), *Looking Back Reaching Forward* (Cape Town: University of Cape Town Press, 2000).

more limited ends. Against this stand the claim that Christian faith is expressed primarily in stories of divine grace and healing instantiated in human encounters, and the acknowledgement that, in situations of entrenched conflict, resources offering practical hope are urgently required.[24]

In another religious context, to take a third example, Aung San Suu Kyi has mounted sustained resistance to the military government of Burma (Myanmar). Despite house arrest and the intimidation of her supporters, she has attracted the support of human-rights organisations and much of the international community through non-violent protest and leadership of the movement for democracy. This was recognised in the award of the Nobel Peace Prize in 1991. Animated by principles of humility, prudence and compassion, her political action is rooted in Buddhist soil. She maintains that it is not power so much that corrupts as fear, a fear that can be intensified in people through repeated violation of human rights by the political authorities. By insisting that her vision and therefore her political struggle are primarily spiritual, she describes the ability of each person to achieve his or her full potential and to enable others to achieve theirs. This Buddhist conviction is expressed politically in 'the struggle of a people to live whole, meaningful lives as free and equal members of the world community'.[25]

Notwithstanding their differences, these three examples illustrate some important features of effective social action informed by religious principles. Protest is rooted in local communities and in the networks of support and activity that they can sustain over long periods of time, often in the face of harassment. A contribution is made not only to political change but to the difficult process of rebuilding societies after traumatic upheaval. Connection is made with political actors and groups outside the religious community, often through the use of human-rights language. This can be crucial to building a consensus that makes change irresistible. And, finally, we are reminded that the mere removal of a bad regime does not itself guarantee the arrival of a peaceful and harmonious society. The work required to create this is often frustrating, interrupted by setback and vulnerable

---

[24] This is explored in John de Gruchy's *Reconciliation: Restoring Justice* (London: SCM, 2002).
[25] Aung San Suu Kyi, *Freedom from Fear* (London: Penguin, 1995), 238.

to bouts of novel conflict. Here again the reinvigoration of civil society is necessary to prevent further forms of convulsion.

Appleby classifies the contribution of religious groups to conflict resolution in three ways.[26] First, there is the mobilisation of protest. Churches, mosques and temples can provide a forum for the expression of dissent through their historical functions and long-standing institutional presence in a community. Often their office-holders are appointed and remunerated by the religious community and are therefore not vulnerable to the economic and political pressures that can be applied to other members of the group. In part, this enabled Martin Luther King to exercise a leadership role in the early stages of the civil-rights movement, and church leaders to provide a focus for dissent in eastern Europe under communist rule.

Second, the 'saturation mode' provides a model for social transformation that often goes unrecognised in headline reports. It is by saturating civil society with agencies of protest, education and change that a religious commitment to transformation can become effective. By operating at different levels and in a variety of contexts, religious groups can create a prevailing climate (to change the metaphor) in favour of just reforms, reconciliation and the rebuilding of community life. Appleby detects this in Northern Ireland, where, through public pronouncements of church leaders, ecumenical initiatives, para-church reconciliation groups such as Corrymeela, and an articulation of the details of political and economic reform, a momentum for change and peace has been generated: 'If sheer exhaustion from thirty years of internecine conflict played no small role in motivating the electorate, the discourse of forgiveness promoted by the churches and religious and cultural groups, which came to permeate the rhetoric of the ratification debate, helped translate popular sentiment into political action for peace.'[27]

Third, the interventionist model that has emerged in recent times, despite its pitfalls, provides some graphic illustrations of the capacity of religious communities for promoting reconciliation and peace. The Sant'Egidio movement, emerging from a post-Vatican II lay movement in Italy, has had success at mediating in Mozambique and elsewhere. Its achievements are born of earning a reputation

---

[26] *The Ambivalence of the Sacred*, 230ff.   [27] Ibid., 238.

for an integrity that commands the trust of all parties, and also for its emphasis upon developing friendships and employing 'secular-friendly' language everywhere. Similarly, Mennonite groups in North America have contributed to facilitating peace efforts on the east coast of Nicaragua and in Bosnia, Croatia and Serbia. Several institutions now offer courses and programmes on mediation, peacemaking and conflict resolution. The obvious danger in this approach lies in its appearing to adopt an attitude of 'We know what's best for you – we'll come and show you.' Yet this may be offset by favouring an 'elicitive' approach in which adaptation to regional cultural factors is stressed alongside the importance of listening, observing and allowing local groups the space in which to develop their own initiatives.

GLOBAL PERSPECTIVES

Each of these cases further confirms the claim that the capacity of a religious community to make a significant public contribution is not dependent upon its functioning as a national or established body in the manner of a Christendom church. In this regard, the experience of non-western churches, to which the majority of Christians world-wide now belong, is instructive. At the end of the nineteenth century over 80 per cent of Christians lived in either Europe or North America. A century later about 60 per cent belong to Africa, Asia, Latin America and the Pacific. Their number rises steadily, while Christian affiliation in Europe dramatically declines.[28] The story of Christianity outside Christendom is not a narrative of sectarian ecclesiology but of deeply instructive ways in which the churches can exercise social significance in education, medicine, welfare and political reform without ever enjoying, and seldom contemplating, the benefits of establishment. For a variety of reasons, establishment was not successfully exported by western missionaries. Churches grew, flourished, took root and became socially significant, usually without aspiring towards a position of religious or political pre-eminence. Much

---

[28] 'Christianity began the twentieth century as a Western religion, and indeed, the Western religion; it ended the century as a non-Western religion, on track to become progressively more so'; Andrew F. Walls, *The Cross-Cultural Process in Christian History* (Edinburgh: T. & T. Clark, 2002), 64.

nineteenth-century Protestant missionary effort resulted from the formation of newly formed voluntary societies rather than through the organisational mechanisms of established churches. These were often led by laypersons. Gathering people from different churches and espousing voluntary principles of liberty and freedom from coercion, their ethos tended to eschew the more constrictive ways of establishment. As a consequence, the transplanting of Christian groups in the non-western world was generally along voluntarist lines. Moreover, even when there was aspiration towards the formation of new national churches this was mostly thwarted by the reality of different political circumstances from those obtaining in Europe. In modern China, the attempt to coordinate religion with socialism is largely the result of political agencies seeking an accommodation. This represents not a Christendom vision in which church and state function as an organic unity, but instead a government initiative to coopt the ambivalent forces of religion for a secular purpose.[29]

The interests of colonial rulers and missionary enterprises were never identical. Across India, for example, the British government did not seek to recreate a Christian nation. Indeed its action may have led to an invigoration of Hinduism. In Algeria, the French legislated against the conversion of Muslims. Throughout the Middle East, churches have a centuries-long history of coexisting with large Muslim populations. Their experience is often neglected in the church history taught in western seminaries, colleges and universities.[30] Within the modern Japanese context, the churches have offered a theological critique of the dangers of an 'ethnocentric and self-righteous nationalism',[31] a critique that must be predicated upon a clear distinction between church and nation. In sub-Saharan Africa, colonial boundaries crossed religious lines, hence rendering nation states religiously plural. Within the Sudan, missionaries complained that the British government encouraged Islamisation. Of course, the colonial powers had their own strategic reasons for doing so, but their ends

---

[29] See Lap Yan Kung, 'What to Preach? Christian Witness in China, with Reference to the Party's Policy of Mutual Accommodation', *Studies in World Christianity* 8 (2002), 206–27.

[30] For a recent study of church and state in this region see Betty Jane Bailey and J. Martin Bailey, *Who Are the Christians in the Middle East?* (Grand Rapids: Eerdmans, 2003).

[31] Yasuo Furuya, 'Epilogue' in Yasuo Furuya (ed.), *A History of Japanese Theology* (Grand Rapids: Eerdmans, 1997), 143.

thus tended to diverge from those of Christian missions. Andrew Walls writes, 'If several generations of missionaries once felt betrayed when a state nominally Christian refused to offer the support they felt due, we now may be humbly grateful that God is kinder than to answer all the prayers of his people.'[32]

Nevertheless, without attempting to emulate the Christendom arrangement, non-western churches did not thereby fail to become socially significant. The contribution to health care, education and poor relief is apparent in sundry ways. The churches could also become vehicles for political protest and reform sometimes against colonial rule. This is not to idealise the non-western experience, and still less to ignore the failure of the church to arrest social disintegration in some situations. Yet it confirms the possibility of a publicly engaged Christianity that does not repose upon the church functioning as national or established in the European sense.

While warning against the dangers of generalising about the complexity of African Christianity, Adrian Hastings notes that by the 1970s the power of the churches was largely locally based and provided alternative structures to those of a political society that was sometimes distrusted by the populace.[33] As sources of information, education and medical care, churches could command grass-roots support. Often this reality had to be faced by governments. Nonetheless, despite the involvement of churches in the maintenance of schools, hospitals, printing presses and radio stations, for most African Christians it is the practices of prayer and worship that are the primary functions of ecclesial life. This liturgical setting decisively shapes the lives of participants and its interaction with the more institutional forms of church life influences the social effects of the faith.

In his discussion of theology and politics in modern Africa,[34] Kwame Bediako notes the initial contribution of churches in mobilising African leadership in the struggle for independence. Since then there has arisen a need to establish more pluralist, consensual styles

---

[32] Walls, *The Cross-Cultural Process in Christian History*, 44.

[33] Adrian Hastings, *A History of African Christianity* (Cambridge: Cambridge University Press, 1979), 263.

[34] Kwame Bediako, 'Christian Religion and African Social Norms: Authority, Desacralisation and Democracy', *Christianity in Africa: the Renewal of a Non-Western Religion* (Edinburgh: Edinburgh University Press, 1995), 234–51.

of politics and he perceives here a theological contribution in understanding political authority as spiritually derived but not as sacral in itself. Its derivation from the sovereignty of God in Hebrew and New Testament tradition resonates with indigenous African notions of spiritual leadership, but political authorities are no longer perceived as possessing an intrinsic sacral quality. This enables a politics to emerge which can challenge on African Christian grounds the claim that multi-party democracy is only a western import. Yet, in arguing theologically for more democratic politics, Bediako resists any attempt to reproduce a new Christendom. All African churches operate within a context of religious pluralism and need to contribute to democratic freedom for all groups and individuals.

A related feature of the translation of European Christianity to other parts of the globe was the better appreciation of other cultures and religions. With hindsight much of this may appear grudging and patronising, but it is clear that many historical attitudes to other faiths had to be abandoned in a first-hand encounter with very different patterns of civilisation. The Westminster Confession had dismissed the possibility that those not professing the Christian religion might be saved, condemning such a proposition as 'most detestable'. Yet as Presbyterian missionaries learned more about the world and its peoples this easy dismissal, along with the doctrine of double predestination, became unthinkable. In reaction to this, the Presbyterian churches of Scotland modified the terms in which they subscribed to the Westminster Confession, explicitly distancing themselves from perceived aspects of its teaching.[35] In doing so, a more positive attitude towards culture in general emerged. The recognition of divine grace as active and present outside the church was now ineluctable.

THE SECULARISATION THESIS

In a post-Christian context, western churches, which once enjoyed considerable national influence, are faced with a temptation that may

---

[35] For example, the 1982 Declaratory Act of the General Assembly of the Free Church affirms the possibility of salvation for those outside the visible church, maintains that there are natural affections and actions which are virtuous and praiseworthy despite human depravity, and disclaims intolerant or persecuting principles. See James L. Weatherhead (ed.), *The Constitution and Laws of the Church of Scotland* (Edinburgh: Board of Practice and Procedure, 1997), 177–8. For further discussion see A. C. Cheyne, *The Transforming of the Kirk: Victorian Scotland's Religious Revolution* (Edinburgh: St Andrew Press, 1983).

prove irresistible. The nature of the temptation, at least according to its critics, is to aspire to a continued national significance but at the price of abandoning what is distinctive in one's contribution. Rather than shaping civil society, the Christian faith simply tracks its shifts and movements, providing spiritual expression for whatever the *Zeitgeist*. The outcome is a steady dilution of 'the faith delivered once for all to the saints'.

This is a point on which those who are charged with school-chaplaincy work sometimes complain. The parish priest or minister continues to exercise a role as chaplain in non-denominational schools, particularly at the primary level, but the ethos of the schools is increasingly pluralist, multi-faith and determined to place all religions on an equal footing. What is thus offered by clergy is often the lowest common denominator, for example reflection on the spiritual quest for meaning, rather than on the Bible, the church or the creeds. The claim that religious observance in schools contributes to spiritual growth is also dubious. An occasional service of worship cannot readily expose a child to the spiritual formation that takes place only over a much longer period of time through immersion and education in the practices of a faith community.

A similar criticism attends the shift in attitude, particularly within our national churches, towards the institution of marriage. This doubtless arises out of pastoral difficulties faced by parish clergy who are asked to conduct marriage services for cohabitees, those seeking remarriage and gay couples. Both the Church of Scotland and the Church of England have published significant reports in the last decade which seek to outline a responsible sexual ethic, particularly in the context of parenting, which is both faithful to the Christian tradition yet pastorally sensitive to changes in attitudes and social practice. Thus *Something to Celebrate* urges the church to look upon those cohabiting as in some sense already on the way to marriage, or in part fulfilling a Christian ideal.[36] Yet the barrage of criticism facing these reports reveals an underlying (though misguided) fear of a sell-out. Too much emphasis is placed, it is said, on sociological findings. There is a moral indifference to the central issues. A loss of theological confidence characterises tentative conclusions. In an

---

[36] *Something to Celebrate: Valuing Families in Church and Society* (London: Church House Publishing, 1995); 'The Theology of Marriage', *Reports to the General Assembly of the Church of Scotland 1994* (Edinburgh, 1994), 257–85.

attempt to accommodate, too much has been compromised. In all these cases the underlying complaint remains the same. Through a misguided desire to retain its social status, the church has neglected its primary tasks of bearing witness, of evangelism, and of faithful discipleship.[37]

The criticism that national churches run the risk of selling-out in a culture of rapid dechristianisation is also fuelled by impatience with pronouncements of church representatives. In seeking to instruct politicians, often on the basis of a centre-left agenda, church leaders are sometimes accused of posturing, of neglecting their pastoral and evangelical tasks, and of following a largely secular agenda. Yet we should note that this criticism is at least in one respect at odds with the previous one. If what is sought is an authentic Christian engagement with social issues then the church will find itself frequently in countercultural mode. This will inevitably excite the reaction that church leaders are posturing in a manner that is unlikely to have little social effect.

Whether this is entirely valid or not, it is indicative of the change in social location that the churches are now experiencing. This change is most troublesome for those denominations which have traditionally enjoyed the benefits and responsibilities brought by state establishment. The terms of partnership between state and church have changed, and in any case the previous arrangement is one that is now recognised to have had deleterious consequences. Moreover, the change in this partnership has come at a time when church theology has become increasingly conscious of the political dimension of faith. Christian responsibility is unavoidably moral, social and political. This closes off any route to sectarian withdrawal at a time of secularisation. Finding itself detached but not withdrawn, Christian social theology must seek new forms of engagement. A route must be charted which embraces evangelical faithfulness but which is comprehending of our current social condition, and this route will need to avoid the perils of demonising the world and of assuming a Christian monopoly upon the truth.

The criticism is sometimes made that theology is too easily captivated by sociological analysis. The view adopted here is the opposite.

---

[37] See the critique of Michael Banner, *Christian Ethics and Contemporary Moral Problems* (Cambridge: Cambridge University Press, 1999), 252–68.

There has been insufficient attention to sociological work, particularly in our theological syllabi, with the result that we make too many assumptions of an impressionistic sort about the nature of the societies in which we live. In a recent study, José Casanova has pointed to interesting ways in which churches continue to make a public contribution at a time of secularisation.[38] The term secularisation itself requires scrutiny. According to Casanova, there are three broad senses in which it can be used and these need to be distinguished.

In one sense, secularisation can refer to the differentiation between functions. Here the processes of science, politics, economics, education and welfare provision achieve greater autonomy and freedom from ecclesiastical control. Considered in this way, secularisation has undoubtedly occurred in many western societies. Direct church control over secular spheres of existence has diminished, with some possible exceptions in the case of church schools, residential homes for the elderly and the hospice movement. The advent of a greater pluralism has ensured that religious affiliation is increasingly irrelevant to the holding of office and the achievement of success in a diversity of fields.

In another sense, secularisation can refer to the inevitable demise of religious belief and practice in societies where this differentiation of functions reaches an advanced stage. Some exponents of the secularisation thesis would see this as a long process which has been under way for centuries, while an increasing number of revisionists point to the stubborn persistence of religion in our social context. Even within western European societies, there is still evidence for widespread religious belief and practice even though this is not expressed by adherence to the institutional church. Relatively few people report that they do not believe in God; the practice of prayer is persistently widespread; and a majority claim still to believe in heaven.[39] Elsewhere in the world, one can point to a resurgence of religious activity in Africa, Latin America, and Asia, particularly within the Muslim world. In this respect, secularisation as the inevitable decline of religion under the conditions of modernity is an increasingly tenuous hypothesis. Indeed, in a recent study, Peter Berger has argued somewhat whimsically that what now requires explanation is the stubbornness of the

---

[38] José Casanova, *Public Religions in the Modern World* (Chicago: University of Chicago Press, 1994).
[39] See Davie, *Europe: the Exceptional Case*, 7.

secularisation thesis amongst western intellectuals. What is needed is not more sociological studies of Islamic communities but analysis of the academic environment inhabited by American professors.[40]

Secularisation, in a third sense, refers neither to the differentiation of functions nor to decline of religion, but rather to the demise of its public significance. It persists, according to the thesis, merely as a harmless epiphenomenon which has now become an optional and leisure-time pursuit, but it lacks social importance. According to Inglehart, the failure of material goods to bring lasting satisfaction will inevitably result in a reversal of spiritual activity in societies whose citizens attain comfortable standards of living. This is the phenomenon of post-materialism. But whether, as Inglehart concludes, this favours more private, non-traditional forms of religious expression is unclear.[41] The older faith traditions may prove capable of adjusting to this new situation. In contrast to this, Casanova's thesis is that religion remains a social force but more through its influence on civil society than through direct engagement with the state and political society. This is argued by reference to a range of examples from Spain, the USA, Poland and Brazil. In each of these cases, the churches have no direct access to the levers of state power, yet their recent contribution to their respective societies is of measurable significance. This works in different ways at the level of civil society. Casanova also notes that the ability of religion to function in a socially effective way depends upon its invigoration of life at the congregational level through worship, education and pastoral support. Without this base, the churches lack sufficient resources to make a distinctive social contribution. The example of Spain is particularly interesting. Here, it is claimed that by abandoning its early alignment with the Franco regime the church reasserted itself in the private and public domains. In doing so, it became a vehicle for democratic reform and individual religious expression.

Within modern pluralist states, Casanova argues that public effectiveness and private appeal will require the distancing of the church from the state. Its status as an established institution will thus tend to diminish its ability to function in a publicly successful manner. Too

[40] Berger, 'The Desecularization of the World', 2.
[41] R. Inglehart, *Modernization and Postmodernization: Cultural, Economic and Political Change in 43 Societies* (Princeton: Princeton University Press, 1997).

closely aligned to government and to an arrangement now adjudged archaic, an established, national church will tend to lack the necessary freedom and space for creative social interaction. In part, this public distrust of large state-like institutions afflicts other bodies including political parties, trade unions and the armed forces. In a more pluralist setting, citizens wish to choose their political, moral and spiritual identity rather than to have this imposed.

Casanova's thesis may require some qualification. An obvious difficulty concerns its applicability to Muslim societies where religion and political life are less clearly differentiated. Even in democratic systems that have achieved a measure of differentiation, the success of Muslim parties takes some explaining. Moreover, the assumption that the differentiation of functions leaves religion to operate in the sphere of civil society assumes that the various sectors of public life are 'non-porous'.[42] This is questionable, since the boundary between civil and political society is fluid. The phenomenon of 'seepage' may be detected in the ways in which religious groups seek directly to influence legislation on the pursuit of embryonic research and animal experimentation, the education system and the regulation of the economy. On the other hand, since this now generally takes place through forming alliances with other groups in civil society rather than through direct access to political power, Casanova's thesis may be judged broadly true and important for much of the Christian world.

The interaction with the different spheres or systems of civil society requires further study by theologians. With his concept of 'structured pluralism', Michael Welker, drawing on the work of Luhmann and others, helpfully points to ways in which the various subsystems of social life are differentiated yet exist in a complex set of relations to one another. A modern society requires both differentiation and interrelationship of its component systems, if it is to avoid a slide into oppression on the one side or anarchy on the other. While differentiation is necessary, the need for an interrelating of systems creates opportunities for public theology.[43]

---

[42] I am indebted here to the argument of David Herbert, *Religion and Civil Society: Rethinking Public Religion in the Contemporary World* (Aldershot: Ashgate, 2003), 54ff.

[43] Michael Welker, 'Christianity and Structured Pluralism', unpublished paper. See also his 'God's Power and Powerlessness: Biblical Theology and the Search for a World Ethos in a Time of Shortlived Moral Markets', in Cynthia L. Rigby (ed.), *Power, Powerlessness and the*

Where does this leave us? It suggests that in ceasing to function as a national institution, the church may nonetheless remain publicly significant. Under the conditions of modernity, the church will increasingly find itself positioned alongside other groups and movements in civil society. While there is a danger that this will lead to a 'sequestration' of religious identity, it provides a way of understanding how the church's social functions may be fulfilled. The capacity of religion to provide moral and spiritual formation, to offer resources for meaning, and perspectives for understanding the values, standards and goals of human life should prevent any constriction of the church to only one limited sphere of civil society. In addition, the particular demands that the church imposes upon its members through the sacrament of baptism set it apart. These indicate that membership of the body of Christ is not commensurate with belonging to other voluntary groups within the civic sphere. The allegiance owed to God defines the commitments that can properly be made elsewhere. In turn, ecclesial loyalty will also become normative for the practice of the individual in other social contexts including the household, the workplace and the political domain.[44]

The older model of church and state as the two dominant institutions cooperating in a close and exclusive partnership is now well past its sell-by date. Secularisation, in the first sense, as the differentiation of functions has rendered this problematic. The church no longer directly controls education, access to political office, or the welfare services. These are in part under the control of the state, and in part influenced by organisations and agencies other than the church. We need increasingly to think of the church as belonging with these other bodies in civil society and seeking to promote its particular vision of the common good through influence, conversation, shared resources and the making of common cause. In doing so, we require to develop a differentiated model for the church's social contribution which leads to neither domination, nor cultural captivity, nor isolation.

Divine (Atlanta: Scholars Press, 1997), 39–55. In this context, Welker makes the significant point that within the scriptural traditions the power of God's Spirit is usually manifested in disempowered communities and individuals.

[44] I am grateful to critical comments of James Skillen that have enabled me both to clarify and to qualify the argument at this juncture.

The following Scottish example provides a concluding illustration. In the years prior to the devolution referendum of 1979, the Church of Scotland in its official reports and pronouncement was consistently in support of some form of home rule within the context of the United Kingdom. This was announced in a rather top-down fashion, it being assumed that the state and other bodies could somehow get on with the business of implementing the proposal. The failure of the public, however, to display sufficient support for devolution in 1979 meant that the opportunity was lost in the closing phases of the Callaghan government. In the traumatic aftermath of the referendum, the church reconsidered its position not with a view to abandoning its earlier policy but in the interests of promoting it more effectively. There then came about a coalition of interest groups – several churches, trades unions, political parties and others – who were committed to devolution and who were able within Scottish society to create the momentum which realised this end with the election of the Blair government in 1997 and a subsequent referendum providing overwhelming support.[45] It will be some time before a full appraisal of this new political arrangement can be undertaken, but the return of the parliament to Edinburgh suggests a different model for the social contribution of the church. It is one that largely confirms Casanova's thesis that different patterns of civic partnership, critical cooperation and provision of moral and spiritual resources are increasingly the means by which the church continues to be publicly significant.

CONCLUSION

In arguing that Christendom has now been superseded, this chapter has sought to contest the conclusion that the only remaining role for religion is that of a private, leisure-time pursuit. The loss of national status does not coincide with the loss of public significance. Attention to the concept of civil society can disclose important ways in which Christian groups *inter alia* can promote the common good and make a constructive public contribution. A variety of recent examples, some

[45] For a recent account of this story set in historical perspective see Neal Ascherson, *Stone Voices: the Search for Scotland* (London: Granta, 2002).

positive and others negative, attest the capacity of religion to make a decisive contribution to national life without reinvoking earlier models of Christendom. Moreover, the possibility of remaining politically significant is already revealed by the experience of the non-western churches, which is often ignored in recent discussion. With increasing scepticism amongst social scientists surrounding the secularisation thesis, the prospects for reasserting the civic impact of faith are not without plausibility.

CHAPTER EIGHT

In the twilight of establishment

It is hardly too much to say that during the twentieth century
Great Britain lost its historic identity as a Protestant nation.

(Peter Clarke)[1]

Young Christians in the Europe of today come to their faith
through individual choice which thrusts them back on the pure
Gospel. So they have a thirst for religious experience and good
teaching.

(John Wilkins)[2]

THE BRITISH CONTEXT

This final chapter ends on a more parochial note by considering the
ongoing debate surrounding establishment in the United Kingdom.
It has been argued already that beyond Christendom a church can
exercise a publicly significant role without functioning as an established, state-recognised church. The conclusions of this chapter are
thus largely anticipated. Indeed, if some sociological analyses are correct it may even be the case that a church's public contribution today
is likely to be greater where its links with the state are kept to a
minimum. By functioning as an institution of civil society in partnership with other groups, churches can continue to be significant in
more pluralist settings where the state cannot be identified with any
one religious party. In any case, citizens in diverse societies prefer to
choose their religious identity rather than to have this institutionally
prescribed. Where a majority exists outside the national church there

---

[1] Peter Clarke, *Hope and Glory, Britain 1900–1990* (London: Penguin, 1997), 161.
[2] *The Tablet*, 20/27 December 2003, 4.

will always be awkward criticisms levelled at the political privileging of one religious institution. This inevitably raises issues about the viability of establishment.

Some attention to terminology is required at the outset. An established church need not be a state church. To be established does not entail state control over the affairs of the church. The term Erastianism is often used to describe a state church, after Thomas Erastus (1524–83), a Swiss theologian and physician who worked in Heidelberg. Asserting that the state had the right to exercise excommunication and church discipline over and above the ecclesiastical authorities, he gave his name to an arrangement in which the church is controlled by the state. Yet establishment need not be Erastian. It more often refers to a partnership between church and state that recognises the integration of civil and church life. This can be marked in a variety of ways. The church may receive special privileges from the state in return for services rendered. These are often financial, perhaps through the levying of church taxes. The services rendered will typically include ministrations to every citizen requesting baptism, marriage or a funeral service, and the provision of a chaplain to a range of civic bodies. Some decisions of the church may require to be ratified or at least acknowledged by the state. The office bearers of the church may require the approval of the state in holding their appointments. The head of state may stand in ceremonial relationship to the courts and services of the church. In surveying modern Europe one finds various manifestations of establishment which have evolved in different ways over time. One of the most recent changes is that initiated in Sweden in 1996 where, through an act of the state, the church gained a greater degree of autonomy, and baptism rather than citizenship became the condition of membership. Yet the church retains a unique place in the constitution. It remains responsible for all burial sites in Sweden. Finances are raised through a fee collected by the state, while the monarch is described as 'the first member' of the Church of Sweden. From a Swedish perspective this new arrangement appears to move in the direction of disestablishment; yet for Anglican commentators it creates a situation not dissimilar to the one that presently obtains in England.[3]

---

[3] See R. Persenius, 'The Year 2000: Disestablishment in Sweden', *Theology* 102 (1999), 177–86; Paul Avis, *Church, State and Establishment* (London: SPCK, 2001), 19–20.

This illustration reveals that establishment is not a univocal concept. It has different meanings across space and time. The same applies to 'disestablishment'. In surveying the British scene, one quickly becomes conscious that (dis)establishment has been an evolving feature of public life. Churches in England and Scotland are established, but in different ways from each other and in a manner that is dissimilar to that of the past. Indeed in the 1970 Chadwick report on *Church and State*, the memorandum of dissent from Miss Valerie Pitt rejected the notion of establishment, partly on the ground that it was an idea without clear sense and could not be coherently stated.[4] Whether or not this is the case, one finds some significant changes in the relationship of church and state over several centuries of English history that suggest it is at least an open-textured concept.

The form of establishment which characterises English public life can be traced back to the arrangements that came into force when Henry VIII seceded from the Roman Catholic Church. Through a series of measures culminating in the Act of Supremacy (1534), Henry assumed control over the English church. Bishops and clergy now owed their appointments, income and freedom to the nation state.[5] The Reformation settlement under Henry and later Elizabeth found theological justification in Hooker's *Laws of Ecclesiastical Polity*. His insistence that the membership of church and commonwealth were coextensive represents an ideal integration of religious and civic life.[6] This powerful vision is deeply appealing in its description of a politically harmonious society animated by the duties and truths of the Christian religion. While church and state have their respective and differentiated functions, under divine providence these operate most effectively in an integrated relationship of mutual recognition. Hooker reflects the view of the magisterial Reformers that every society must be shaped by its religious commitments. It is thus not so much a question of 'whether establishment' as 'which establishment'.

---

[4] Valerie Pitt, 'Memorandum of Dissent', *Church and State: Report of the Archbishop's Commission* (London: Church Information Office, 1970), 69.

[5] 'The Church of England within two short years passed from being an England-located branch of a great trans-national company with headquarters in Rome to being a department of state whereby the monarch in Parliament catered for the religious welfare of his subjects'; Colin Buchanan, *Cut the Connection: Disestablishment and the Church of England* (London: Darton, Longman & Todd, 1994), 13.

[6] Hooker, *Of the Laws of Ecclesiastical Polity*, ed. McGrade, Book VIII.1.2, 130. Hooker goes on to argue for the relative autonomy of church and state in a manner reminiscent of Luther and Calvin. Although firmly committed to establishment, he is at pains to avoid Erastianism.

Adrian Hastings remarks that 'Hooker's vision is so satisfying for the moderate nationalist, his tone so judicious, his style so elegant that even into the twentieth century it has been hard (for Anglicans) to recognise that it was a misleading vision, neither theologically nor factually well grounded.'[7]

The establishment arrangement was threatened on two fronts. First, should the monarch ever become a Roman Catholic it would break down. This happened on two occasions; once in the reign of Mary Tudor (1553–8) and again in the time of James II (1685–9). Eventually, following the overthrow of James II and the accession of William of Orange, the laws of succession and the coronation oath were changed to ensure that no Roman Catholic could again succeed. In securing a Protestant succession, moreover, the Act of Settlement (1701) prevented the monarch from marrying a Roman Catholic. A second threat to the nature of establishment came in the form of the church itself. What if the church were dominated by a party which objected to the arrangement and desired a greater freedom or change of direction in matters of church government, liturgy and doctrine? This effectively happened when the Puritan party secured power and beheaded Charles I in 1649. Following the restoration in 1662, efforts to reintegrate the dissidents failed, and instead of a policy of assimilation a policy of toleration was pursued. Dissenters were tolerated but certain privileges or rights were denied them. Throughout the eighteenth century, only the members of the established church could pursue a career in Parliament, hold municipal office, obtain a commission in the armed forces, gain admission to Oxbridge or teach there.[8] Only those belonging to the establishment, indeed, could be buried in the cemetery surrounding the parish church. A lower social status was thus accorded to nonconformists and dissenters, for example Baptists, Methodists and Independents; still lower was the status of many Roman Catholics and Jews. Nonetheless, the policy of toleration required an adjustment of Hooker's vision. The full integrity of

---

[7] Adrian Hastings, *Church and State: the English Experience* (Exeter: University of Exeter Press, 1991), 22.

[8] These arrangements were under strain through much of the eighteenth century with loopholes being found in the case of Dissenters holding political office. This is explored by Stewart J. Brown, *The National Churches of England, Ireland and Scotland, 1801–1846* (Oxford: Oxford University Press, 2001), 1–92.

church and society was lost. The latter lacked the cohesion expressed in the ideal of a comprehensive allegiance to the national church.

While Scotland after the Reformation of 1560 had a national, established church it was shaped by a different set of historical circumstances. Although not part of the original programme of the reformers, the commitment to Presbyterian church government that emerged later in the sixteenth century disturbed relations between crown and church. Lacking the ability to appoint bishops who could rule without reference to church courts, the monarch seemed significantly disempowered. This led to a series of struggles throughout much of the seventeenth century, and a resultant political suspicion of Episcopalianism. Freedom from royal control was advocated by theologians and church leaders, but this was mostly for the sake of maintaining the Reformed church as the religious expression of Scottish identity. This necessitated a clear distinction of functions and powers such as that presupposed in Andrew Melville's celebrated rebuke to James VI in 1596 at Falkland Palace. Informing the monarch that the church was the kingdom of Christ, he added 'whose subject King James the Sixth is, and of whose kingdom not a king, nor a lord, nor a head, but a member'.[9] Yet if the Church of Scotland was to be free, it was in order to function as an established Protestant church north of the border. Hence the struggle with successive monarchs was not for the end of a more tolerant and religiously diverse society, but for maintaining the identity of Scotland as a unitary Reformed country. Eventually, this was secured through the succession of William of Orange, whose confidant and advisor for many years was William Carstares, a leading Scottish Presbyterian divine. Early in the following century, a condition of the union of Parliaments would be the state's guarantee of Presbyterianism as the established form of religion in Scotland. Subscription to this form of church government and to the Westminster Confession were (and still are) required of all elders and ministers.

The union of Great Britain and Ireland produced a political establishment that curiously was not coextensive with any single religious establishment. While this arrangement has been viewed as creating

---

[9] Cited in J. H. S. Burleigh, *A Church History of Scotland* (Oxford: Oxford University Press, 1960), 204–5.

a pan-Protestant Britain on which subsequent imperial achievement was founded,[10] it lacked stability, particularly with respect to the situation in Ireland but also in England and Scotland. Throughout the eighteenth century, traditions of dissent had grown in England with Baptists, Independents, Quakers and Presbyterians showing a marked vitality. In Scotland, the issue of patronage was a running sore, the right of the landowner to impose a minister upon a charge without reference to the wishes of the church being widely resented. Despite vigorous efforts to maintain establishment through the United Kingdom, a series of measures was adopted in the nineteenth century that would lead eventually to disestablishment in Ireland, while delivering a greater measure of pluralism in England and Scotland. With Catholic emancipation in 1829, following the Tests and Corporations Act of the previous year, parliamentary office was now open to members of the Free Churches and Roman Catholics. The Dissenting Marriages Act in 1836 enabled those outside the Church of England to hold a religious marriage service. Shortly thereafter, they were permitted access to parish cemeteries. In 1830 Jews were allowed to conduct business in the city of London and to be called to the bar. The new University of London was open to non-Anglicans, as was Oxbridge later in the century. In 1871 disestablishment eventually took place in Ireland.

Scotland was covered by much of this legislation and in 1852 religious tests were abolished for all university professorial appointments other than chairs of divinity. The Disruption of 1843 had already breached the cohesion of the national church, though to a lesser extent this had already occurred with the secessions of the previous century. The splintering of the national church was largely on account of disputes over whether landowners had the right to appoint ministers against the wishes of congregations. In 1843 about one third of ministers and members departed the 'auld Kirk' to form a rival national church, the Free Church of Scotland, thus producing a proliferation of Victorian steeples in every town and city, a sight still visible today. In the aftermath of this, the principle of spiritual independence was essential to the identity of those Presbyterians outside the established

[10] Linda Colley, *Britons: Forging the Nation 1707–1837* (New Haven: Yale University Press, 1992).

church. Only by the latter's recognition of it was reunion achieved. By the end of the nineteenth century, there were three strong Presbyterian denominations in Scotland with Episcopalianism now also growing in strength. Reunions and schisms would continue into the following century. Indeed the fissures within Scottish Presbyterianism are sometimes depicted in textbooks by a diagram resembling a complex drainage system. It has given rise to the apocryphal story of the Scot who was shipwrecked and marooned on a desert island. When he was finally rescued, they discovered that he had built two churches. 'Why two?' he was asked. Gesturing, he replied 'That's the one I don't go to.'

The curious manner in which the British state spawned different, evolving and pragmatic establishments throughout the realm is poignantly illustrated by Queen Victoria's decision in 1873 to receive the sacrament at Crathie Kirk in the Scottish highlands.[11] The Queen, as head of state, was expected to worship in the established Church of Scotland when residing north of the border. Although a member and supreme governor of the Church of England, Victoria held the Scottish Kirk dear to her heart and regarded Norman MacLeod, one of its leading figures, as her counsellor in the years following Albert's death. Such was her earlier sense of disappointment at not receiving communion along with her Scottish subjects at Crathie that she resolved to participate in the celebration of the sacrament in 1873. This was after much anxiety and discussion on the part of her advisors who believed that it might upset a delicate arrangement. Could she recognise the ministry of those who had not been ordained by a bishop? And, although monarch, could she receive the sacrament in a church to which she had not been admitted in the required manner as a communicant member following a course of instruction in the Christian faith? The queen's action thus threatened not one but two establishments to which as head of state she was committed. In the event, Victoria communicated each year and without fuss. There was little lasting public reaction and ecclesiastical life continued much as before. Since then, monarchs and members of the royal household

---

[11] This is explored by Owen Chadwick, 'Sacrament at Crathie 1873', in Stewart J. Brown and George Newlands (eds.), *Scottish Christianity in the Modern World* (Edinburgh: T. & T. Clark, 2000), 177–98.

have followed a similar pattern without apparent disruption to either establishment.

What is the moral of the story? Perhaps it is the pragmatism that accompanies much of public life in the United Kingdom. Whatever anomalies establishment generates, if public opinion is relaxed about these arrangements, then they will be tolerated and even welcomed. This may also give the lie to suggestions that our current constitutional arrangements are so tightly woven that to remove one thread would lead to the unravelling of the whole garment. Such reasoning may be particularly relevant to the Act of Settlement, one piece of legislation that Catholics continue to find offensive and that ought to be repealed. Whether the monarch's role could be adjusted to allow him or her to be described as the defender of faith or faiths, rather than defender of *the* faith, is less certain. There are at least two problems here. How can one be a defender of several faiths, some of which contradict others on significant matters of belief? If it only implies defending their civil liberty to worship and freely to associate in our society, then presumably the monarch already does this. Second, if the intention is to extend the protection of the queen or king to other faiths in a way analogous to that currently attaching to the Church of England then it stumbles on the problem that this is almost certainly not an arrangement that other churches, let alone other faiths, desire. Some exponents of establishment think almost intuitively that if the same provision could be extended to other churches and religions then their objections might be met. But the objection is frequently one of principle. According to this, the alliance between faith and state is inappropriate given the spiritual independence of the former, and the need for the latter to reflect a pluralism that must include secularists and sceptics.

In Scotland, the process of reunion in the Presbyterian churches culminated in 1929 with the union of the Church of Scotland and the United Free Church. This union brought about a new form of establishment, in which the church was recognised by the state as exercising a national and historic role. In the terms of the 1921 Act of the Church of Scotland, the freedom of the church in all matters spiritual was recognised. This was formally expressed in the fourth Declaratory Article of the united church. The state in establishing the Church of Scotland thus eschewed any right to involvement in its government. The presence of the monarch or her representative at the General Assembly of the Church of Scotland is symbolic of this arrangement. She or he is seated not within the court of the church but in one of the visitors' galleries above the court. When Mrs Thatcher delivered her famous 'Sermon on the Mound' in 1988, she did so not by right *ex officio*, but only as a guest of the Lord High Commissioner, the Queen's representative, and at the invitation of the Assembly.

Throughout the twentieth century significant developments in the establishment arrangement have taken place in England and Wales. The Church in Wales was disestablished in 1914, at about the same time as began the diminishing of parliamentary control over the affairs of the Church of England. In 1919 the National Assembly of the Church of England was created as a forum for discussing matters which had previously been debated solely in parliament. This existed alongside the Convocations of Canterbury and York, the historic elected assemblies of the clergy. Yet the Assembly still required parliamentary approval, and in 1927–8 the Commons twice rejected a revised prayer book. This precipitated renewed discussion of the church–state relationship and led to greater ecclesiastical autonomy. It led to a shift of attitude in leading church figures, most notably Hensley Henson, who, having formerly championed establishment, now led the charge against it as Bishop of Durham. He famously compared the established Church of England to 'a magnificent roof ravaged by the death-watch beetle, yet masking by its splendid appearance a fatal though unheeded weakness'.[12] His fundamental objection was that parliamentary obstruction of church measures was an infringement of 'the crown rights of the Redeemer', an expression that had been familiar to Scottish ears at least since the Disruption.

The 1950s and 1960s saw the Anglican church exert greater control over its own affairs, and in 1970 the Church Assembly and Convocations were merged to bring about the General Synod. Parliament granted the church control over worship and doctrine in 1974, and two years later the present method of appointing bishops was agreed. A Crown Appointments Commission set up by the General Synod now passes two names to the Prime Minister. He or she can choose

---

[12] Hensley Henson, *Bishoprick Papers* (Oxford: Oxford University Press, 1946), 7.

either candidate or request an alternative nomination, before making a final recommendation to the monarch.

This cursory tour of the history of establishment reveals a process of gradual but significant weakening in the course of four hundred years. Access to political office, university education and the professions has ceased to be dependent upon one's ecclesiastical allegiance. It has to be conceded that relatively few complaints are heard from the leaders of other churches and other faith communities about present arrangements. On account of this, the status quo persists. There has been recent debate in Scotland about whether a residual sectarianism persists, but it seems that, Celtic–Rangers games notwithstanding, for the most part the discrimination of former years is now behind us.[13] What then are we to make of contemporary arguments for and against establishment? With a succession of books and articles on the subject recently appearing, the discussion continues.

There are several recurrent arguments in support of disestablishment. The first concerns the integrity of the church and its mission. Symptomatic of this is concern over Prime Ministerial involvement in the appointment of Anglican bishops. It is argued that this infringes the freedom of the church to organise its own affairs in faithfulness to God. In particular, if the pastoral leadership of the church is subject to political interference, this can compromise the responsibility of the church to heed the call of God in the appointment to episcopal office. This is a powerful argument which is backed by a long theological tradition that has distinguished carefully the different provinces of civil and ecclesiastical rule. Guided by the Holy Spirit, the church owes its highest allegiance to Christ and not to Caesar. This claim for 'the crown rights of the Redeemer' was made repeatedly in discussions about the extent of establishment in Scotland, England and Ireland in the nineteenth century. According to Keble's Assize sermon preached in the University Church, Oxford, in 1833, the church as catholic and apostolic is to be distinguished from every department of

---

[13] See Tom Devine (ed.), *Scotland's Shame: Bigotry and Sectarianism in Modern Scotland* (Edinburgh: Mainstream, 2000).

state. Improper parliamentary interference in the life of the church is perceived as inconsistent with its apostolic succession.[14] Despite minimal state involvement today, this argument continues to be rehearsed. It is worth exploring in a little more detail.

According to defenders of Prime Ministerial participation in diocesan appointments, the organic unity of church and society is recognised appropriately in this system. The bishop performs an important civic function within the diocese to which he is appointed. Hence it is important that he have the support and trust of the civic authorities. In any case, it will be pointed out that the Prime Minister's involvement is minimal – normally, he will select from two names passed to him or her by the Crown Appointments Commission, a body under the jurisdiction of the General Synod. To this, it can be added that the involvement of the Prime Minister is to be welcomed as a lay contribution to the government of the Church. Thus, instead of perceiving Downing Street's participation as political interference, it can be constructed as a broadening of church government.

However, there are formidable objections to this position. If the Church of England through a process of consultation, prayer and deliberation has reached the conclusion that it wishes to nominate a particular candidate to exercise episcopal or archiepiscopal leadership, on what grounds could a Prime Minister overrule this recommendation and select an alternative candidate? (It is believed that during Mrs Thatcher's premiership this happened on two occasions.) Either these would be theological grounds, in which case the government would be informing the church that its own procedures for selecting office-bearers were flawed and that it knew the mind of God better than the church.[15] Or else, the rejection of the church's nomination would be on political grounds, in which case we would have a clear

---

[14] 'What answer can we make henceforth to the partisans of the Bishop of Rome, when they taunt us with being a mere Parliamentarian Church?'; John Keble, *'National Apostasy Considered'*, *Sermon Preached before His Majesty's Judges of Assize* (Oxford, 1833), 2.

[15] The related remarks of Donald MacKinnon following the appointment of the Archbishop of Canterbury in 1960 are still worth quoting: 'No one has yet suggested in so many words that the Patronage Secretary has replaced the Holy Ghost in the Church of England's understanding of the proper method for choosing its chief pastors; but its practice encourages the belief that such a substitution has taken place, or that we shall soon hear that the passages in the Fourth Gospel relating to the "Other Advocate" are to be demythologized in terms of the gift of such a functionary'; *The Stripping of the Altars* (London: Collins, 1969), 31.

instance of illicit Erastian interference.[16] To these objections, two further rejoinders are possible. One is the pragmatic gesture that this is a price worth paying for an arrangement that is generally beneficial on both sides. This is a response that is honest but appears to concede the relative weakness of the position. A second is that recourse to the Prime Ministerial veto can 'stop the church running away with itself'. This last point smacks of desperation. Even worse, it reflects an earlier cap-doffing age that always assumed that our political masters knew what was best for us. Their paternal wisdom was to be respected, even when this conflicted with our own benighted assumptions.

Related to arguments about Prime Ministerial input to the appointment of bishops is the role of the monarch. Indeed many of the arguments for the sacramental, sacral and metaphysical role of the monarch in contemporary Britain reside within the general neighbourhood of arguments for an established church. It is not the purpose of this discussion to explore these arguments in any detail. But it should be noted that the notion that the office and person of the monarch in some special way mediate the presence of God is more akin to the panegyric of Eusebius than to the desacralised concept of kingship that one finds in the Old Testament and in Jesus' encounter with Pilate. At a time when some non-western theologians are seeking to mobilise these Hebraic traditions to promote more democratic and participatory forms of government, a return to such notions, however benign, seems untimely. Although the Queen displays publicly a strong sense of Christian vocation, the future of the monarchy is not well served by inflating its metaphysical significance. In any case, it is not clear that its defence need be protective of church establishment as this currently stands. Ian Bradley, in his recent study, concludes that the future of a sacred, spiritual monarch may be better served by a looser affiliation to the Church of England than the title 'Supreme Governor' indicates. He argues that the need for the monarch to relate positively to all religious groups in a multi-faith society can be better facilitated by an abridged establishment through greater stress on the spiritual independence of the church, as in Scotland.

---

[16] In fairness, it can be pointed out that the Prime Minister functions in this process more as the sovereign's first minister than as the leader of a political party. Yet these roles are not readily divisible in our constitutional arrangements. The current process is set out by Avis, *Church, State and Establishment*, 72–3.

This is developed through a series of suggestions as to how a future coronation ceremony might be organised.[17]

An appointments process in which the exercise of Prime Ministerial discretion was prevented would not in itself bring about disestablishment. It would merely be a further modification to an arrangement that has already been adjusted in recent times. A system in which the church appointed its bishops in much the same way as it now exercises autonomy in other matters would not lead to disestablishment. It would bring the Church of England closer to the model of establishment that functions in Scotland, a model that was commended by the Chadwick report of 1970 and is frequently adverted to by defenders of establishment in England.[18] Here the church is established in the sense that the state recognises its historic right to function as the national church but acknowledges its freedom and independence in all spiritual matters. This will be examined in more detail below.

Other commentators on church life have claimed that the church's responsibility to engage in prophetic criticism of society and the government will inevitably be blunted by state involvement in the appointment of its leaders, or indeed the granting of any privileges or status by the state to the church. This distinct possibility is not to be underestimated. The trappings of privilege, status and proximity to the powerful are still apparent; the coopting of church representatives by vested interests has not ceased to be an unfamiliar phenomenon. This was explored in a famous essay by Donald MacKinnon on 'Kenosis and Establishment': 'Where England is concerned, the passing of Establishment as we have known it would surely lead to a day in which episcopal lawn sleeves would cease to flutter in the breeze as their wearer bestowed the diocesan benediction upon the latest Polaris submarine. Here we should find sheer gain without any loss at all.'[19] In the case of Scotland, one can record a succumbing

---

[17] *God Save the Queen* (London: Darton, Longman & Todd, 2002), 194ff. For another recent defence of the monarchy in relation to its spiritual significance see N. T. Wright, 'God and Caesar, Then and Now', first in a series of lectures on *God, Church, Crown and State* delivered at Westminster Abbey on 22 April 2003; www.westminster-abbey.org/event/lecture/archives/020428_tom_wright.html.

[18] *Church and State: Report of the Archbishop's Commission*, 65.

[19] 'Kenosis and Establishment', in *The Stripping of the Altars*, 32. Commenting on this essay, Rowan Williams has recently remarked that he doubts whether anything very much has changed since MacKinnon delivered his Gore lecture; *On Christian Theology*, 234.

to similar temptations. The attempt of the Moderator of the General Assembly in 1953 to participate in the coronation ceremony, together with the unusually obsequious bow he made to the new monarch, provoked expressions of disgust amongst Presbyterians north of the border.[20]

For MacKinnon, the dangers of establishment are most acute in the temptation of the church to offer its moral support to the state whenever it declares war. This was most apparent, at any rate, until the First World War in the frequent fusion of the language of Christ's sacrifice with that of military service. Nonetheless, some recent history suggests that this process of cooption and assimilation is not inevitable for the established church. The bishops in the House of Lords have not infrequently been critical of government legislation. Archbishop Robert Runcie, though conservative by instinct, displayed no little courage in pronouncements which were quietly though deeply critical of the Thatcher government, particularly at the thanksgiving service to mark the end of the Falklands War. Throughout the 1980s the General Assembly of the Church of Scotland was consistently opposed to Thatcherite domestic policy as well as investment in the Trident nuclear submarine programme. And on a further range of issues – bio-medical ethics, euthanasia, urban decay, social justice, the debt of developing countries, asylum seekers – national church leaders have often developed lines of thinking that have distanced them from government policy. Most recently, moral doubts were raised by the Archbishop of Canterbury alongside other church leaders over the war on Iraq in 2003. Once again, the thanksgiving service was devoid of all triumphalist tendencies. A variety of trends may be detected here: the greater politicisation of theology since 1945; a stronger sense of the countercultural nature of Christian witness; the loosening of ties between church and national identity; a deeper sympathy with

---

[20] Ian Henderson later wrote: 'The part allotted to the Moderator at the Coronation was pathetic in its brevity. He had to say a few words and hand a Bible to the Queen. Much more serious was the fact that during its performance he, as the representative of the Church of Scotland, knelt in a place of worship, but did not kneel to God'; *Power without Glory: a Study in Ecumenical Politics* (London: Hutchinson, 1967), 111. In fairness to James Pitt-Watson, it should be noted that to the dismay of some of his more conservative colleagues he was amongst those who spoke against the government during the Suez crisis in 1956. Cf. MacKinnon, *The Stripping of the Altars*, 80.

the arguments of pacifism; and a keener awareness of the ecumenical and international dimension of the body of Christ.[21]

The strongest argument for disestablishment appeals to the growing dissociation of the population at large from the beliefs and practices of the Church of England. With the traditional markers of Christian identity all in decline, the case for maintaining establishment becomes increasingly anachronistic. Historically, this has been met by the claim that there is a reservoir of implicit support for Anglicanism throughout the country. 'He who is not against us is for us.' This works in a variety of ways including provision of rites of passage, civic ceremonies, pastoral support in times of crisis, the management of church schools, the public pronouncements of bishops, and the maintenance of the great medieval cathedrals with their fine traditions of worship. The national church, it is argued, still commands the loyalty of broad sections of the community who regard themselves however minimally as 'CofE'. With its established identity, the church can remain open at the boundaries to differing shades of commitment and to a wide spectrum of needs. As serviceable, accessible, evocative, worthy of respect and tolerant, Anglicanism has a particular vocation to the people of England.[22] Although probably the strongest argument for retention of establishment in some form, this has been seriously weakened by the dissociation noted above. While it could be rehearsed with some plausibility in the 1980s, it is not clear that this remains the case into the twenty-first century. The incredulity of a younger writer such as Theo Hobson is instructive in this regard.[23] The world of the arts and literature and the popular culture of today's youth seem remote from this residual sense of a national Anglican identity. Citing the examples of Roger Scruton, Alan Bennett and A. N. Wilson, he points out that many of those

---

[21] These issues are explored in George Moyser (ed.), *Church and Politics Today: the Role of the Church of England in Contemporary Politics* (Edinburgh: T. & T. Clark, 1985), and Martin, *Does Christianity Cause War?*, 102ff.

[22] This is the thesis of John Moses in *A Broad and Living Way: Church and State, a Continuing Establishment* (Norwich: Canterbury Press, 1995), 226ff. The expression 'a broad and living way' is derived from Gladstone. A similar defence of establishment can be found in John Habgood, *Church and Nation in a Secular Age* (London: Darton, Longman & Todd, 1983).

[23] Theo Hobson, *Against Establishment: an Anglican Polemic* (London: Darton, Longman & Todd, 2003).

who yearn for something like an Anglican order do so wistfully and nostalgically, not through conviction but more from an aesthetic loss of something that once lent dignity and order to the social world of England. A church that persists in perceiving itself in those terms will prove detached and alien from the concerns of those yet to reach middle age.

ESTABLISHMENT IN SCOTLAND

One frequently encounters the claim that the Scottish model, or something resembling it, is the way ahead for England.[24] This requires further scrutiny. Commentators are divided over whether the Church of Scotland (the Kirk) should be characterised as established at all. In a recent BBC2 television series 'The Sword and the Cross' it was baldly asserted that the price of Presbyterian reunion in 1929 was the disestablishment of the Church of Scotland. And a leading historian of the period has declared that the Scottish church is national and free, but neither established nor disestablished.[25] Yet this judgement is not at all straightforward. It is true that the Church of Scotland is spiritually independent in that it exercises exclusive control over its own affairs, endowments and appointments. As we have already noted, the state has no role in the government of the church or capacity for interference in the decisions of its courts regarding 'matters spiritual'. This is recognised by the Church of Scotland Act of 1921 in acknowledging the position of the Kirk in terms of its Articles Declaratory. Moreover, it is clear that this is not a status that Parliament confers; it is merely ratified or confirmed. This Act provides a model of 'negotiated freedom' by which church and state may reconfigure their relative independence from and relationship to one another. (In this respect at any rate, it may provide a way forward for the Church of England.[26]) The Articles that are recognised by the state include Article III:

This Church is in historical continuity with the Church of Scotland which was reformed in 1560, whose liberties were ratified in 1592, and for whose security provision was made in the Treaty of Union of 1707. The continuity

---

[24] This is argued by Adrian Hastings, Paul Avis, Ian Bradley and Tom Wright amongst others.
[25] Douglas M. Murray, *Rebuilding the Kirk* (Edinburgh: Scottish Academic Press, 2000), 280.
[26] See Colin Buchanan, *Cut the Connection*, 198.

and identity of the Church of Scotland are not prejudiced by the adoption of these Articles. As a national Church representative of the Christian Faith of the Scottish people it acknowledges its distinctive call and duty to bring the ordinances of religion to the people in every parish of Scotland through a territorial ministry.[27]

In upholding this article, the Church of Scotland Act (1921) effectively recognises the Kirk as the national church north of the border. In this respect, it may be considered established, though not in the sense that the state grants this status to the church. The reality of Scottish establishment is signified by a series of provisions that have not historically been extended to other churches. The sovereign or her representative, the Lord High Commissioner, attends the General Assembly of the Church of Scotland each year. Not since the Silver Jubilee celebrations of 1977 has the Queen herself been present, although the Prince of Wales was appointed Lord High Commissioner in 2000. Residing at Holyrood Palace, the Lord High Commissioner, from a gallery above the floor of the Assembly, addresses delegates and commissioners, by invitation rather than right, at the start and conclusion of its proceedings. He or she is also involved in sundry other engagements and receptions during that same week. The Prince of Wales' remarks to the 2000 General Assembly seem to confirm the impression of the Church of Scotland as established: 'I could not be more proud to stand before you this morning as Lord High Commissioner . . . because this Office is a precious symbol of the long history which has bound together Church and Sovereign for nearly 450 years in a relationship of shared responsibility in their care for the people of Scotland.'[28] As this might suggest, the Kirk continues to function in a manner analogous to that of other established European churches. It provides a chaplaincy service to civic bodies, hosts national ceremonial occasions usually in the High Kirk, otherwise known as St Giles' Cathedral, in Edinburgh, while its clergy generally function as chaplains to non-denominational schools throughout the country. The

---

[27] The Articles Declaratory are reprinted in Weatherhead, *The Constitution and Laws of the Church of Scotland*, 159ff. On the issue of establishment, Weatherhead wisely asserts that 'it is best to understand the Church in terms of what the Declaratory Articles actually say, rather than seeking to fit it into outmoded and misleading categories'; 18.

[28] Quoted by Bradley, *God Save the Queen*, 193. The implication in this remark that the Church of Scotland did not exist until 1560 is unfortunate as it undermines its claim to catholicity.

Queen appoints royal chaplains to minister to her household when in Scotland – these are drawn from the ranks of the Kirk. By maintaining a parish system, moreover, the Church of Scotland continues to provide a service of ministration to the population at large, including weddings and funerals. (In the case of baptisms, its legislation has tended to be more restrictive.)

The Church of Scotland Act (1921) explicitly notes the right of other Christian Churches in Scotland to be protected by the law in the exercise of their spiritual functions. Moreover, the use of the indefinite article in the expression 'as a national Church' may suggest that other churches could also operate as national institutions. Yet *de facto* it is hard to resist the impression that this was not the intention of those who framed the article nor the subsequent outcome of its adoption. John White, one of the leading architects of church union in 1929, clearly regarded the united institution as constituting the national church in continuity with the Reformation of 1560 and the Treaty of Union in 1707. Although not a matter of law, the conferral of various privileges by the state upon the church remained customary. This did not infringe upon the freedom of other churches, but retained for the united Church all the privileges of the 'auld Kirk' prior to the Union. Thus those more voluntarist members of the United Free Church who happily assumed that something like disestablishment was taking place in the Church of Scotland Act were deceived. In a revealing letter, Lord Sands wrote to John White in 1922 that 'the privileged position as the national established Church remains just where it was. It would be injudicious to tell them this and it is best to let them talk.'[29]

There are three further problems with this position today which together require the amending of Declaratory Article III. In this way, the Church of Scotland should properly distance itself from its problematic claim to be the proper religious expression of Scottish national identity. First, it is now recognised that the successful drive towards Presbyterian reunion was interlinked with some vicious anti-Catholic propaganda throughout the 1920s. The campaign for reunion was in part a revival of older notions of Scotland as a covenanted Protestant nation. This prompted an attack on the Catholic population which had increased mainly as a result of Irish immigration, particularly in

---

[29] Quoted by Murray, *Rebuilding the Kirk*, 106.

the west of Scotland, during the latter part of the nineteenth century. Condemning the 'menace' of an alien race with its different creeds and practices, a report to the General Assembly of the Church of Scotland in 1923 marked the start of a campaign intended to reduce the influence of the Roman Catholic population. If necessary, this would entail repatriation.[30] By the late 1930s the campaign had largely ground to a halt. It was based on inflated statistics about Irish immigration; it failed to reckon with the integration of the descendants of immigrants into the political, social and economic life of Scotland; while the emergence of a younger generation of Scottish church leaders with more ecumenical insights brought a fresh set of concerns before the General Assembly. Although much has changed since the 1920s, there is embedded within the Kirk's constitution the claim that Scotland is in effect a unitary Protestant nation. By amending Declaratory III and abandoning this pretension, the Church of Scotland could formally distance itself from the intolerance of its past. This would represent a creative political and ecumenical gesture, and one that could contribute to a rethinking of the Kirk's identity and mission in the new century.[31]

A second reason for disquiet is the relationship of the Church of Scotland to the new Scottish Parliament. Although privileged by the 1921 Act passed at Westminster, the Church of Scotland does not appear to enjoy any favourable status in relation to Holyrood, nor has it sought any. It is clear that, for the most part, the Scottish Parliament is anxious to treat church and other faith groups on an equal footing. Shortly before its appearance, Johnston McKay could write:

It is clear that those preparing for a Scottish Parliament expect it to be even-handed not only as between Christian denominations but as between different faiths. In an ecumenical multi-cultural Scotland, the traditional status of the Church of Scotland as the national Church is irrelevant to the role which the communities of faith can play.[32]

---

[30] For an account of this episode see Stewart J. Brown, 'Presbyterians and Catholics in Twentieth-Century Scotland', in Brown and Newlands (eds.), *Scottish Christianity in the Modern World*, 255–81.

[31] This argument is articulated by Will Storrar in *Scottish Identity: a Christian Vision* (Edinburgh: Handsel, 1990), 202–25.

[32] 'Is The Kirk Still Relevant? Home Truths about Influence as a National Institution', in Kernohan (ed.), *The Realm of Reform*, 63.

Scottish identity is now expressed in terms of citizenship rather than ethnicity or religion, thus belying earlier notions that it was bound up with a commitment to Protestantism. Here again the modern condition of Scottish society militates against the earlier sense of the Kirk as uniquely expressive of Scottishness. Whether historically accurate or not, the semi-popular notion that the Kirk's General Assembly acted as a mouthpiece for the nation in the absence of a Scottish Parliament is now redundant.

Third, there are the statistical data, already noted, that reveal the growing dissociation of Scottish society from the beliefs and practices of the national church. Only a small minority attend public worship on a regular basis. A steady decline in the number of baptisms and church weddings is apparent. The identification of the population at large with their local parish church is diminishing. Without a robust commitment from a significant section of society at grass-roots level, the rhetoric of 'the church at the heart of the community' sounds hollow. In any event, it is grossly unfair to other Christian groups to suggest that only national or parish churches have the concerns of the community at heart. The age of establishment is drawing to a close. Neither the United Kingdom nor Scotland can be described, except residually, as Protestant countries. Since the Reformation, the Kirk has been presented as the authentic expression of Scottish national identity. This is no longer tenable and it is time to move forward to a church life that must inevitably be more voluntarist, congregational, countercultural in part, and engaged in new patterns of mission.

Of course, the amendment or repeal of Declaratory Article III would not in itself bring about a transition to a new era in the life of the Church of Scotland. Yet it would signal to other Christian groups, especially Roman Catholics, that the Kirk no longer presumes to express uniquely the religious identity of Scotland. It would offer a formal commitment to a pluralist and tolerant Scotland, while also contributing to a process in which the Kirk perceived its future neither as a retrieval of the past nor as an attempt to prevent further erosion of its national status. This would be a future, moreover, in which a more balanced and positive appropriation of the past might become possible in spite of the self-loathing that frequently informs caricatures of Calvinism in the media today.

TWILIGHT VISION

Although the arguments against establishment seem pretty strong, it is not altogether clear what disestablishment would entail in our current situation.[33] In this respect, some qualification to the foregoing is required. For example, it is argued, by the Liberal Democrat party and the *Guardian* newspaper, that a disestablished church would provide necessary recognition that Britain is now a multi-faith, pluralist society. Failure to take this step is thereby presented as an offence to the integrity and citizenship of Muslims, Hindus, Jews and others. This is sometimes accompanied by the observation that if we were starting afresh, no one would ever dream of proposing the current set of arrangements.[34]

The argument for equality amongst faiths is convincing to most people when expressed in these terms. Yet upon closer inspection some problems emerge. If it implies the removal of religious discourse and conviction from the public domain then it is problematic for reasons outlined in earlier chapters. Where do our political commitments come from, if not our deepest convictions about God, human persons and the nature of society? A secular liberalism based upon autonomy provides a basis that is much too thin to sustain public life. Moreover, a constitution which attempts to keep religion out of public life may result in many of the absurdities and anomalies that blight debates in the USA about the interpretation of the First Amendment. Behind arguments for equality there lurks a new form of establishment, the establishment of the secular which prohibits the intrusion of religious convictions in public debate. It is partly on account of this fear, that leaders of other churches and faith communities express a preference for something like current forms of establishment. In a recent multi-faith symposium on church and state only the Buddhist spokesperson came out firmly against the establishment of the Church

---

[33] This is the fundamental weakness of Hobson's *Against Establishment*. Although succeeding in showing why all the arguments for establishment no longer quite work, he seems unclear as to what a disestablished Anglican church would look like.

[34] This argument is in fact quite disingenuous. What is really absurd is the notion that any society could reconstitute itself *de novo* as if history, tradition, customs and mores could be discarded in favour of some abstract, rootless set of intuitions about how we should comport ourselves. It is yet another illusion generated by secular liberalism.

of England.[35] Others perceived the status quo as one in which they already enjoyed full civil liberties while also sensing that their particular allegiances were closer to those of an inclusive Anglicanism than an intolerant secularism. A state which acknowledges the higher authority of spiritual and moral realities is one which is to be preferred to secular alternatives. It is this consideration that finally convinces an anti-Erastian Catholic writer like Adrian Hastings that it is better to maintain a form of weak establishment than to move towards less acceptable alternatives. Hastings offers one of the most convincing recent defences of establishment. He argues that we should not misread today's situation out of a belated remorse for yesterday's.[36] The present form of weak establishment, he writes,

challenges the secular monism which is in great danger of dominating our world far too powerfully. It is for this reason that I believe many religious non-Christians – Hindus, Muslims, Sikhs and Jews – as well as many non-Anglican Christians like myself actually prefer some establishment to remain as a public symbol of the importance of religion, of belief in god, of the limits of Caesar's sovereignty. No age has needed such a symbol more.[37]

The spectre of a militant secularism is more worrying to religious minorities, it seems, than the protection offered by current arrangements. The example of France, where the right of Muslim women to wear headscarves in civic institutions is currently under threat, provides an alternative configuration of religion and state that does not seem generally to commend itself to the majority within the UK. This illustrates an earlier argument of this study to the effect that there is no ideal secular arrangement that limits religion to a private sphere by banishing it from the public. Within the USA and elsewhere, this 'hard secularism' is in trouble. We should beware, therefore, of the blithe assumption that there exists some clean, *Guardian*-led alternative down the road of disestablishment.

However, this residual support for something like establishment – it might better be understood as misgivings about the consequences of full disestablishment – should not be seen as endorsement of every existing provision, nor as a reluctance to contemplate a further

---

[35] Tariq Modood (ed.), *Church, State and Religious Minorities* (London: Policy Studies Unit, 1997).
[36] Hastings, *Church and State*, 64.   [37] Ibid.

evolution of current arrangements. Hastings, in the aforementioned study, has no wish to see continued political involvement in episcopal appointments. And representations from minority faith groups and non-established churches to the Wakeham Commission were all opposed to the status quo governing religious representation in the upper chamber.[38]

The example of the Church in Wales after disestablishment draws attention to the ways in which some of the earlier regime must inevitably persist.[39] The church will continue to be faced with the need of significant sectors of the population at large for some spiritual facility. Although only a minority of the population explicitly identifies with established churches through membership and attendance, in the case of death at least we remain a recognisably Christian nation. About 90–95 per cent of funeral services[40] are still conducted by Christian clergy, and in the majority of cases these are the parish clergy of the Church of England and the Church of Scotland. The Christian funeral persists as an almost universal rite of passage although, as noted earlier, it too may be undergoing some 'postmodern' adjustments.[41] It also has a public dimension with the organisation of services by the national churches at times of crisis and public mourning. This has been analysed in some detail by sociologists.[42] The services following the Piper Alpha, Hillsborough, Lockerbie, Dunblane, Paddington and Hatfield disasters were held by the representatives of our national churches. They involved other Christian denominations and in some occasions other faith communities. These were inclusive, civic events but also acts of Christian worship which attested the virtues of faith, hope and love. The funeral service of Diana, Princess of

---

[38] See Hobson, *Against Establishment*, 44.

[39] This is explored by Keith Robbins, 'Establishing Disestablishment: Some Reflections on Wales and Scotland'; in Brown and Newlands (eds.), *Scottish Christianity in the Modern World*, 231–54.

[40] This is the recent estimate of Calum Brown. However, this high percentage may reflect little more than the lack of available alternatives. Following the example of register-office weddings, the public provision of a secular funeral service would provide a welcome increase in choice for bereaved families while also releasing hard-pressed clergy from some thankless work.

[41] The emergence of post-Christian approaches to death and funeral rites is increasingly apparent. See Douglas J. Davies, *Death, Ritual and Belief*, 2nd edition (London: Continuum, 2002).

[42] E.g. Davie, *Religion in Britain since 1945*, 74–92.

Wales, was a national, civic event which blended elements of folk and Christian religion. It gathered the country together in a way that surprised many. Yet without the contribution of the Church of England and the focal point of Westminster Abbey this could not have happened, and without the richness of the Christian tradition and its liturgy much of this public grief would probably have degenerated into maudlin sentiment. These events correspond to what happens thousands of times each day across the country through the provision of Christian funeral services.[43] In this respect, there remains a grain of truth in T. S. Eliot's remark that a society does not cease to be Christian until it has positively become something else.[44]

It is difficult to see how even in a disestablished future the churches could decline such requests for assistance in domestic and civic settings. Educational institutions, hospitals and the armed forces will continue to maintain chaplaincy services. While these ought to be shared with other churches and faiths, again it is hard to see how disestablishment in England and Scotland can or ought to lead to a withdrawal from these fields of service. It is significant that after presenting a robust case for disestablishment, Colin Buchanan reflects on what would be left within the life of the Church of England. His list of resources and functions is surprisingly rich, suggesting that even in a disestablished, post-Christian setting the past would continue to determine present and future social reality.[45] George Lindbeck has recently written:

I once welcomed the passing of Christendom . . . but now I am having uncomfortable second thoughts. The waning of cultural Christianity might be good for the churches, but what about society? To my chagrin, I find myself thinking that traditionally Christian lands when stripped of their historic faith are worse than others. They become unworkable or demonic . . . From this point of view, the Christianization of culture can be in some situations the churches' major contribution to feeding the poor, clothing the hungry and liberating the imprisoned. So it was in the past and, given the disintegration of modern ideologies, so it may be at times in the future.[46]

---

[43] It is this aspect of established church life that is the focus of much recent defence. See Wesley Carr, 'A Developing Establishment', *Theology* 102 (1999), 2–10.

[44] T. S. Eliot, *The Idea of a Christian Society* (London: Faber, 1939), 13.

[45] Buchanan cites the following: a nationwide organisation, the standing of the episcopate, the church's material resources, its custodianship of medieval buildings, and its concern for life in society; *Cut the Connection*, 76ff.

[46] George Lindbeck, *The Church in a Postliberal Age* (London: SCM, 2002), 7.

Nonetheless, while acknowledging this significant point, the church ought at least to function in ways which recognise clearly that its civic role is neither its primary purpose nor the leading principle for the organisation of its life, worship and doctrine. If this analysis is correct, then the best response of our churches to establishment may be to remain relaxed about its ongoing decline. There will continue to be residual effects, opportunities and responsibilities arising from the age of establishment but we should not pretend that these are embers that can be rekindled to return the nation to a glowing era of Protestant Christianity. Although there is no disestablished utopia awaiting us, adjustments to the status quo should be adopted willingly rather than reluctantly. These include minimally for the Church of England an end to all political involvement in the appointment of church leaders, and for the Church of Scotland formal repeal of its claim to be the expression of an indigenous Protestant identity. The public contribution of the Christian faith will continue in multiple ways, but no longer focused on maintaining an organic unity of society and church. To suggest that disestablishment will create sects in place of national churches is misleading, if not scaremongering.

CONCLUSION

The crown tower of King's College Chapel in Old Aberdeen is depicted on the front cover of this book. It represents a closed crown underneath a cross. Originally constructed in 1500, it is a tribute to James IV of Scotland but also to the church with whom he founded the university some five years earlier. The closed crown is thought by some commentators to be imperial rather than royal, thus suggesting the full power and autonomy of the Scottish king within his land. Whether or not the appearance of the cross above the crown is intended to portray the superiority of spiritual to temporal power, the crown tower is a powerful testimony to the unity of state and church in the late Middle Ages. Indeed, Bishop Elphinstone, the founder of the university, functioned in effect as secretary of state to the monarch.[47]

---

[47] For an account of the history of the chapel see Jane Geddes (ed.), *King's College Chapel, Aberdeen, 1500–2000* (Leeds: Northern Universities Press, 2000).

Politics, society and church life have all undergone dramatic changes in the course of five centuries. The ties of church to state, represented in the long-running establishment provision, have been loosened and now partly severed in late modernity. What remains of this arrangement can reasonably be expected to suffer further diminution in the century ahead. The complex interweaving of systems that constitute a modern western society has ended the earlier alignment of ecclesiastical and political rule. With the differentiation of functions, the church now finds itself in an altered social location. Yet, although more detached from political society, it has not ceased to be publicly significant. Our social systems cannot be entirely autonomous since questions about values, standards, and the nature of human persons are all inevitably embedded within the assumptions that inform practices, policies and decisions. Faith communities that continue to offer meaning, vision and an account of human well-being will provide a necessary contribution not only to their own adherents, but also to wider public debates about how we should organise our common life.

Within this more complex, differentiated setting, the social contribution of the church will itself be varied. Discernment will be required on when to offer support for change, to contest existing practice, to engage in dialogue, and to form alliances. In different ways, the church will find itself functioning both as lubricant and irritant within the systems of its host society. This public voice of the church will require to be established upon a strong congregational base. Apart from this, it will sound increasingly hollow and strident, while lacking the resources in energy, intellect and personnel to participate effectively in the public domain. The theological assets of Scripture and tradition will require exploitation to offer a convincing response to developments in the socio-political world. Older forms of triumphalism that assumed that the church 'knew best' will have to be eschewed. Christ is not owned or monopolised by the Christian community. Divine wisdom can be found in other places. The doctrine of sin, moreover, should also caution against an easy complacency or the perennial temptation to social acquiescence in exchange for being accorded status or granted a hearing.

In a recent study of the civil-rights movement in the USA, David Chappell has drawn attention to the contribution of the religious left.[48] This differed from mainstream liberalism in that it grew from theological roots, particularly in the black churches. With their knowledge of the prophetic traditions of Scripture and the Augustinian account of human nature, the leaders of this group, especially Martin Luther King Jr, had a sober estimate of human nature and the practice of politics. According to Chappell, this actually made them more effective politically. The sources on which they drew provided a measure of independence that prevented their being overly indebted to any political philosophy or regime. By standing on this ground and learning how to translate religious insights into a language accessible to a wider constituency, they proved themselves well equipped for effective social engagement.[49] Diaspora Jewish communities also have much to offer in this context. With their dialogical traditions and capacity for transposing the ethical claims of their faith, they could offer practical insight and wisdom to their host society, even if this was often ignored or unheeded.

With the end of Christendom, western societies have severed in important respects their earlier connections with the Christian churches. Although the parish system is still recognisable in much of Europe, this will surely come under increasing strain in the coming decades. In this changing context, much of what has been written about the theology of the state is now anachronistic. The dominant and exclusive partnership of monarch and church is no longer the setting for configuring the relationship of the ecclesial to the civil. However, the future of the churches should not be represented in purely or even mainly countercultural terms. The allure of a distinctive, even exotic, faith community with its own traditions and resources witnessing to (and usually against) the regnant liberal order will prove irresistible to some. Yet the church has a stake in pervasive features of modern, liberal society, and in any case the act of appropriating its own resources will reflect the hermeneutic position of its members in other systems. Nevertheless, as we have seen, there are significant

---

[48] David L. Chappell, *A Stone of Hope: Prophetic Religion and the Death of Jim Crow* (Chapel Hill: University of North Carolina Press, 2004).

[49] In view of this, it has been suggested by one recent commentator that although religion should not be practised in public schools, children ought to be taught theology for the sake of understanding its social contribution; David Brooks, 'One Nation, Enriched by Biblical Wisdom', *New York Times*, 23 March 2004. I am grateful to Don Shriver for this reference.

resources in Scripture and tradition for understanding ways in which Christian communities are publicly significant and can make a positive contribution to the well-being of society, without attempting to be in charge or speaking as the only moral voice.

Partly by appeal to earlier scriptural themes, but also by attention to the experience of the non-western church, the argument has been advanced that in terms of its position in civil society the church can continue to make a contribution to the differentiated spheres of modern life. Often this will take place in partnership and conversation with other groups, movements and organisations. This is not an attempt to reinvigorate an older model of the national church, and still less a form of civil religion. Ecclesiologically, our future resides in recognising the primacy of voluntary, congregational and gathered communities. Only as this occurs on the ground will Christian theology find the necessary empirical expression and institutional base from which wider social engagement can take place.

To return finally to the dichotomy posed at the outset: the danger of assimilation or captivity is the loss of evangelical and catholic identity, whereas the danger of withdrawal or isolation is the absence of any contribution to the common good. Both need to be eschewed. At a time of crisis for secular liberalism the church may make a constructive though critical contribution by drawing upon its own account of the dominion of God. There remains here the ineluctable duty of seeking the welfare of the city in faithfulness to this God. Admittedly, the church's public status has to be earned in conversation with other groups, in service to its host society, and in a critical support of its institutions and political state. Clinging to establishment is futile; it represents a failure to recognise current cultural trends, especially amongst the younger generations. And in any case, the study of history reveals that there never was a golden age of church–state integrity. But beyond establishment and the wane of Christendom, there is a future that can be enlivened by the rich social theology of Scripture and the church's traditions.

Bibliography

Ahlers, Rolf, *The Barmen Declaration of 1934: the Archaeology of a Confessional Text* (Lewiston, NY: Edwin Mellen, 1986).

Allison, Dale C., *Jesus of Nazareth: Millenarian Prophet* (Minneapolis: Fortress Press, 1998).

Althaus, Paul, *The Ethics of Martin Luther* (Philadelphia: Fortress Press, 1972).

Appleby, R. Scott, *The Ambivalance of the Sacred: Religion, Violence, and Reconciliation* (New York: Rowman & Littlefield, 2000).

Aquinas, Thomas, *Selected Political Writings*, ed. A. P. D'Entrèves (Oxford: Blackwell, 1959).

   Summa Theologiae, Blackfriars edition (London: Eyre & Spottiswoode, 1745/75).

Armstrong-Brown, Sue, *The Eczema Solution* (London: Vermilion, 2002).

Asch, Ronald G., *The Thirty Years War: the Holy Roman Empire and Europe 1618–48* (Basingstoke: Macmillan, 1997).

Ascherson, Neal, *Stone Voices: the Search for Scotland* (London: Granta, 2002).

Augustine, *City of God*, in Alexander Roberts and James Donaldson (eds.), *Nicene and Post-Nicene Fathers*, revised edition (Peabody, MA: Hendrickson, 1994), vol. II, 1–511.

   Treatise Concerning the Correction of the Donatists, in Alexander Roberts and James Donaldson (eds.), *Nicene and Post-Nicene Fathers*, revised edition (Peabody, MA: Hendrickson, 1994), vol. IV, 633–51.

Avis, Paul, *Church, State and Establishment* (London: SPCK, 2001).

Bailey, Betty Jane and J. Martin Bailey, *Who Are the Christians in the Middle East?* (Grand Rapids: Eerdmans, 2003).

Bainton, Roland, *The Medieval Church* (London: Nostrand, 1962).

Banner, Michael, *Christian Ethics and Contemporary Moral Problems* (Cambridge: Cambridge University Press, 1999).

Barclay, John, *Jews in the Mediterranean Diaspora* (Edinburgh: T. & T. Clark, 1996).

Barnes, Timothy D., *Constantine and Eusebius* (Cambridge, MA: Harvard University Press, 1981).

Barth, Karl, 'The Christian Community and the Civil Community', *Against the Stream: Shorter Post-War Writings* (London: SCM, 1954), 13–50.

— *Church Dogmatics*, ed. and trans. G. W. Bromiley and T. F. Torrance, 4 vols. (Edinburgh: T. & T. Clark, 1956–75).

— *The German Church Conflict* (London: Lutterworth, 1965).

— *Letters 1961–68* (Grand Rapids: Eerdmans, 1981).

Bax, Douglas (trans.), 'Barmen Declaration', *Journal of Theology for Southern Africa* 47 (1984), 78–81.

Baylor, Michael (ed.), *The Radical Reformation* (Cambridge: Cambridge University Press, 1991).

Bediako, Kwame, *Christianity in Africa: the Renewal of a Non-Western Religion* (Edinburgh: Edinburgh University Press, 1995).

Belhar Confession, www.warc.ch/pc/20th/02.html

Bellamy, Richard, *Liberalism and Pluralism: Towards a Politics of Compromise* (London: Routledge, 1999).

Bellamy, Richard and Martin Hollis, 'Consensus, Neutrality and Compromise', in Richard Bellamy and Martin Hollis (eds.), *Pluralism and Liberal Neutrality* (London: Frank Cass, 1999), 54–78.

Berger, Peter, 'The Desecularization of the World: a Global Overview', in Peter Berger (ed.), *The Desecularization of the World: Resurgent Religion and Global Politics* (Grand Rapids: Eerdmans, 1999).

Berlin, Isaiah, *Four Essays on Liberty* (London: Oxford University Press, 1969).

Bethge, Eberhard, *Dietrich Bonhoeffer* (London: Collins, 1970).

Biggar, Nigel, 'Social Withdrawal: Is Stanley Hauerwas Sectarian?', in Mark Thiessen and Samuel Wells (eds.), *Faithfulness and Fortitude: in Conversation with the Theological Ethics of Stanley Hauerwas* (Edinburgh: T. & T. Clark, 2000), 141–60.

Board of Social Responsibility (Church of England), *Something to Celebrate: Valuing Families in Church and Society* (London: Church House Publishing, 1995).

Bonhoeffer, Dietrich, *The Cost of Discipleship* (London: SCM, 1948).

— *Letters and Papers from Prison*, 3rd edition enlarged (London: SCM, 1971).

Borg, Marcus, *Conflict, Holiness and Politics in the Teaching of Jesus*, 2nd edition (Harrisburg, PA: Trinity Press International, 1998).

Bornkamm, Heinrich, *Luther's Doctrine of the Two Kingdoms* (Philadelphia: Fortress Press, 1966).

Bowlin, John, 'Augustine on Justifying Coercion', *Annual of the Society of Christian Ethics* 17 (1997), 49–70.

Bradley, Ian, *God Save the Queen* (London: Darton, Longman & Todd, 2002).

Brakelmann, Günter, 'Barmen V – ein historisch-kritischer Rückblick', *Evangelische Theologie* 45 (1986), 3–20.

Brierley, Peter (ed.), *UK Christian Handbook of Religious Trends*, vol. III (London: Christian Research, 2003).

Brown, Callum G., *The Death of Christian Britain: Understanding Secularisation, 1800–2000* (London: Routledge, 2001).

Brown, Stewart J., 'Presbyterians and Catholics in Twentieth-Century Scotland', in Stewart J. Brown and George Newlands (eds.), *Scottish Christianity in the Modern World* (Edinburgh: T. & T. Clark, 2000), 255–81.

The National Churches of England, Ireland and Scotland, 1801–1846 (Oxford: Oxford University Press, 2001).

Brown, William P. (ed.), *Character & Scripture: Moral Formation, Community and Biblical Interpretation* (Grand Rapids: Eerdmans, 2002).

Bruce, F. F., 'Render to Caesar', in E. Bammel (ed.), *Jesus and the Politics of His Day* (Cambridge: Cambridge University Press, 1984), 249–64.

Bruce, Steve, *Religion in Modern Britain* (Oxford: Oxford University Press, 1995).

Brueggeman, Walter, *Theology of the Old Testament* (Grand Rapids: Eerdmans, 1997).

Buber, Martin, *On Judaism* (New York: Schocken Books, 1967).

Buchanan, Colin, *Cut the Connection: Disestablishment and the Church of England* (London: Darton, Longman & Todd, 1994).

Bultmann, Rudolf, *The Gospel of John*, trans. G. R. Beasley-Murray (Oxford: Blackwell, 1971).

Burleigh, J. H. S., *A Church History of Scotland* (Oxford: Oxford University Press, 1960).

Busch, Eberhard, *Karl Barth* (London: SCM, 1976).

'Church and Politics in the Reformed Tradition', in Donald McKim (ed.), *Major Themes in the Reformed Tradition* (Grand Rapids: Eerdmans, 1992), 180–95.

Calvin, John, 'Defensio Orthodoxae Fidei De Sacra Trinitate contra Prodigiosos Errores Michaelis Serveti Hispani', *Calvini Opera* (Brunsvigae: 1863), vol. VIII, 452–643.

Institutes of the Christian Religion, trans. F. L. Battles (Grand Rapids: Eerdmans, 1986).

Cameron, Averil, *Christianity and the Rhetoric of Empire* (Berkeley: University of California Press, 1991).

Cameron, James, 'Scottish Calvinism and the Principle of Intolerance', in B. A. Gerrish (ed.), *Reformatio Perennis: Essays on Calvin and the Reformation in Honour of Ford Lewis Battles* (Pittsburgh: Pickwick Press, 1981), 113–28.

Cameron, James K. (ed.), *The First Book of Discipline* (Edinburgh: St Andrew Press, 1972).

Campbell, W., 'The Scottish Westminster Commissioners and Toleration', *Records of the Scottish Church History Society* 9 (1947), 1–18.

Carr, Wesley, 'A Developing Establishment', *Theology* 102 (1999), 2–10.

Carter, Stephen, *The Culture of Disbelief* (New York: Basic Books, 1993).

Casanova, José, *Public Religions in the Modern World* (Chicago: University of Chicago Press, 1994).

Castellio, Sebastian, *Concerning Heretics*, ed. Roland Bainton (New York: Columbia University Press, 1935).

Chadwick, Owen, 'Sacrament at Crathie 1873', in Stewart J. Brown and George Newlands (eds.), *Scottish Christianity in the Modern World* (Edinburgh: T. & T. Clark, 2000), 177–98.

Chappell, David L., *A Stone of Hope: Prophetic Religion and the Death of Jim Crow* (Chapel Hill: University of North Carolina Press, 2004).

Charles, Rodger, SJ, *Christian Social Witness and Teaching: the Catholic Tradition from Genesis to Centesimus Annus* (Leominster: Gracewing, 1998).

Cheyne, A. C., *The Transforming of the Kirk: Victorian Scotland's Religious Revolution* (Edinburgh: St Andrew Press, 1983).

Church of Scotland, 'The Theology of Marriage', *Reports to the General Assembly of the Church of Scotland 1994* (Edinburgh, 1994), 257–85.

Clarke, Peter, *Hope and Glory, Britain 1900–1990* (London: Penguin, 1997).

Clements, Keith, 'Community in the Ethics of Dietrich Bonhoeffer', *Studies in Christian Ethics* 10 (1997), 16–31.

Cochrane, Arthur C., *The Church's Confession Under Hitler* (Philadelphia: Westminster Press, 1962).

Coffey, John, *Persecution and Toleration in Protestant England 1558–1689* (Harlow: Longman, 2000).

Coleman, Janet, *A History of Political Thought from Ancient Greece to Early Christianity* (Oxford: Blackwell, 2000).

Colley, Linda, *Britons: Forging the Nation 1707–1837* (New Haven: Yale University Press, 1992).

Crossan, John Dominic, *The Historical Jesus: the Life of a Mediterranean Jewish Peasant* (San Francisco: HarperCollins, 1991).

Cunningham, Agnes (ed.), *The Early Church and the State* (Philadelphia: Fortress Press, 1982).

Curran, Charles, *Catholic Social Teaching, 1891–Present: a Historical, Theological and Ethical Analysis* (Washington, DC: Georgetown University Press, 2002).

Davie, Grace, *Religion in Britain since 1945: Believing without Belonging* (Oxford: Blackwell, 1994).

  Europe: the Exceptional Case, Parameters of Faith in the Modern World (London: Darton, Longman & Todd, 2002).

Davies, Douglas J., *Death, Ritual and Belief*, 2nd edition (London: Continuum, 2002).

Devine, Tom (ed.), *Scotland's Shame: Bigotry and Sectarianism in Modern Scotland* (Edinburgh: Mainstream, 2000).

Dickens, A. G. and Whitney R. D. Jones, *Erasmus the Reformer* (London: Methuen, 1994).

Dunn, James D. G., *Romans* (Texas: Word Books, 1988).

Dworkin, Ronald, *Sovereign Virtue: the Theory and Practice of Equality* (Cambridge, MA: Harvard University Press, 2000).

Eliot, T. S., *The Idea of a Christian Society* (London: Faber, 1939).

Elliot, Neil, 'Romans 13: 1–7 in the Context of Imperial Propaganda', in Richard A. Horsley (ed.), *Paul and Empire: Religion and Power in Roman Imperial Society* (Harrisburg: Trinity Press International, 1997), 184–204.

'Paul and the Politics of Empire', in Richard Horsley (ed.), *Paul and Politics* (Harrisburg, PA: Trinity Press International, 2000), 17–39.

Epistle to Diognetus, in Alexander Roberts and James Donaldson (eds.), *Ante-Nicene Fathers*, revised edition (Peabody, MA: Hendrickson, 1994), vol. I, 25–30.

Ericksen, Robert P., *Theologians under Hitler* (New Haven: Yale University Press, 1985).

Fergusson, David, *Community, Liberalism and Christian Ethics* (Cambridge: Cambridge University Press, 1998).

'Reclaiming the Doctrine of Sanctification', *Interpretation* 53 (1999), 380–90.

Fitzmyer, Joseph, *Romans* (London: Chapman, 1992).

Flannery, Austin (ed.), *Vatican II: Conciliar and Post-Conciliar Documents* (Dublin: Dominican Publications, 1975).

Flannigan, Kieran, 'Theological Pluralism, Religious Pluralism and Unbelief', in Ian Hamnett (ed.), *Religious Pluralism and Unbelief: Studies Critical and Comparative* (London: Routledge, 1990), 81–113.

Forrester, Duncan B., 'Luther, Calvin and Hooker', in Leo Strauss and Joseph Cropsey (eds.), *History of Political Philosophy* (Chicago: Rand McNally, 1963), 277–323.

Beliefs, Values and Policies: Conviction Politics in a Secular Age (Oxford: Oxford University Press, 1989).

On Human Worth (London: SCM, 2001).

Furuya, Yasuo (ed.), *A History of Japanese Theology* (Grand Rapids: Eerdmans, 1997).

Garnsey, Peter, 'Religious Toleration in Classical Antiquity', in W. J. Shiels (ed.), *Persecution and Toleration* (Oxford: Blackwell, 1984), 1–27.

Geddes, Jane (ed.), *King's College Chapel, Aberdeen, 1500–2000* (Leeds: Northern Universities Press, 2000).

George, Timothy, *The Theology of the Reformers* (Nashville: Broadman Press, 1988).

Gill, Robin, *Churchgoing and Christian Ethics* (Cambridge: Cambridge University Press, 1999).

Gillespie, George, *Whole Severity Reconciled with Christian Liberty* (London, 1645).

Goertz, Hans-Jürgen, *The Anabaptists* (London: Routledge, 1996).

Goldhagen, Daniel, *Hitler's Willing Executioners: Ordinary Germans and the Holocaust* (New York: Alfred Knopf, 1996).

Gray, John, *Mill on Liberty: a Defence* (London: Routledge & Kegan Paul, 1983).

Liberalism, 2nd edition (Buckingham: Open University Press, 1995).

Two Faces of Liberalism (Oxford: Polity Press, 2000).

Green, Clifford (ed.), *Karl Barth: Theologian of Freedom* (Edinburgh: T. & T. Clark, 1989).

Greer, Rowan, *Broken Lights and Mended Lives: Theology and Common Life in the Early Church* (University Park, PA: Pennsylvania State University, 1986).

Grell, Ole Peter and Bob Scribner (eds.), *Tolerance and Intolerance in the European Reformation* (Cambridge: Cambridge University Press, 1996).

Gruchy, John W. de, 'Barmen: Symbol of Contemporary Liberation?', *Journal of Theology for Southern Africa* 47 (1984), 59–71.

Christianity, Art and Transformation: Theological Aesthetics in the Struggle for Justice (Cambridge: Cambridge University Press, 2001).

Reconciliation: Restoring Justice (London: SCM, 2002).

Guignon, Charles B. and David R. Hiley, 'Biting the Bullet: Rorty on Private and Public Morality', in Alan Malachowski (ed.), *Reading Rorty* (Oxford: Blackwell, 1990), 339–64.

Gustafson, James, 'The Sectarian Temptation', *Proceedings of the Catholic Theological Society of America* 40 (1985), 83–94.

Habgood, John, *Church and Nation in a Secular Age* (London: Darton, Longman & Todd, 1983).

Haldane, John, 'The Individual, the State and the Common Good', in Ellen Frankel Paul, Fred D. Miller Jr and Jeffrey Paul (eds.), *The Communitarian Challenge to Liberalism* (Cambridge: Cambridge University Press, 1996), 59–79.

Harak, Simon, *Virtuous Passions: the Formation of Christian Character* (New York: Paulist Press, 1993).

Harris, Margaret and Colin Rochester (eds.), *Voluntary Organisations and Social Policy in Britain: Perspective on Change and Choice* (London: Palgrave, 2001).

Harris, Margaret, 'Civil Society and the Role of UK Churches: an Exploration', *Studies in Christian Ethics* 15 (2002), 45–59.

Hart, H. L. A., *Essays in Jurisprudence and Philosophy* (Oxford: Oxford University Press, 1983).

Hastings, Adrian, *A History of African Christianity* (Cambridge: Cambridge University Press, 1979).

    Church and State: the English Experience (Exeter: University of Exeter Press, 1991).

Hauerwas, Stanley, *In Good Company* (Indiana: University of Notre Dame Press, 1995).

    Sanctify Them in the Truth: Holiness Exemplified (Edinburgh: T. & T. Clark, 1998).

Hauerwas, Stanley and Charles Pinches, *Christians among the Virtues: Theological Conversations with Ancient and Modern Ethics* (Notre Dame: University of Notre Dame Press, 1997).

Hayek, F. A., *Constitution of Liberty* (New York: Legal Classics Library, 1999).

Henderson, Ian, *Power without Glory: a Study in Ecumenical Politics* (London: Hutchinson, 1967).

Henson, Hensley, *Bishopprick Papers* (Oxford: Oxford University Press, 1946).

Herbert, David, *Religion and Civil Society: Rethinking Public Religion in the Contemporary World* (Aldershot: Ashgate, 2003).

Herman, Arthur, *The Scottish Enlightenment: the Scots' Invention of the Modern World* (London: Fourth Estate, 2002).

Hill, Christopher, 'Tolerance in Seventeenth-Century England: Theory and Practice', in Susan Mendus (ed.), *The Politics of Toleration: Tolerance and Intolerance in Early Modern Life* (Edinburgh: Edinburgh University Press, 1999), 27–44.

Hobbes, Thomas, *Leviathan*, ed. Richard Tuck (Cambridge: Cambridge University Press, 1996).

Hobson, Theo, *Against Establishment: an Anglican Polemic* (London: Darton, Longman & Todd, 2003).

Hollenbach, David, *Justice, Peace and Human Rights: American Catholic Social Ethics in a Pluralistic World* (New York: Crossroad, 1990).

    The Common Good and Christian Ethics (Cambridge: Cambridge University Press, 2002).

Hooker, Richard, *Of the Laws of Ecclesiastical Polity*, ed. Arthur Stephen McGrade (Cambridge: Cambridge University Press, 1989).

Horn, Nico, 'From Barmen to Belhar and Kairos', in Charles Villa-Vicencio (ed.), *On Reading Karl Barth in South Africa* (Grand Rapids: Eerdmans, 1988), 105–19.

Horsley, Richard A., 'Rhetoric and Empire – and I Corinthians', in Richard A. Horsley (ed.), *Paul and Politics* (Harrisburg, PA: Trinity Press International, 2000), 72–102.

    Jesus and Empire: the Kingdom of God and the New World Disorder (Minneapolis: Fortress Press, 2003).

Hunsinger, George, *How to Read Karl Barth* (Oxford: Oxford University Press, 1991).

Huntington, Samuel P., *The Clash of Civilizations and the Remaking of the World Order* (London: Touchstone, 1998).

Inglehart, R., *Modernization and Postmodernization: Cultural, Economic and Political Change in 43 Societies* (Princeton: Princeton University Press, 1997).

Jüngel, Eberhard, *Christ, Justice and Peace: Towards a Theology of the State in Dialogue with the Barmen Declaration* (Edinburgh: T. & T. Clark, 1992).

Käsemann, Ernst, *Romans* (Grand Rapids: Eerdmans, 1980).

Keane, John, *Global Civil Society?* (Cambridge: Cambridge University Press, 2003).

Keble John, *'National Apostasy Considered', Sermon Preached before His Majesty's Judges of Assize* (Oxford, 1833).

Kee, Alistair, *Constantine Versus Christ: the Triumph of Ideology* (London: SCM, 1982).

Kerr, David, 'Christianity and Islam: "Clash of Civilizations" or "Community of Reconciliations?" Questions for Christian–Muslim Studies', *Studies in World Christianity* 8 (2002), 81–98.

King, Preston, *Toleration* (London: Allen & Unwin, 1976).

Kirkpatrick, Frank G., *The Ethics of Community* (Oxford: Blackwell, 2001).

Kohen, Arnold S., *From the Place of the Dead: Bishop Belo and the Struggle for East Timor* (Oxford: Lion Books, 1999).

Kung, Lap Yan, 'What to Preach? Christian Witness in China, with Reference to the Party's Policy of Mutual Accommodation', *Studies in World Christianity* 8 (2002), 206–27.

Kyi, Aung San Suu, *Freedom from Fear* (London: Penguin, 1995).

Lapide, Pinchas, '"No Balm in Barmen?" A Jewish Debit Account', *Ecumenical Review* 45 (1984), 423–36.

Lehmann, Paul, 'Of Faithfulness, Responsibility and the Confessional State of the Church', in Hubert G. Locke (ed.), *The Barmen Confession: Papers from the Seattle Assembly* (Lewiston, New York: Edwin Mellen, 1986), 21–58.

Lincoln, Andrew, 'From Sabbath to Lord's Day: a Biblical and Theological Perspective', in D. A. Carson (ed.), *From Sabbath to Lord's Day* (Grand Rapids: Zondervan, 1982), 343–412.

Lindbeck, George, *The Nature of Doctrine* (London: SPCK, 1984).

The Church in a Postliberal Age (London: SCM, 2002).

Lindsay, Mark R., *Covenanted Solidarity: the Theological Basis of Karl Barth's Opposition to Nazi Antisemitism and the Holocaust* (New York: Peter Lang, 2001).

Little, David, 'Reformed Faith and Religious Liberty', in Donald McKim (ed.), *Major Themes in the Reformed Tradition* (Grand Rapids: Eerdmans, 1984), 196–213.

Lochhead, David, *The Dialogical Imperative* (London: SCM, 1988).

Lochman, Jan Milic, *Signposts to Freedom: the Ten Commandments and Christian Ethics* (Minneapolis: Augsburg, 1982).

The Faith We Confess: Towards an Ecumenical Dogmatics (Edinburgh: T. & T. Clark, 1984).

The Lord's Prayer (Grand Rapids: Eerdmans, 1990).

Locke, John, *Second Treatise on Civil Government* (*c.* 1681), in *Political Writings* (Harmondsworth: Penguin, 1993), 261–387.

'A Letter Concerning Toleration' (1685), in *Political Writings* (Harmondsworth: Penguin, 1993), 390–436.

Lohse, Bernhard, *Martin Luther's Theology: Its Historical and Systematic Development* (Edinburgh: T. & T. Clark, 1999).

Luther, Martin, 'On Secular Authority', in Harro Höpfl (ed.), *Luther and Calvin on Secular Authority* (Cambridge: Cambridge University Press, 1991), 1–43.

MacIntyre, Alasdair, *After Virtue* (London: Duckworth, 1981).

Whose Justice? Which Rationality? (London: Duckworth, 1988).

'Toleration and the Goods of Conflict', in Susan Mendus (ed.), *The Politics of Toleration: Tolerance and Intolerance in Modern Life* (Edinburgh: Edinburgh University Press, 1999), 133–55.

MacKinnon, Donald, *Borderlands in Theology* (London: Lutterworth, 1968).

The Stripping of the Altars (London: Collins, 1969).

Macmurray, John, *Reason and Emotion* (London: Faber & Faber, 1935).

Conditions of Freedom (Canada: Ryerson Press, 1949).

Madison, James, Alexander Hamilton and John Jay, *The Federalist Papers*, ed. Isaac Kramnick (Harmondsworth: Penguin, 1987).

Mahoney, Jack, SJ, *The Making of Moral Theology: a Study of the Roman Catholic Tradition* (Oxford: Oxford University Press, 1987).

'Subsidiarity in the Church', *The Month*, November 1988, 968–74.

Markus, Robert A., *Saeculum: History and Society in the Theology of St Augustine* (Cambridge: Cambridge University Press, 1970).

Marsilius of Padua, *Defensor Pacis*, translated and introduced by Alan Gewirth (Toronto: University of Toronto Press, 1980).

Martin, David, *Does Christianity Cause War?* (Oxford: Oxford University Press, 1997).

Martyrdom of Polycarp, in Alexander Roberts and James Donaldson (eds.), *Ante-Nicene Fathers*, revised edition (Peabody, MA: Hendrickson, 1994), vol. I, 39–44.

Mayer, Wendy and Pauline Allen, *John Chrysostom* (London: Routledge, 2000).

McGrath, Alister, *Reformation Thought*, 3rd edition (Oxford: Blackwell, 1999).

McKay, Johnston, 'Is the Kirk Still Relevant? Home Truths about Influence as a National Institution', in Robert D. Kernohan (ed.), *The Realm of Reform: Presbyterianism and Calvinism in a Changing Scotland* (Edinburgh: Handsel, 1999), 57–68.

McMullen, Christine, 'Cohabitation and Marriage', *Crucible*, January–March 2001, 42–53.

Meeks, Wayne, *The First Urban Christians: the Social World of the Apostle Paul* (New Haven: Yale University Press, 1983).

   The Moral World of the First Christians (London: SPCK, 1986).

   The Origins of Christian Morality (New Haven: Yale University Press, 1993).

Meier, John, *A Marginal Jew*, vol. ii (New York: Doubleday, 1994).

Mendus, Susan, *Toleration and the Limits of Liberalism* (London: Macmillan, 1989).

Mendus, Susan (ed.), *The Politics of Toleration: Tolerance and Intolerance in Modern Life* (Edinburgh: Edinburgh University Press, 1999).

Meyer, Ben F., *The Aims of Jesus* (London: SCM, 1979).

Mill, John Stuart, *On Liberty*, ed. David Bromwich and George Kateb (New Haven: Yale University Press, 2003).

Miller, Patrick D., 'The Good Neighborhood: Identity and Community through the Commandments', in William P. Brown (ed.), *Character & Scripture: Moral Formation, Community and Biblical Interpretation* (Grand Rapids: Eerdmans, 2002), 55–72.

Modood, Tariq (ed.), *Church, State and Religious Minorities* (London: Policy Studies Unit, 1997).

Moltmann, Jürgen, *On Human Dignity* (London: SCM, 1984).

Moses, John, *A Broad and Living Way: Church and State, a Continuing Establishment* (Norwich: Canterbury Press, 1995).

Mount, Eric, Jr, *Covenant, Community and the Common Good* (Cleveland: Pilgrim Press, 1999).

Moyser, George (ed.), *Church and Politics Today: the Role of the Church of England in Contemporary Politics* (Edinburgh: T. & T. Clark, 1985).

Muddiman, John, 'The Resurrection of Jesus as the Coming of the Kingdom – the Basis of Hope for the Transformation of the World', in Robin Barbour (ed.), *The Kingdom of God and Human Society* (Edinburgh: T. & T. Clark, 1993), 208–23.

Murray, Douglas M., *Rebuilding the Kirk* (Edinburgh: Scottish Academic Press, 2000).

Nicholls, David, *Deity and Domination: Images of God and the State in the Nineteenth and Twentieth Centuries* (London: Routledge, 1989).

Niebuhr, H. Richard, *Christ and Culture* (New York: Harper, 1951).

Niemöller, Gerhard, *Die erste Bekenntnissynode der Deutschen Evangelischen Kirche zu Barmen*, vols. I–II (Göttingen: Vandenhoeck & Ruprecht, 1959).

Nozick, Robert, *Anarchy, State and Utopia* (Oxford: Blackwell, 1975).

Nussbaum, Martha, *Sex and Social Justice* (Oxford: Oxford University Press, 1999).

   Women and Human Development: the Capabilities Approach (Cambridge: Cambridge University Press, 2000).

O'Brien, David J. and Thomas A. Shannon (eds.), *Catholic Social Thought: the Documentary Heritage* (Maryknoll: Orbis, 1992).

O'Donovan, Oliver, *The Desire of the Nations* (Cambridge: Cambridge University Press, 1996).

O'Donovan, Oliver and Joan Lockwood O'Donovan, *From Irenaeus to Grotius: a Sourcebook in Christian Political Thought* (Grand Rapids: Eerdmans, 1999).

Oberman, Heiko, 'The Travail of Tolerance: Containing Chaos in Early Modern Europe', in Ole Peter Grell and Bob Scribner (eds.), *Tolerance and Intolerance in the European Reformation* (Cambridge: Cambridge University Press, 1996), 13–31.

Origen, *Against Celsus*, in Alexander Roberts and James Donaldson (eds.), *Ante-Nicene Fathers*, revised edition (Peabody, MA: Hendrickson, 1994), vol. XIV, 395–669.

Pagan, Ann, *God's Scotland: the Story of Scottish Christian Religion* (Edinburgh: Mainstream, 1988).

Paris, Peter J., 'Moral Exemplars in Global Community', in Max L. Stackhouse and Don S. Browning (eds.), *God and Globalization*, vol. II: *The Spirit and the Modern Authorities* (Harrisburg: Trinity Press International, 2001), 191–219.

Parker, Geoffrey (ed.), *The Thirty Years War* (London: Routledge, 1984).

Persenius, R., 'The Year 2000: Disestablishment in Sweden', *Theology* 102 (1999), 177–86.

Pilgrim, Walter E., *Uneasy Neighbors: Church and State in the New Testament* (Minneapolis: Fortress Press, 1999).

Pitt, Valerie, 'Memorandum of Dissent', *Church and State: Report of the Archbishop's Commission* (London: Church Information Office, 1970).

Plant, Raymond, *Politics, Theology and History* (Cambridge: Cambridge University Press, 2001).

Potter, Philip, 'Barmen – An Ecumenical Response', *Ecumenical Review* 45 (1984), 421–3.

Preuss, Horst Dietrich, *Old Testament Theology*, vol. II (Edinburgh: T. & T. Clark, 1996).

Putnam, Robert, *Bowling Alone: the Collapse and Revival of American Community* (New York: Simon & Schuster, 2000).

Quillet, Jeannine, 'Community, Counsel and Representation', in J. H. Burns (ed.),*Cambridge History of Medieval Political Thought c. 350–c. 1450* (Cambridge: Cambridge University Press, 1988), 520–72.

Rahner, Karl, *Theological Investigations*, vol. III (London: Darton, Longman and Todd, 1967).

Rawls, John, 'Justice as Fairness: Political Not Metaphysical', *Collected Papers* (Cambridge, MA: Harvard University Press, 1999), 388–414.

Raz, Joseph, *The Morality of Freedom* (Oxford: Oxford University Press, 1986).

Ricoeur, Paul (ed.), *Tolerance between Intolerance and the Intolerable* (Providence, RI: Berghahn, 1996).

Rist, John, *Augustine: Ancient Thought Baptized* (Cambridge: Cambridge University Press, 1994).

Robbins, Keith, 'Establishing Disestablishment: Some Reflections on Wales and Scotland', in Stewart J. Brown and George Newlands (eds.), *Scottish Christianity in the Modern World* (Edinburgh: T. & T. Clark, 2000), 231–54.

Rowland, Christopher, 'Reflections on the Politics of the Gospels', in Robin Barbour (ed.), *The Kingdom of God and Human Society* (Edinburgh: T. & T. Clark, 1993), 224–41.

Rutherford, Samuel, *A Free Disputation against Pretended Liberty of Conscience* (London, 1649).

Ruthven, Malise, *A Satanic Affair: Salman Rushdie and the Rage of Islam* (London: Chatto & Windus, 1990).

Sacks, Jonathan, *Faith in the Future* (London: Darton, Longman & Todd, 1995).

   The Politics of Hope (London: Jonathan Cape, 1997).

   The Dignity of Difference: How to Avoid the Clash of Civilizations (London: Continuum, 2002).

Sandel, Michael, *Liberalism and Its Critics* (Oxford: Blackwell, 1984).

Scholder, Klaus, *The Churches and the Third Reich*, vols. I–II (London: SCM, 1987–8).

   A Requiem for Hitler and Other Perspectives on the German Church Struggle (London: SCM, 1989).

Schottroff, Luise, '"Give to Caesar What Belongs to Caesar and to God What Belongs to God": a Theological Response of the Early Christian Church to Its Social and Political Environment', in Willard M. Swartley (ed.), *The Love of Enemy and Nonretaliation in the New Testament* (Louisville: John Knox Press, 1992), 157–76.

Shandley, Robert R. (ed.), *Unwilling Germans? The Goldhagen Debate* (Minneapolis: University of Minnesota Press, 1998).

Smit, Dirkie, 'A Status Confessionis in South Africa?', *Journal of Theology for Southern Africa* 47 (1984), 21–46.

Sonderegger, Katherine, *That Jesus Christ Was Born a Jew: Karl Barth's Doctrine of Israel* (University Park, PA: Pennsylvania State University Press, 1992).

Stackhouse, Max with Peter Paris (eds.), *Religion and the Powers of the Common Life* (Harrisburg, PA: Trinity Press International, 2000).

Stephens, W. P., *The Theology of Huldrych Zwingli* (Oxford: Oxford University Press, 1986).

Storrar, Will, *Scottish Identity: a Christian Vision* (Edinburgh: Handsel, 1990).

Stout, Jeffrey, *Ethics after Babel* (Cambridge, MA: Clarke, 1988).

Taylor, Charles, *The Ethics of Authenticity* (Cambridge, MA: Harvard University Press, 1991).

'The Politics of Recognition', in Amy Gutman (ed.), *Multiculturalism* (Princeton: Princeton University Press, 1994), 25–73.

Tertullian, *Apology*, in Alexander Roberts and James Donaldson (eds.), *Ante-Nicene Fathers*, revised edition (Peabody, MA: Hendrickson, 1994), vol. III, 17–55.

On Idolatry, in Alexander Roberts and James Donaldson (eds.), *Ante-Nicene Fathers*, revised edition (Peabody, MA: Hendrickson, 1994), vol. III, 61–76.

On Prescription Against Heretics, in Alexander Roberts and James Donaldson (eds.), *Ante-Nicene Fathers*, revised edition (Peabody, MA: Hendrickson, 1994), vol. III, 243–65.

A Treatise on the Soul, in Alexander Roberts and James Donaldson (eds.), *Ante-Nicene Fathers*, revised edition (Peabody, MA: Hendrickson, 1994), vol. III, 181–235.

Thiemann, Ronald, *Religion in Public Life: a Dilemma for Democracy* (Washington, DC: Georgetown University Press, 1996).

Tracy, David, *The Analogical Imagination* (London: SCM, 1981).

Troeltsch, Ernst, *The Social Teaching of the Christian Churches*, trans. Olive Wyon, 2 vols. (Louisville: Westminster/John Knox, 1992).

Tutu, Desmond, *The Rainbow People of God* (London: Doubleday, 1994).

No Future without Forgiveness (London: Rider, 1999).

Vallely, Paul (ed.), *The New Politics: Catholic Social Teaching for the Twenty-First Century* (London: SCM, 1998).

Verba, Sidney, Kay Lehman Schlozman and Henry Brady, *Voice and Equality: Civic Voluntarism in American Politics* (Cambridge, MA: Harvard University Press, 1995).

Vile, John R., *A Companion to the United States Constitution and Its Amendments* (Westport: Praeger, 1997).

Villa Vicencio, Charles and Wilhelm Verwoerd (eds.), *Looking Back Reaching Forward* (Cape Town: University of Cape Town Press, 2000).

Vitoria, Francisco de, *Political Writings*, ed. Anthony Pagden and Jeremy Lawrence (Cambridge: Cambridge University Press, 1991).

Walls, Andrew F., *The Cross-Cultural Process in Christian History* (Edinburgh: T. & T. Clark, 2002).

Walzer, Michael (ed.), *Toward a Global Civil Society* (Oxford: Berghahn Books, 1995).

On Toleration (New Haven: Yale University Press, 1997).

Weatherhead, James L. (ed.), *The Constitution and Laws of the Church of Scotland* (Edinburgh: Board of Practice and Procedure, 1997).

Welker, Michael, 'God's Power and Powerlessness: Biblical Theology and the Search for a World Ethos in a Time of Shortlived Moral Markets', in Cynthia L. Rigby (ed.), *Power, Powerlessness and the Divine* (Atlanta: Scholars Press, 1997), 39–55.

Wendel, F., *Calvin* (London: Collins, 1963).

Wengst, Klaus, *Pax Romana and the Peace of Jesus Christ* (London: SCM, 1987.

Wilkins, John (ed.), *Understanding Veritatis Splendor* (London: SCPK, 1994).

Williams, Bernard, 'Toleration, a Political or Moral Question?', in Paul Ricoeur (ed.), *Tolerance between Intolerance and the Intolerable* (Providence, RI: Berghahn, 1996), 35–48.

Williams, Rowan, *On Christian Theology* (Oxford: Blackwell, 2000).

Wolterstorff, Nicholas, 'Why We Should Reject What Liberalism Tells Us about Speaking and Acting in Public for Religious Reasons', in Paul Weithman (ed.), *Religion and Contemporary Liberalism* (Notre Dame: University of Notre Dame Press, 1997), 162–81.

Wright, David, 'The Kirk: National or Christian?', in Robert Kernohan (ed.), *The Realm of Reform: Presbyterianism and Calvinism in a Changing Scotland* (Edinburgh: Handsel Press, 1999), 31–40.

Wright, N. T., *Jesus and the Victory of God* (London: SPCK, 1996).

'God and Caesar, Then and Now', first in a series of lectures on *God, Church, Crown and State* delivered at Westminster Abbey on 22 April 2003. www.westminster-abbey.org/event/lecture/archives/020428_tom_wright.html

Yoder, John Howard, *The Politics of Jesus*, 2nd edition (Grand Rapids: Eerdmans, 1994).

'How H. Richard Niebuhr Reasoned: a Critique of *Christ and Culture*', in Glen H. Stassen, D. M. Yeager and John Howard Yoder (eds.), *Authentic Transformation: a New Vision of Christ and Culture* (Nashville: Abingdon Press, 1996), 31–90.

Index